Tolerance

Between Forbearance and Acceptance

Hans Oberdiek

ROWMAN & LITTLEFIELD PUBLISHERS, INC.
Lanham • Boulder • New York • Oxford

ROWMAN & LITTLEFIELD PUBLISHERS, INC.

Published in the United States of America
by Rowman & Littlefield Publishers, Inc.
4720 Boston Way, Lanham, Maryland 20706
www.rowmanlittlefield.com

12 Hid's Copse Road
Cumnor Hill, Oxford OX2 9JJ, England

British Library Cataloguing in Publication Information Available

Library of Congress Cataloging-in-Publication Data

Oberdiek, Hans, 1937–
    Tolerance : between forbearance and acceptance / Hans Oberdiek.
        p. cm.
    Includes bibliographical references and index.
    ISBN 0-8476-8785-6 (alk. paper) — ISBN 0-8476-8786-4 (pbk. : alk. paper)
        1. Toleration. I. Title.

    BJ1431 .O24 2001
    179'.9—dc21

                                                            00-069043

Printed in the United States of America

♾™ The paper used in this publication meets the minimum requirements of American
National Standard for Information Sciences—Permanence of Paper for Printed Library
Materials, ANSI/NISO Z.39.48-1992.

To
Seamus, Meghan, and Kate
and
Elena, Isabel, Benjamin, and Matthew
and
Henry, Virginia, and Peter

May they enjoy a world as vibrant as it is tolerant

Contents

Preface

Recent studies of tolerance vary widely in their aims. Some concentrate solely on clarifying what tolerance is and is not. Others defend or, more often, ardently criticize the idea that tolerance is an important value. I build on these discussions but make what I hope is a distinctive contribution to the question of the place of tolerance in the contemporary world, for I embed a defense of tolerance within a certain kind of liberal theory, one that takes *personal autonomy*, not *individualism*, to be central. This connects my account with older forms of liberalism. These are not classical "libertarian" forms but, rather, are like those championed in the late nineteenth and early twentieth centuries by, for instance, L. T. Hobhouse.[1] This connects my defense with a late nineteenth- and early twentieth-century notion of autonomy, such as the self-realizationist position of Hastings Rashdall.[2] And this idea, in turn, is prefigured in passages found in John Stuart Mill's *On Liberty*,[3] especially those invoking the views of Baron von Humbolt.[4]

I choose to avoid the term "self-realization" because it too readily suggests that there is a "self" (like an acorn) waiting to be "realized" or actualized into what it is destined to become if only properly cultivated. I favor John Dewey's more open-ended notion of self-direction and his recognition that there are various diverse, even conflicting, experiments in living that call for, and develop, distinctive characters.[5] Dewey agrees with Aristotle and Mill that our lives go well only when we give full expression to distinctive human powers and with Mill that each of us has our own peculiar powers and capacities. He stresses, however, what both glide over, if not ignore altogether, namely, that we both shape, and are shaped by, our culture, community, and civilization.

The good of any human life consists in the living of it. Joseph Raz skillfully develops the kernel of this idea in *The Morality of Freedom*.[6] For those of us living in contemporary, pluralistic, and multicultural societies, a deep, constitutive part of a good life is that we all have the opportunity to bc (part) authors of our own lives. I will elaborate in detail what I take this to mean in chapter 8. Intuitively, however, the idea is clear enough. Each of us is not only the principal character in the lives we live but also—if we are persevering and fortunate—principal coauthor of the dramas that are our lives. Others help write our lives—parents and friends, for example. Equally important, the contextual background is already given by our culture, language, traditions, epic tales, occupational concerns, and so on. Unlike theatrical dramas, however, there are no dress rehearsals—though life provides a lucky few with second acts.

I will argue that we need toleration (the practice) and tolerance (virtue) if we are to express our individuality, at least in the pluralistic, multicultural world in which most members of the "first world" live. Liberals true to their beliefs will strive to protect the possibility of people, differently situated, developing their own distinctive ways of life by advocating tolerance and embedding practices of toleration in the institutions of government and society.

One way liberals advocate this is by urging the state to adopt the principle of strict neutrality. As long as no one is harmed or no one's fundamental rights are violated, the state should keep hands off, tolerating what those controlling the state find disgusting, deplorable, or even debased. This for a long time has been the most prevalent defense of toleration by liberals, partly because it reflects U.S. constitutional jurisprudence regarding the First Amendment (freedom of religion, assembly, and expression) and Fourteenth Amendment (due process and equal protection of the laws). It is found, for example, in the writings of American philosophers John Rawls,[7] Robert Nozick,[8] Ronald Dworkin,[9] Brian Barry,[10] and a Canadian, Will Kymlicka,[11] among others. This defense has its virtues. It also has its limitations. And one in particular stands out; namely, it cannot move beyond a grudging defense of toleration, beyond mere tolerance, for it sees tolerance as little more than forbearance, as putting up with what is disgusting, deplorable, or debased in order to establish a system of well-ordered political liberties that treats everyone evenhandedly, without regard to their particular conceptions of the good.

The latter position and the constitutional jurisprudence it reflects are not to be dismissed or despised. The protection of free expression and guarantee of due process and equal protection of law constitute an enormous accomplishment. Many emerging democracies strive, with mixed success, to become nations of well-ordered political liberties. Still, there is something missing, for the understanding of tolerance it begets always tempts one to place a "mere" before the word "tolerance," as I have done in the previous paragraph. To supply what is missing, I offer a more robust defense of tolerance, one that lets us see that tolerance amounts to more than mere forbearance, one that invites us to explore the terrain that lies between mere forbearance and full acceptance.

To do so, I need to embed my account in a version of political liberalism with greater resources than those found in Rawls, Dworkin, and the others just mentioned. I call the version I defend *substantive* liberalism.[12] While sharing a common history with liberalisms that emphasize strict neutrality or fair procedures, it allows citizens to make substantive arguments about what is worth pursuing *and to enlist the support of the state in favoring what is good.* It is a more *comprehensive* liberalism in two respects. It does not advocate "epistemic abstinence"[13] (Rawls), and it is not "rights-based" (Dworkin). At the same time, it is modest in its aspirations, avoiding the obvious vices of political views that would use the coercive powers of the state to enforce approved ways of life. In defending tolerance as embedded in substantive liberalism, I hope to show that it can be much more than merely "putting up with" what one finds deplorable. While it does not require us to *accept* what we tolerate or pass by what we tolerate in respectful silence, it strongly encourages us to explore the terrain between forbearance and full acceptance, exploring possibilities of mutual understanding and accommodation along the way.

Tolerance seems at once both necessary and impossible—necessary, because living in an intolerant world is intolerable; impossible, because living in a world that tolerates the intolerable is also intolerable. I introduce some of the complexities, puzzles, and paradoxes of tolerance in chapter 1 but then elaborate on them more extensively in chapter 2. To unravel them we need to clarify the differences between *tolerance* and *toleration,* draw even finer distinctions among different shades of tolerance (chapter 3), and then spell out the circumstances in which tolerance arises (chapter 4). The intolerable is the subject of chapter 5. In thinking about tolerance and its limits, we will see that it is imperative to keep in mind the centrality of intolerance. *It* is the dog that wags, tolerance the tail that is wagged.

In chapter 6, I discuss toleration in the thought of Thomas Aquinas and John Locke. I select Aquinas both because his use of "tolerance" shows its long history and because his views on toleration are both usefully similar and different from those of John Locke. In a brief historical interlude, I consider the views of three European thinkers—Michel de Montaigne, René Descartes, and Baruch Spinoza—as they try to make room for religious toleration on the Continent.

I explore Locke's famous defense of toleration in detail because it sets the stage for all subsequent discussions. It does so not because it was the first systematic examination of toleration in English or because its logic is unassailable. Locke's *Letter on Toleration* did, however, exert enormous influence over subsequent thinking about toleration, and not just among (or even primarily among) philosophers. Locke's argument has a directness and power that force us to confront fundamental questions. An understanding of the controversy Locke's famous *Letter* engendered in his own day shows the strengths and limitations of his way of addressing tolerance and its limits.

In chapter 7, I consider Michael Walzer's argument that regimes of toleration are varied in their singularity and that no successful regimes have mandated that we adopt tolerance as an attitude or virtue. While I raise several objections to Walzer's own account, he does offer a contemporary, grudging defense of toleration not far from Locke's original account. But can we not move beyond "mere" tolerance to something richer and more attractive?

It is to that question that I turn in chapter 8. There I provide a defense of tolerance as a virtue, a defense that grounds it in substantive liberalism. This defense does not so much compete with as complement nonliberal considerations advanced for regimes of toleration. I hope to show that tolerance need not have the negative, static implications many think it has, that it is something more than *mere* or *bare* toleration. Those who possess tolerance as a virtue, I will argue, are compelled to engage those whom they tolerate in ways that create the possibility of transforming their relationship. That, in turn, will stimulate a reassessment of some implied objections to tolerance broached earlier and to several new objections (chapter 9). In a short final epilogue, I will suggest what the understanding of tolerance advanced throughout the book can and cannot do.

My intellectual debts are many. Since 1980, the C. and J. B. Morrell Trust has funded research into toleration at the University of York. Many excellent studies of toleration owe their origins to the trust, especially the work of Susan Mendus and her colleague, John Horton. Their influence is readily apparent, especially in chapter 4 ("The Circumstances of Tolerance"). I have learned much from Joseph Raz's seminal work, *The Morality of Freedom.* Whether he would be happy with the direction I take or the arguments I make I do not know. I have also learned much from George Sher's *Beyond Neutrality: Perfectionism and Politics.*[14] Michael Walzer's *On Toleration* comes in for heavy criticism, but I owe much to his deft discussion of various "regimes of toleration."[15] Charles Taylor's essays on social and political philosophy always cause one to reflect more deeply on whatever his subtle hand touches.[16]

I also owe a debt of gratitude to colleagues at Swarthmore College, who responded to a very early version of some distinctions and arguments made here: Robin Wagner-Pacifici, Richard Schuldenfrei, Barry Schwartz, and Braulio Munoz. I presented early versions of the core ideas at Albright College, where I received helpful criticisms, as I did when I spoke at Bryn Mawr College. A more recent version was presented at Reading University in England, where Jonathan Dancy permitted me to look at an unpublished paper of his on tolerance. Several convivial but probing conversations with James Griffin deepened my understanding of how a questioning turn of mind fits into a defense of tolerance. I also learned much by giving a series of lectures on tolerance to participants at a Soros Open Society summer institute in Kiev, where younger philosophers and social scientists seek to rebuild the moribund system of higher education from the shambles of the former Soviet Union.

Several generations of Swarthmore students have also helped me think through the meaning and implication of tolerance, both practically and philosophically. Three recent students deserve special recognition since we worked through some of the literature on tolerance together: Jessica McFarland, Matthew Hellman, and Douglas Berger, all from the class of 1998. Over the years I have learned much from lengthy philosophical conversations with my colleagues, Hugh Lacey and Richard Eldridge. They are everything one could want in philosophical colleagues, as warmly supportive as they are critical. And John Oberdiek's suggestions were especially helpful in chapter 8. Michael Krausz has been a constant support in seeing this project to completion. And Constance Hungerford's sharp editorial eye and continuing encouragement made this book possible.

NOTES

1. L. T. Hobhouse, *Liberalism* (New York: Henry Holt, 1911).

2. Hastings Rashdall, *The Theory of Good and Evil: A Treatise on Moral Philosophy*, 2 vols. (Oxford, 1907).

3. John Stuart Mill, *On Liberty* (London: J. W. Parker and Son, 1859); *On Liberty: In Focus*, ed. John Gray and G. W. Smith (London: Routledge, 1991); *On Liberty*, ed. David Spitz (New York: W. W. Norton, 1975).

4. Wilhelm Freiherr von Humbolt, *The Sphere and Duties of Government*, trans. J. Coulthard (London: Trübner, 1854).

5. John Dewey, *Human Nature and Conduct: An Introduction to Social Psychology* (New York: Henry Holt, 1922); *Experience and Nature* (Chicago: Open Court Publishing, 1925); *Individualism: Old and New* (New York: Minton, Balch, 1930); *Intelligence in the Modern World: John Dewey's Philosophy*, ed. Joseph Ratner (New York: Modern Library, 1939).

6. Joseph Raz, *The Morality of Freedom* (Oxford: Clarendon Press, 1986).

7. John Rawls, *A Theory of Justice* (Cambridge, Mass.: Harvard University Press, 1971).

8. Robert Nozick, *State, Anarchy, and Utopia* (New York: Basic Books, 1974).

9. Ronald Dworkin, "Liberalism," in *A Matter of Principle* (Cambridge, Mass.: Harvard University Press, 1988).

10. Brian Barry, *Justice as Impartiality* (New York: Oxford University Press, 1995).

11. Will Kymlicka, *Liberalism, Community, and Culture* (New York: Oxford University Press, 1989).

12. What I propose sometimes goes by the name "weak perfectionism." In chapter 8, I give reasons for rejecting that term. In fairness, the political philosophies of Rawls and Dworkin are not without substance. My complaint is that they preach far too much abstinence when it comes to the place of defending values in political and social life.

13. Joseph Raz, "Facing Diversity: The Case of Epistemic Abstinence," in *Ethics in the Public Domain* (Oxford: Clarendon Press, 1994).

14. George Sher, *Beyond Neutrality: Perfectionism and Politics* (Cambridge: Cambridge University Press, 1997).

15. Michael Walzer, *On Toleration* (New Haven, Conn.: Yale University Press, 1997).

16. Charles Taylor, *Sources of the Self: The Making of the Modern Identity* (Cambridge, Mass.: Harvard University Press, 1989); *Multiculturalism: Examining the Politics of Recognition*, ed. Amy Gutmann (Princeton, N.J.: Princeton University Press, 1994); *Philosophical Arguments* (Cambridge, Mass.: Harvard University Press, 1995).

Chapter 1

Tolerance: An Impossible Virtue?

When the Berlin Wall fell and the Soviet Union dissolved, many hoped for a "new world order," an order distinguished by significant reduction in internecine bloodshed. It would be replaced by continued growth of democracy, mutual concern, and respect for differences. So far, it has not worked out that way. In the former Yugoslavia, neighbors who once lived in peace, even intermarried—Serbs, Croats, Bosnian Muslims, Kosovar Albanians, and Gypsies—are now at each other's throats. Northern Ireland remains bitterly divided between Protestants and Catholics, internal strife or mutual enmity marks several former Soviet republics, and large-scale massacres have taken place not only in Rwanda but elsewhere around the world. There is nothing new in this, only additional instances of conflict, strife, and hatred. Long before the Berlin Wall went up or came down, people have found it difficult to live together peacefully, unless coerced into a false harmony to do so.

Many things create deep divisions. Material interests, such as water rights or market access, can set people against each other. Cultural animosities sometimes serve as proxies for these. Demanding protection of a group's cultural heritage, for example, seems a less squalid reason for oppression than economic advantage. Behind high-minded and sentiment-filled demands, we often find selfish interests. Those grasping for power have their own self-interested reasons for turning small differences, disquieting suspicions, and minor irritations into major confrontations.

Still, although all animosities and strife have material consequences, not all have their roots in material concerns, greed, or narrow self-interest. Appeals to racial purity, linguistic superiority, cultural traditions, sacred places, and the sacred history of the nation continue to create deep divisions. Nor are hostilities limited to race or religion or to distinct linguistic, cultural, and geographical groups. *Any* difference, it seems, can produce hatred between and among peoples. Hatreds sometimes arise largely, though never simply, because one group cannot stand what another feels, thinks, or does. Such bitter animosities may so blind

1

parties to a dispute that they cannot see that they are jeopardizing both their own enlightened self-interest and what they hold most dear, as the terrible example of religious war proves. Opportunistic ideologues are skilled at cynically blowing on the coals of racial, ethnic, or cultural hatreds to further their own interests. Once ignited, publics often become so inflamed that they consume even themselves, often including those whose fanaticism or cynical grab for power initially lit the match.

Animosity, loathing, and abhorrence reveal themselves not only in atrocities, though that is common enough. They manifest themselves through sneers, petty humiliations, discrimination, persecution, and oppression. Each breeds anger and resentment and a powerful urge to retaliate. This, in turn, adds to greater suspicion, fear, distorted thinking, and twisted emotions on all sides. People may continue to *be* neighbors but not live *as* neighbors. Although they live next door, there is nothing neighborly about their relations, as the miles of shiny razor wire separating Catholics and Protestants in Northern Ireland attests.

Such hatred and bitterness corrosively eats away at what commonly cements communities together. Without the mortar of respect, trust, and tolerance, brick scrapes against brick. The result is familiar. Those locked in enmity yearn not only to be free from the hated other but to smash them to smithereens. Where those with power cannot keep the despised completely oppressed, they may yield to the temptation to rid themselves of the contemptible altogether, to make them "disappear."

A curious feature of some deep-seated animosities is that, from the outside, they often look unfathomable, even faintly ridiculous. From the outside, individuals or groups locked in hatred may seem like two peas in a pod. From the inside, however, the similarities only highlight remaining differences, differences that come to assume monumental importance. Oddly enough, great differences do not always breed the same intense animosity as do small ones.

From our present perspective, for example, the antagonism among various Protestant denominations in seventeenth-century England seems incredible. Surely, we think, it was mad to let such seemingly minor doctrinal differences matter *so much*. Is it really worth fighting over whether one is baptized as an infant or an adult? Yet we also know that, at the time, differences such as this were regarded as supremely important. An entire theology was implicated and therefore God's will on earth. To have allowed other persuasions to flourish without resistance would have been to abandon one's own deepest convictions to do God's work. It would also have seriously endangered one's own soul. Martin Luther's (perhaps apocryphal) reply to his inquisitors deserves quoting in full: "Here I stand, I can do no other. It is not safe for a man to violate his conscience. God help me." Nor was it only theological doctrine that divided English Protestants. The ways in which they thought churches should be governed or precisely how one should worship also sometimes led to persecution and bloodshed.

Many who hate and despise each other strike even outsiders as pervasively different: different in race, ethnicity, language, religion, metaphysical commitments, kinship systems, aesthetic sensibilities, sexual practices, and customs. Christian Serbs and Muslim Kosovar Albanians, for example, differ in religion, ethnicity, and language, as do Hindu Tamils and Buddhist Sinhalese in Sri Lanka. Class and caste distinctions also lead to bitter antagonisms. These kinds of deep and often divisive differences are neither new nor rare. Modern weaponry coupled with ancient savagery, however, can make them especially brutal when they erupt in violence, though machetes remain brutally effective.

Why difference, whether trivial or substantial, should make *such* a difference in how we see and act is deeply puzzling. Many answers suggest themselves, but none is fully convincing. Further, there is no reason to expect that there will be a single answer or even one set of interrelated answers, however intellectually satisfying that might be. One explanation is the apparent need of many in-groups to define themselves against an out-group: "We are 'we' because we differ from 'you'." The more we resemble you, the greater the need to find *some* differences, however seemingly trivial, to distinguish ourselves and justify ourselves as distinctive—and superior. But why the need to feel superior?

"The nonidentity of discernibles" entails that, given any two things, there must be *some* discernible difference between them, or there would not be two things, only one. It trivially follows that if we speak of Serbs and Croats, Baptists and Methodists, Tutsis and Hutus, straight and gay, and so on, there will be discernible differences. These can be, again, especially from the outside, exceedingly small: Tutsi and Hutu, for instance. Yet, whether great or small, discerned differences can drive deep wedges between communities. Each looks across the gap separating them with suspicion, fear, and anger that can explode in violence.

Yet we also know that widely divergent groups have lived in peace and harmony for generations, even in places now torn apart by mutual enmity. If anything, living in peace is the norm. Otherwise, the world would have been consumed by hatred long ago. Just as we oil squeaky wheels, so distinctions that grow into tension and conflict catch our attention.

Deep and pervasive differences alone are, however, not enough to explain the harm groups inflict on each other. Nor can it explain why, after generations of peaceful coexistence, neighbors turn on each other with such viciousness. We know, historically, which differences seem to have led to the greatest hostility, namely, religion, race, ethnicity, gender, and customs. We do not, however, have anything like an adequate sociological explanation of why *these* engender such animosities. An "other," as noted previously, helps define who we are in terms of whom we are not: We are Scots, not English; Christians, not Jews; straight, not gay. The Inuit, who were isolated from other human beings for centuries, have the same name for themselves as for humans generally, namely, "Inuit." There was no human "other" to stand in contrast. The mechanism of defining oneself in terms of others, however, is not well understood. Although speculative explanatory theories abound, none has garnered widespread support. Fortunately, finding answers to what causes perceived differences to become transformed into sources of hatred belongs more to the social sciences than to philosophy, though philosophers have speculated endlessly about it.

Whether the differences among warring groups are slight or great, the degree of animosity in the world remains high. Whether it is higher or lower than before the end of the Cold War is difficult to say. Some suggest that the two superpowers kept ethnic, cultural, and racial hatreds in check, preventing them from spilling over into violence. This might explain peace in Yugoslavia under Tito. Elsewhere, however, the superpowers were only too happy to stir up trouble, as in Africa and Southeast Asia. Undeniably, however, bigotry, narrow-mindedness, fanaticism, and prejudice pervade today's world. A catalog of differences festering into malice in the United States alone could itself fill a book. Even when the enmity has not turned violent—and it has done that often enough—it has crippled the targets of hatred and society as a whole. One could compile lists for nation after nation, community after community. Everywhere there are pleas for reconciliation and—where that fails—*toleration* and *tolerance*.

While we need research to find out what causes contempt and hatred between various groups and what allows them to reconcile and live together harmoniously, the need for toleration (the act of tolerating) and for tolerance (the attitude or virtue)[1] will not thereby disappear. Simply knowing what causes what does not mean that we can control the causes. Bare toleration will sometimes be all we can expect—or should want. No one wishes to live in a homogeneous or lobotomized world, a world without difference, passion, and commitment. Yet we think it is reasonable to expect, even demand, that individuals and diverse groups[2] *at least* tolerate each other.

But, we quickly add, not tolerate *all* differences. It would be unreasonable—worse, utterly wrong—to demand that we should tolerate *every* divergent attitude, belief, or practice. No one, we think, should tolerate cruelty or slavery just because it happens at a comfortable remove. Can we not say the same about racist, sexist, and homophobic attitudes? We should not aspire to exchange unthinking bigotry for mindless toleration of everything.

We therefore need to sort out what tolerance implies, the circumstances in which it arises as a live option, and when it is (and is not) defensible, for understanding the *limits* of tolerance is part of understanding the scope of its justification. So far, tolerance has resisted any consistent or agreed-on analysis and defense. It has proven to be—as the subtitle of an excellent anthology on it implies—"an elusive virtue."[3] One contributor calls it highly "paradoxical."[4] Another goes so far as to say that it is "an impossible virtue."[5]

Tolerance and toleration appear elusive not only because of their apparent impossibility but also because of their apparently inherent *instability*. Tolerance seems to occupy a no-man's-land between intolerance on the one hand and complete acceptance on the other. That is, it seems to exist in an unstable moment like that between the point at which, when looking at the familiar duck/rabbit drawing, we can *only* see the duck and then, in the blink of an eye, can *only* see the rabbit. Tolerance seems equally unstable, equally fleeting. It either collapses back into intolerance or swiftly moves to acceptance or at least indifference. In the *Republic,* Socrates says of opinion that it rolls around between ignorance and knowledge, being neither one nor the other and impossible to pin down. Tolerance seems like that. We simply cannot seem to make it stand still long enough to pin it down.

Nor does everyone accept that tolerance is a good thing, and certainly not that it should be elevated to the status of a virtue, that is, as a morally desirable character trait. Some think that tolerance either requires or leads us to become skeptics, doubters, or indifferent spectators to our own lives. Someone who did not suffer from doubt was the French priest, then bishop, Jacques Bossuet (1627–1704). In 1598, the Edict of Nantes granted Protestants in France the right to worship openly. When it was revoked in 1685, Protestant pastors were forced to renounce their calling or face severe punishment, including death. Bossuet gave a classic defense of intolerance in threatening the Protestant clergy: "I have the right to persecute you," he said, "because I am right and you are wrong."[6] There is no lack of certainty or indifference here, and that, some critics say, is a good thing, for tolerance, they argue eats away at the very things that give our lives meaning and substance. If tolerance is a good at all, it pertains only to the small, insignificant things in life. It will otherwise sap the strength of our deepest convictions.

Others reject tolerance because it does not go far enough. It is a half measure for the powerful and arrogant, who preach tolerance provided that they—and they alone—decide who and what to tolerate. What we need to do, these critics say, is move beyond tolerance and toleration to respect and positive appreciation of deep differences, to recognize and celebrate difference. For this to happen, however, we will have to move beyond the pretensions of contemporary liberal thought with its emphasis on individualism, rights, means–end rationality, and selves emptied of all meaning but that which they can provide on their own. We must move to a new, perhaps postmodern, sensibility.

If tolerance is not universally celebrated as a virtue or attitude, neither is toleration universally recommended as an act or practice. If we truly believe that our own way of life is best, why should we tolerate—that is, put up with—inferior, maybe corrupt, ways? Champions of toleration themselves do not show forbearance to absolutely everything. They, too, draw lines. They just draw them at different places. The language of tolerance and toleration, critics conclude, simply masks different judgments about where those lines should be drawn.

This is an essay in social and political philosophy. I will, therefore, largely ignore questions of tolerance arising in interpersonal relations. I will occasionally use examples drawn from this sphere because of their familiarity. Clearly, this is possible only if we deploy the notions of tolerance and intolerance in similar ways. I believe that we do. Nor is this surprising, for interpersonal moral reflection and social and political reflections are not radically discontinuous, though there are important differences of focus and emphasis. Justice and rights generally figure less prominently in interpersonal affairs than in social and political ones, while boorish or insensitive behavior figure less importantly in social and political affairs than in interpersonal ones.

This is not to say that considerations in one sphere are absent from the other. In our personal relations, we are often as deeply concerned about the social and political attitudes of people we know well as we are of their actions. We may find it difficult, for instance, to sustain a friendship with someone whom we know harbors bigoted thoughts or expresses racial antipathy even if he never otherwise *acts* on his thoughts and antipathy. Politically speaking, this may be largely (though not completely) beneath notice; in our personal interactions, it looms large.

Philosophers only interpret the world, Marx famously says, adding that the point is to change it. That philosophers only interpret the world means no more than that they are doing their job. They are ill-equipped to do more and are likely to make a mess of things when they try. Gaining a better philosophical understanding of appeals to tolerance may help us understand both the possibilities and the limits of intelligent change.

Philosophers introduce novel terms or ideas into public discourse at their peril; usually, they work with words, phrases, and notions already in use. They shape and refine existing currency, both old and new, and return them brightly polished to contemporary service as if freshly minted. This does not mean that philosophers simply tidy up ordinary language. They also systematically explore not only the linguistic conditions for a term's application but also its connections with related concepts. The aim is not dictionary making but conceptual clarification and understanding. Sometimes a philosopher can transform our understanding of the meaning, implications, and justifications for ready-at-hand terms. This might mean taking a word or phrase already in use and giving it a more central place in our thinking. Or it might mean reshaping language and so what we think. Words then take on new meaning and importance.

Most words in ordinary language (or even learned discourse, such as medieval Latin) do not have a precise sense, unless someone deliberately assigns one. Many words, especially those that do not name common objects (and even here the exceptions abound), are marked by ambiguity and vagueness, at least until they are used in a specific context. This is both understandable and unproblematic. Words are tools. We do things with them. Provided that they get the job done, we are not always too fussy about giving them a precise sense. Just as we use screwdrivers as levers and as punches, so we use ordinary words in a variety of ways, usually connected but often straying from their original employment. If it matters, we can always assign a word or phrase an exact sense, as we do in science, mathematics, and certain phrases in legal contracts. Often, however, it does not matter, and we get on perfectly well without precise definitions.

Context often removes ambiguity and vagueness. When engineers discuss "tolerances" of a particular fitting, for instance, we are not thrown into hopeless confusion. This example illustrates an important point, for in a certain context, a word that might be vague or generally ambiguous can have a precise meaning. The danger lies only in thinking that it always has the same precise sense in all contexts. We need to remind ourselves, moreover, that we simply do not always need precision. Everyone can distinguish day from night and dusk from both, but is there unanimity about when dusk begins and ends? And how, precisely, does dusk differ from twilight? Everything just said is true of the word "tolerance." As we will see in chapter 6, it has been around a long time.

NOTES

1. I will distinguish these terms more finely in chapter 3. Usually, however, they can be used interchangeably because the context makes clear which is meant.

2. "Groups" is not a happy word choice. I use it to refer to varied social groupings, such as families, communities, ethnic groups, castes, religions, political parties, pressure groups, unions, and the state. It would be tedious to provide this list, or portions of it, repeatedly. A group, incidentally, need not be institutionalized, as will be discussed later.

3. See the collection of essays in David Heyd, ed., *Toleration: An Elusive Virtue* (Princeton, N.J.: Princeton University Press, 1996).

4. John Horton, "Toleration as a Virtue," in *Toleration,* ed. Heyd, 28–43.

5. Bernard Williams, "Toleration: An Impossible Virtue?" in *Toleration,* ed. Heyd, 18–27.

6. Quoted in Susan Mendus, *Toleration and the Limits of Liberalism* (Atlantic Highlands, N.J.: Humanities Press International, 1989), 7.

Chapter 2

Puzzles and Paradoxes of Tolerance

TOLERATION AS AN IMPOSSIBLE VIRTUE

The basic dilemma of toleration, Bernard Williams contends, is that we need it only for the intolerable.[1] This is no mere paradox: It is an outright impossibility. If something is intolerable, then we should not tolerate it. Yet tolerance, Williams contends, calls for just that. The impossibility arises because of contradictory premises. If tolerant practices are defensible, it is only because they further or protect some substantive good. Specifically, Williams argues, it must be the good of *individual autonomy*. Williams interprets autonomy in its Kantian form, a form that locates man's glory and burden in his power as a freely willing, rational being. What elevates man above the animals, according to Kant, is our freedom to act from laws that we legislate for ourselves. Because these laws flow from our rationality, however, they will be the same for every free, rational being. Because of our animality, however, we will often be tempted to violate them, especially when it serves our selfish, private ends to do so. Duty requires us nonetheless to obey the laws we have willed for ourselves: We never escape our autonomy.

But whether we identify the good as autonomy or some other value, we know that whatever value we adopt, it is contestable or, rather, actually contested and rejected by some, often many. In contesting autonomy (or any substitute) as a prime value, toleration will also be contested, for its fate is linked to whatever has prime value. "The practice of toleration," Williams concludes, "cannot be based on a value such as individual autonomy and also hope to escape from substantive disagreements about the good. . . . This really is a contradiction."[2]

Williams observes that toleration exists both as a *practice* and as an *attitude*. A university, for instance, could have the practice of tolerating ethnic diversity, even if few in the university were particularly tolerant in attitude. If the practice of toleration involves contradictions, Williams believes, the attitude fares even worse, for it relies on a special, Kantian demand that "one should rise not only above

9

one's own desires but above one's desires to secure the fullest expression of one's own values."[3] This really is an impossible demand. If this is the price of being tolerant, the cost is outrageously high. Why should Jill abandon the fullest expression of her own values just to tolerate Jack's giving expression to his? Tolerance starts to look not just impossible but self-abnegating. It seems to demand that we turn ourselves into doormats.

In demanding tolerance, Williams continues, we ask people to lose one thing but keep something else. Specifically, we ask that people lose their desire to suppress or drive out detested beliefs. They are said to be able to keep (in exchange?) their own beliefs—beliefs that gave them the desire now to be suppressed in the first place. As Williams notes, "There is a tension here between one's own commitments and the acceptance that other people may have other, perhaps quite distasteful commitments: the tension that is typical of toleration, and which makes it so difficult."[4] And risky, he might have added, for although tolerance is supposed to be based on more than skepticism and indifference, it may lead to this and so weaken one's own commitments.

Williams does grant a weak, transitional defense of the practice (but not the attitude or virtue) of toleration in terms of *skepticism, indifference, the "broad church" view,* and *Hobbesian equilibrium.* After the wars of religion in the sixteenth and seventeenth centuries, Williams writes, some became skeptical that any denomination embodied God's truth. Although only a few became agnostics or atheists, many doubted whether the "truths" proclaimed by each denomination were knowable. Since no one could know which, if any, of the denominations on offer had the truth, it was only reasonable to urge everyone to adopt a tolerant stance to all (Protestant) denominations. Others developed what Williams calls the "broad church view." According to this view, the wars of religion forcefully taught that God does not mind how people worship or precisely which creed they believe. God requires only that people worship in good faith and within certain broad (again, Protestant) limits. This courtesy was later extended to Catholics and eventually to non-Christians, too.

About other subjects, and occasionally religion as well, many people "slide toward indifference."[5] That is, they no longer care, for example, about the religious affiliations or gender orientations of their neighbors. Indifference, however, is not tolerance. As Williams points out, if I do not care what other people eat, I do not act tolerantly by not interfering in their lives. I just do not care. The question of "allowing" them to eat what they wish does not even arise.

We need a tolerant attitude only to give us the resolve not to lash out at those with whom we are in deep disagreement. As we become increasingly indifferent to anything but what happens in our own small world, Williams suggests, occasions for toleration arise less and less often. The image he conjures up as we finish his essay is that of the stereotypical rug merchant in a Middle Eastern bazaar—utterly indifferent to the strange goings-on of everyone around him— provided only that he can carry on his business without too much nuisance.

Hobbesian equilibrium is nothing more than a modus vivendi, a simulacrum of toleration. Protestants and Catholics (and Protestants and Protestants) might once have intensely desired to vanquish each other. After exhausting themselves in endless bloodshed, however, they eventually settled instead for peaceful coexistence. It was the best deal either side could get. This story—not always with this happy ending—recurs around the world (e.g., Northern Ireland, Rwanda, Cyprus, and Israel). Williams regards such Hobbesian equilibria as one way of practicing toleration. It is, however, unprincipled (in, as it were, a good sense) and/but does not manifest a tolerant attitude.

Toleration as a modus vivendi or Hobbesian equilibrium, then, recommends itself as a messy, unprincipled but often effective way to keep hostile individuals and groups from each other's throats. After he was filmed being beaten up by the Los Angeles police and after several days of race riots, Rodney King appeared on television to plead, "Can't we just get along?" The thought here is not that we respect or care for each other but simply that we stop brutalizing attacks. The modus vivendi argument for tolerance appears to rob tolerance of its justification as a separate virtue. It comes to look less like a virtue and more like an invisible substitute for razor wire. We will return to this defense of toleration in chapter 7 when we examine the views of Michael Walzer.

These considerations, then, offer a sort of justification of toleration, but only as a practice, and even then these defenses are highly attenuated. These defenses vary with shifting knowledge, interest, and power. It is not surprising, therefore, that it is so difficult—even impossible—to arrive at a satisfactory, full-blown defense of toleration as a practice or virtue. Tolerance, Williams speculates, is likely to end in history's rubbish bin, for as modernity's principal creation—the international commercial society—washes over the world, skepticism will rule, not only about religion but about all claims to "exclusivity" that cause great harm—and where not skepticism, indifference. Still, in the interim, Williams concedes, tolerant practices have a place, for despite their "awkwardness," they will remain important if we are to live peacefully with each other. In that limited degree, the practice is possible. We will, however, have to abandon any grand Kantian justification for the inculcation of tolerance as a virtue. For Williams, however, this loss is not to be regretted but welcomed.[6]

TOLERATION AS PARADOXICAL

Susan Mendus, whose many thoughtful writings on tolerance have informed this study, provides one statement of toleration's paradox:

> [N]ormally we count toleration as a virtue in individuals and a duty in societies. However, where toleration is based on moral disapproval [as opposed to mere dislike], it implies that the thing tolerated is wrong and ought not to exist. The question which then arises is why . . . it should be thought good to tolerate.[7]

The paradox arises because we appear to believe both that we have conclusively good reasons *against* tolerating a given attitude, belief, action, practice, person, or way of life—and equally compelling reasons *for* doing so. This is not because the reasons are equally balanced, at least not at the same level of reasoning. Instead, we are confident that we are right and they are wrong, but that for reasons of a different kind we should let them alone. This seems highly paradoxical, even irrational, and, a critic might add, clearly wicked, for if we are confident in our reasons, why should we tolerate anything that opposes our beliefs, attitudes, or practices? Why allow people to do that or believe that which we know is hideously wrong or deeply misguided? Is not this the paradoxical position of tolerating the intolerable, the "basic problem" of tolerance identified by Williams?

In response to this paradox, some have deliberately rejected toleration as either attitude or practice. We have already cited Bishop Bossuet's vivid remark that "I have the right to persecute you because I am right and you are wrong." This unequivocally avoids the paradox, but in a way that almost everyone would find objectionable. The trick will be to unravel the paradox so that those like Bossuet can confidently affirm their faith and moral commitments without feeling the need to act intolerantly toward those with whom they are profoundly at odds.

There is a further paradox. What is the difference, in practice, between *tolerating* the intolerable—which we seem to be asking Bossuet to do—and *accepting* it? Is not demanding that Bossuet tolerate Protestants tantamount to demanding that, as a matter of public acknowledgment, he must also accept their beliefs, ways of worship, and so on? Not "accept" in the sense of converting to Protestantism but "accept" in the sense of admitting that Protestantism is either as good as or nearly as good as Catholicism. We often do accept differences in this sense. One person, say, firmly believes that the best of classical music is superior to the best of jazz yet fully accepts that jazz is good.

May we force Bossuet to take this stance to Protestantism? But then, as far as outward behavior goes, it will look to all the world as if he accepts that Catholicism and Protestantism are equally good. Surely this places him in an untenable position. But why stop here? If we wish to ensure that French Protestants are truly tolerated, why even allow Bossuet to *voice* his objections? After all, if thought is father to the deed, then surely expressing one's thoughts might father many intolerant deeds, at least to the extent that he persuades others. Were it possible— and maybe with modern techniques of "reeducation" it now is—would it not be best to stop Bossuet from harboring his bigoted thoughts in the first place? But now tolerance, which presents itself as the mildest of demands, seems to take a sinister turn—a turn to oppression of those who think in nonprescribed ways. And what is this, paradoxically, but intolerance?

Yet another puzzling paradox about tolerance is this. No one can (or should) tolerate *everything*. Advocates of toleration always have in mind toleration of *this,* not toleration of *that.* Today many people, for example, call for tolerance to homosexuals and homosexual conduct. But this is disingenuous, say critics, for in their heart of hearts, these same people do not believe that there is anything whatever wrong with homosexuality. Were they honest, therefore, they would call for acceptance, not tolerance. Advocates of toleration, in short, simply wish to impose their own tastes and values on everyone else under the guise of tolerance. They do so because they know they cannot convince most people that homosexuality, say, is a good way to live. Realizing this, they fall back on toleration. In their own eyes, however, it is only as a second-best, stopgap position. They will advocate toleration until "bigots" change their minds, give up, become indifferent, or die out.

This disingenuousness, not to say hypocrisy, is easily shown, for those who proudly call themselves tolerant do not take kindly to admonitions that *they* show the same tolerance to what others accept but that they strongly believe to be unjustifiable. In England, for instance, many deplore fox hunting. Others find it not only acceptable but also an invigorating, character-building sport. For opponents of fox hunting, to be told to "show some tolerance" would outrage them. Because of its cruelty, opponents cannot tolerate fox hunting. They will not, however, allow a similar argument to be used by opponents of homosexuality, namely, that because of its perverted nature or sinfulness, it ought not be tolerated. So it seems that advocates of toleration are in the disreputable position of holding that *others* should willingly tolerate what they approve but that they need not return the favor. Surely this is as incoherent, arrogant, and unreflective.

This type of example shows, furthermore, that tolerance is not doing any real work. The work that tolerance pretends to do is done offstage, out of sight, by other considerations. It is done when we make our original moral judgments about the relative merits of fox hunting, homosexuality, smoking in public places, religious or moral belief, and even whole ways of life. Once our judgments are firmly arrived at, tolerance appears on stage to urge forbearance by those (in its eyes) too bigoted or blind to see the truth of the tolerator's own views. Or perhaps we should say that tolerance does not do any *honest* work. It does indeed do real work. This is the work of disguising the true views of those that urge toleration; namely, we should replace tolerance with indifference or acceptance.

If we are honest, therefore, we will see that tolerance is neither an attitude nor a virtue we should acquire, nor is it always desirable as a practice. Instead, we must recognize that, at best, tolerant practices are a second-best accommodation we make with those who—in our eyes—stubbornly or blindly refuse to see that there is nothing wrong with what we demand that they tolerate. Perhaps the object of toleration is not *ideal* (even by our own lights) but clearly well within the domain of acceptability, such that refusal to tolerate manifests intolerance. As a modus vivendi, or unprincipled accommodation, then, toleration gets some support, but not as a core moral virtue. And this was just the point made by Bernard Williams.

Tolerance might be a virtue if we adopt the outlook that none of our commitments can (or should) run deeply, save maybe to family and friends. Our commitments, in this view, are best understood as growing out of subjective preferences, not unlike our preferences for various foods. Just as Jack prefers his vegetables stir-fried and Jill boiled, so Jack prefers his religion Roman Catholic and Jill Hindu. Of course, the comparison need not be this simplistic. For example, religious preferences are typically bound up with a whole way of life and not as easily changed as our culinary predilections. It is much harder for a Catholic to develop a taste for Hinduism than to develop a taste for curry. Sometimes, of course, food preferences are integral to one's religion. For an observant Jew to develop a taste for pork involves far more than merely finding it tasty. Subjectivism itself can be more sophisticated than these brief remarks suggest. Philosophers in the past fifty years have been adept at elaborating and defending various forms of "noncognitivism" in ethical theory. John Mackie[8] and Simon Blackburn,[9] for example, hold that we "project" or "spread" our subjective feelings and attitudes onto the world—and then read them back off, as if they were there. Those seeing the tape of Rodney King's beating, for example, felt revulsion. They then "spread" or "projected" that revulsion onto the beating. The revulsion thus became attached to the beating. In describing it, then, we say that *the beating itself* was revolting. Since people by and large have similar responses to the same event—at least within the same moral community and when they agree on the "facts"—we can all agree that the beating of Rodney King was intolerable. Yet if we reflect *philosophically* on what we are doing, we see that we are, in the end, just projecting or spreading our own subjective responses onto the world. It is as if the world exists in black and white, but our moral community generally sees the world through rose-colored glasses. We attribute the tint to the world, not to us.

The caveat "in our moral community" is important, for different moral (religious and so on) communities may be equipped with spectacles of many different tints. Consequently, they project significantly different colors onto the same black-and-white world. Philosophical sophistication may save us from coming to blows over our disputed judgments about the (moral) colors of the world. We need only to point out to each other the tints of our respective spectacles. Once we accept projectivism (or any other form of emotivism or subjectivism, for that matter), we will realize how misguided it is to have fierce disputes over what is, in the end, just a clash of subjectively held attitudes or perspectives. We need not change our particular judgments of right and wrong, good and bad, beautiful and ugly, but we will realize that they rest on shifting sands.

If we accept this understanding of how our deepest values are grounded, it then seems puzzling why we need tolerance, for we do not typically tolerate differences that grow out of subjective preferences. We simply accept that we have different preferences; what is there to tolerate? Just as it seems irrational to get upset about, let alone oppress, those whose taste in food and music differs from ours, so it would seem irrational to become enraged because others do not share our preferences in religion, the borders of our ancestral homeland, or sexual proclivities. The reply is that many subjectively based preferences are quite unlike those we have regarding food or music. Some, like those regarding religion, we hold with great passion and commitment. Since we know historically that such passionate commitments can spill over into persecution of those who do not share the same religious outlook, tolerance is important. One might add, however, that even when held strongly, such passionate commitments are more like our devotion to the home team. We will recognize, after a little reflection, that—however much we want our team to win—there are fans of other teams with equal but opposite loyalties. "Fans," after all, is short for "fanatics." Because we know that our fanaticism grows out of nothing more than deep-seated subjective responses that we spread onto the object of our passion, it seems crazy to attack other fans who have the same passion, except for a different team. Now, if everyone recognized this, we would not need toleration. We need it only because we cannot get everyone to grasp this simple truth.

The strength of our commitments, on this view, has little to do with their rational grounding. To talk about "depth of conviction," for instance, is simply a euphemism for strength of commitment. All commitments float near the surface of subjectively held attitudes. I can explain why I root for the home team—for example, I immerse myself in news about it, avidly follow its fortunes, grew up with it, lived with it, attended games with my father as a child, and so on—but I would not even pretend that it is *wrong* for you to be equally devoted to your team. Anyone who does simply does not understand what it is to be a fanatical supporter of the home team.

Or of any other commitments, for, the subjectivist argues, what has just been said extends to *all* our most valued commitments: to religion, morality, tribe, clan, ethnicity, country, family, and friends. I have my religion (morality, country, and so on), and you have yours. It is only sensible, therefore, that we interact civilly. There is no more way for me to convince you that my religion is superior to yours than that you could convince me that your team is superior to mine. You will support your religion (country and so on) as I will mine. And the explanation will be much the same. We each immerse ourselves in our religion, grew up with it, and so on. The only reasonable thing for us to do when we confront each other on the soccer pitch or religious (national and so on) forum is, perhaps wryly, recognize each other's respective subjectively based loyalties. Only those who fail to see the subjective bases of their commitments need to practice toleration.

Strictly speaking, even this does not follow, for suppose it is part of the story of my "home" religion or nation to believe that it has a "manifest destiny." Will not my strongly held commitments, then, provide me with reasons to dominate those whose subjective responses clash with mine? Of course, some "home" commitments might be more latitudinarian. We might have been brought up with something like the broad church view. And then we might argue that there would be less strife and cruelty in the world if we acted tolerantly to others. That may be true, but it cannot be anything more, in the end, than the subjective stance some people find congenial and others do not. If any subjectivist claims that tolerance is something *everyone* of whatever persuasion should adopt, then he would be unjustifiably privileging tolerance by claiming (contrary to his avowed position) that it has some transsubjective basis. But if toleration does have an objective basis, then it would be exceedingly odd if it were the *only* one that did. And then we would be back in the fix that subjectivism was supposed to dissolve in the first place.

If, on the other hand, *everything* we cherish rests, in the end, on mere subjective preference, then so too does a cherished commitment to toleration. Why should that be any different? And just as there may be an explanation but no justification for any of our other commitments, so there might be an explanation but no justification for our commitment to toleration. You might be tolerant because you were raised that way; I might be intolerant because I was raised differently or have an "authoritarian personality." Whatever the explanation, you are in no position *justifiably* to demand that I become more tolerant. You may *make* the demand (e.g., because you were brought up to do so), but my resistance would be equally explicable. You may even be in a position of power or influence to bring it about that I become more tolerant. But *should* I be more tolerant? Well, *should* I root for your home team? Neither one of us is *entitled* or *justified* to the loves and loyalties we have. I am prepared to die for my cause, you for yours, and that's an end to it. They are simply facts about us that need to be *explained.* If it is a fact about us that we tend to be intolerant of difference, then that is without need or possibility of justification. To invoke toleration here would be utterly gratuitous.

The support tolerance draws from subjectivism, therefore, turns out to be shaky indeed. Yet matters are worse when we look at them from the point of view of those who do believe that their strong commitments are nonsubjectively grounded, those like Bossuet. The subjectivist, a defender of Bossuet might say, is deeply *attached* to his team, religion, and so on, but attachment by itself provides no compelling reason to tolerate this or that attachment. Presumably, Bossuet did not question the attachments or commitments as such of French Protestants. Instead, he fervently believed that they rested on false and sinful foundations, foundations that posed a threat to what he considered the only true religion.

But now the problem is this. If we move away from subjective attachments and grant that some commitments can be deeply *grounded* (and not merely *explained*), have we not squeezed toleration out of the picture in another way? Where we believe our commitments are correctly grounded, it will be unjustified to tolerate opposed, falsely grounded commitments. Contemporary scientists, for instance, do what they can to keep the teaching of creation science out of the school curriculum. Does that make them intolerant? Their firm opposition is grounded in what they take to be the objectively based discoveries of natural science. Their antagonism to creation science, they contend, is neither a matter of opinion nor flowing from subjective preferences. They base it on hard fact, they argue, and highly confirmed theory. To allow creation science to be taught in the schools, therefore, is intolerable. So, it is wrong to accuse them of intolerance just because they will not tolerate the intolerable. If there is a difference between contemporary scientists and Bossuet, it seems to be only that secular westerners are far more inclined to think that science, not religion, is the objective source of knowledge. The structure of the argument, however, is identical. If we think that Bossuet was unjustified in grounding his opposition in the claim that "I am right and you are wrong," then it seems not only fair but also logical that we say the same of scientists who lobby to prevent the teaching of creation science in schools.

So we have the following paradox. If we adopt some version of subjectivism, we may be able to defend toleration as unprincipled yet necessary—unprincipled because there is no compelling reason everyone should be tolerant, necessary (only) because too many people do not see that subjectivism is the only philosophically defensible position. Subjectively grounded attachments might lead us to tolerant policies, but only if that is one of our attachments or if we do not have the stomach to wage all-out war to see that our attachments triumph. If we adopt some form of objectivism, we may be able to provide principled justifications of our commitments but not of our commitment to toleration, for our commitment to toleration seems to clash with our commitment to the truth. Deeply grounded commitments will, it seems, *necessarily* exclude competing commitments because they are false. Neither subjectivism nor objectivism, therefore, seems to offer a promising defense of tolerance.

TOLERATION AS UNSTABLE

The paradoxes, maybe the impossibility, of tolerance explains why so many find tolerance inherently unstable, for it appears to occupy a no-man's-land between willingness to persecute and complete acceptance, or at least utter indifference. If not Bossuet himself, one can imagine many French Catholics moving quickly from Bossuet's own position of intolerance to not caring much whether anyone is Catholic or Protestant, for there seems to be no natural stopping point on the scale that moves from intolerance to complete indifference. Williams's phrase "sliding into indifference" captures this point nicely. We find ourselves on a slippery slope indeed when adopting either tolerant practices or attitudes.

It is as if we unilaterally disarm once we become tolerant. It is simply not realistic, the critic charges, to believe that we can maintain our own commitments in the face of widespread departures from them. Either we will ourselves become accepting or indifferent—or retreat to the psychological security of intolerance.

TOLERANCE AS UNDESIRABLE

This is closely connected with the contention that tolerance—so far from being a virtue—is a vice foisted on the world by hegemonic liberalism. The agenda, not always hidden, of those advocating greater tolerance is nothing more than making the world safe for liberalism. If we claim to know that our beliefs are true, attitudes sound, and our way of life best, why should we tolerate those that we sincerely believe, that we *know,* are deeply mistaken—maybe even corrupt and depraved? By advocating tolerance, the argument continues, we are being urged to adopt a generally skeptical stance, to doubt our deepest convictions.

If proponents of toleration can get us to doubt the truth of what we believe or the soundness of our practices, they will succeed in turning us into timid, tentative believers. This will have the desired effect of getting us to tolerate that which we previously abominated. How can we not tolerate divergent beliefs or practices when we have no confidence in our own? Gradually, the critic continues, we will lose confidence even in ourselves. This is something other than skepticism or indifference. It is the unhappy state where doubt will so fill us that a generalized tolerance will become our only refuge. Sowing the seeds of doubt is an effective way of turning us into a society of (self-)Doubting Thomases. As we come to lack confidence in our own judgments about the worthiness of this or that, it will only be natural for us to let all contenders struggle for recognition and acceptance. We surely would not be in any position to impose our doubt-plagued judgments on anyone else. Although doubt itself is not an argument for tolerance, it is likely to slide not only into indifference but diffidence.

Once we become tolerant—even if we initially hold onto our own commitments—it will not take long before the acid of skepticism and doubt eats away at our confidence. We will lose that which now gives our lives meaning and substance. Instead, we will become jaded and rootless, without a sense that our lives any longer have a center. Tolerance, the argument continues, is just a genteel way for liberals to undermine the solidarity that comes with utter and complete commitment to one's religion, ethnic community, nation, and so on. Tolerance is fine for liberals, the critic continues, since they seem to celebrate their distance from any deep commitments. Liberals, however, have no right to foist it on the rest of us.

Some object to tolerance for other reasons. No one likes being tolerated; most resent it. To be tolerated is to be an object of contempt, condescension, or patronizing suffocation. Jews, for example, rightly resent being tolerated. What they demand is not tolerance but full acceptance. The alleged virtue of tolerance encourages tolerators to indulge a groundless, smug complacency celebrating their own superiority. While it is surely better to be tolerated than persecuted, at least persecutors regard those whom they persecute as *worth* persecuting. The tolerant often like to present themselves as showing great forbearance and largeness of soul by not letting on how offensive, childlike, or otherwise deficient they find the objects of their toleration. What is worse, their position as tolerators—which is solely because of their power—is so often completely unearned. It is the self-proclaimed prerogative of the arrogantly powerful.

Some charge that toleration is little more than a genteel way for "the establishment"—especially the *liberal* establishment—to repress and exclude those on the fringes of "acceptable" society. They are not permitted to participate as full equals in the give-and-take of everyday politics but must hope that they will be granted the small mercy of toleration. Today we associate this charge with the right, but it comes from the left as well, as we will see in chapter 9.

I will address these concerns later. Here I will remark only that these criticisms of "pure tolerance" raise the type of problems we can expect any *defense* of tolerance will have to confront. Given that tolerance of absolutely everything is out of the question, how do we judge what deserves the protective umbrella of toleration and what does not? If knowledge is not to be had—at least not in enough hard cases to matter—then how and where will we draw the line between the tolerable and the intolerable?

MULTICULTURAL CRITICISMS OF TOLERANCE

Multiculturalists raise a different criticism. Tolerance not only appears arrogant but is so, for it assumes that one group in a society—namely, the one that has so far held power and shaped the broader culture—is entitled to pass judgment on "lesser" groups. Conversations about toleration are held by and for those controlling the society: Can we, they ask, tolerate this lesser group, religion, dissident, or cultural expression—or does it pose too great a threat to our hegemony? Advocates of tolerance argue that we do not have to worry. Either there is no real threat to our continued control of cultural forms or the threat is better handled through a regime of toleration. Opponents disagree. This disagreement, however, is no more than an intense family dispute, for neither party to the disagreement will countenance for a moment the possibility that they, collectively, should lose their privileged position within their society to shape it to their liking.

Multiculturalists respond by saying that to avoid such arrogance we must move "beyond tolerance," not in the sense of accepting what we disapprove but in a deeper, richer way. This way is not always evident, but the main outlines are clear enough. Neither the practice of toleration nor the tolerant attitudes go far enough, argue some, because they self-satisfiedly settle for putting up with so-called inferior beliefs, religions, people, and so on. No one, we have seen, relishes being tolerated. Not only does anyone not like being "put up with," but those taking pride in their generous forbearance have themselves no legitimate claim to their self-awarded superiority. Once we recognize, as multiculturalists would have us do, that no culture has the truth, or that no culture has the whole truth, or that cultures express the truth in extraordinarily different ways, we will come to respect all cultures. And the same holds for other differences (e.g., sexual orientation and ethnic identity).

This departs from Williams's "broad church" view insofar as it urges more than simple tolerance. Part of respecting difference, the multiculturalist continues, is both to see it as our equal and to see in it values missing from what we treasure. We will see that humanity can share a common core while developing in ways that will enrich our own lives, if only we are open-minded. When we see how much good can be found in different languages, belief systems, and folkways and aesthetic, religious, and moral sensibilities, we will celebrate these differences and become grateful that they exist alongside and mingle with our own.

The move from tolerance to respect to celebration may be imperceptible, but it is real and powerful. We need only to free ourselves from the "grand narratives of the Enlightenment"[10] that sees the story of man as the triumph of scientific reason over superstition, emotion, and religion. The condescension that tolerance implies rests on a modern self-image of the superiority of scientific, economic rationality. We must move beyond tolerance, beyond modernity's pretensions.

This movement of thought and attitude will show up in how we teach. No longer, for instance, will we teach our children to tolerate the curious ways of the Amish or the odd appearance of Hasidic Jews. We will teach them to respect them as living equally good lives, lives that may be superior to ours in certain respects and surely lives from which we can learn. To do this, we will have to learn about them, and then (we can hope) we will celebrate the fact that we live in the same world as they. We will learn their customs, sing their songs, and maybe (if they permit us to do so) attend their religious services. This will not be mere cultural tourism because they will ask us to respect and celebrate their ways of life, to take delight in the fact that we live in such a richly variegated world, even take part in their folkways. Doors will open so that members of other cultures can fully participate in our common public life. More important, representatives of every culture will be positively encouraged to participate in politics, business, higher education, and other institutions that shape our society.

Not every culture, however, will find itself respected and celebrated, for some cultures, or at least subcultures, may be extraordinarily cruel or nasty. Or, more likely, though not especially cruel, they may not themselves celebrate, respect, or even tolerate cultural differences. At the very least, they would like to be left alone; at the most, they would like themselves to control the society of which they are a minority. And therein lies a recurring paradox: Must we respect or celebrate intolerant cultures? If we do, then it seems that we are betraying our commitment to living in a multicultural world; if we do not, then it seems that we are being intolerant. This might arise pointedly in a teaching situation. Is a school justified, for example, in obliging its students to respect, appreciate, and celebrate that which the students are taught at home and church is an abomination in the sight of God? This looks precisely like the criticism leveled against those whom multiculturalists purposed to move beyond, namely, the criticism that they, too, are only too willing to impose their ideological stance on everyone else.

CONCLUSION

Since my aim is to clarify, explain, and defend tolerance as virtue and practice, I must show that it is not as elusive as alleged. More than that, I must show that tolerance is not impossible, irredeemably paradoxical, or undesirable. Given recent doubts and puzzles, this will not be easy, especially because the doubts and criticisms arise from so many sides and take so many forms. To succeed, we must journey into the thickets of language, moral reflection, and political philosophy.

NOTES

1. Bernard Williams, "Toleration: An Impossible Virtue?" in *Toleration: An Elusive Virtue*, ed. David Heyd (Princeton, N.J.: Princeton University Press, 1997), 18.

2. Williams, "Toleration," in *Toleration*, ed. Heyd, 24–25.

3. Williams, "Toleration," in *Toleration*, ed. Heyd, 26.

4. Williams, "Toleration," in *Toleration*, ed. Heyd, 19–20.

5. Williams, "Toleration," in *Toleration*, ed. Heyd, 21.

6. For a blistering attack on Kantian morality, see Bernard Williams, *Ethics and the Limits of Philosophy* (Cambridge, Mass.: Harvard University Press, 1985).

7. Susan Mendus, *Toleration and the Limits of Liberalism* (London: Macmillan, 1989), 18–19.

8. John Mackie, *Ethics: Inventing Right and Wrong* (New York: Penguin Books, 1991).

9. Simon Blackburn, *Spreading the Word: Groundings in the Philosophy of Language* (Oxford: Oxford University Press, 1984).

10. Alasdair MacIntyre is the inspiration for much of the talk about "narratives" and "the Enlightenment Project," though he himself has not embraced the more exuberant forms of multiculturalism, let alone postmodernism. See Alasdair MacIntyre, *After Virtue*, 2nd ed. (Notre Dame, Ind.: University of Notre Dame Press, 1984); *Whose Justice? Which Rationality?* (Notre Dame, Ind.: University of Notre Dame Press, 1988); and *Three Rival Versions of Moral Inquiry: Encyclopaedia, Genealogy, and Tradition* (Notre Dame, Ind.: University of Notre Dame Press, 1990).

Chapter 3

Shades of Tolerance

Bernard Williams holds that tolerance is an impossible virtue because we are required to tolerate the intolerable. Yet he acknowledges that the practice of toleration will remain necessary for the indefinite future:

> [T]he practice of toleration has to be sustained not so much by a pure principle resting on a value of autonomy as by a wider and more mixed range of resources. Those resources include an active skepticism against fanaticism and the pretensions of its advocates; conviction about the manifest evils of toleration's absence; and, quite certainly, power, to provide Hobbesian reminders to the more extreme groups that they will have to settle for coexistence.[1]

Toleration is indeed indispensable for any decent society—or at least for societies encompassing deeply divergent ways of life. Highly homogeneous societies, which are increasingly rare, may be able to dispense with tolerance or greatly reduce its centrality. Most of the world cannot. Toleration is indispensable, especially if we live in pluralist, multicultural societies seeking to be free of oppression, violence, and indignities.

DISTINGUISHING TOLERANCE FROM TOLERATION

Williams doubts, however, whether we need to cultivate tolerance as a virtue. So far, "tolerance" and "toleration" have been used interchangeably, and for the most part it does not matter. Still, there is a grammatical point to be made differentiating them that yields one small and one larger philosophical point: "Toleration" is transitive. That is, it requires an object. If I tolerate something, it always makes sense to ask what it is that I tolerate. The emphasis is on what is tolerated. Knowing what is tolerated, however, tells us little about underlying attitudes. In particular,

23

it tells us nothing about why or whether someone regards tolerating what he does as virtuous or merely the least of several possible evils.

"Tolerance," on the other hand, may be either transitive or intransitive. Fotion and Elfstrom[2] point out that when we say that someone is tolerant, we may be saying either that one has a particular attitude to what one tolerates or that one has a certain character trait; that is, that one is a tolerant person. Building on this distinction, Fotion and Elfstrom go on to say, "Tolerating is the combination of a negative attitude to something with the restraint from acting in accordance with this attitude."[3] As "tolerance" refers mainly to one's attitude or character trait, however, one can still possess the attitude or trait even if one does (or does not) occasionally act as an intolerant person would.

Similarly, persons, institutions, or societies can tolerate this or that without it being true that they are tolerant. A person can espouse a regime of toleration without being especially tolerant. More generally, people may grudgingly put up with many things without us being in the least tempted to describe them as tolerant. We would be obliged to say of such people only that they tolerated this or that, not that they were tolerant. The same is true of institutions and whole societies. For example, to the extent that the medieval church tolerated Jews, it does not follow from that fact alone that we can characterize the church as tolerant, for to be tolerant, the church's response would have had to have been of a certain sort, to have exhibited a certain set of attitudes and dispositions to Jews.

The small philosophical moral of the story is this: Toleration points to what is (or is not) tolerated; tolerance points primarily to one's attitude or character trait in tolerating. Further, as a character trait, someone who is tolerant (or intolerant) tends to exhibit that attitude or character trait to many things. Optimism provides a useful analogy. Optimists tend to look on the bright side of many things; pessimists do not, even though on rare occasions pessimists may be optimistic and optimists pessimistic. So, too, with the virtues. Generous people typically act generously, though not always, and ungenerous people typically act ungenerously, though not always. The same is true of tolerance. Later we will see that Michael Walzer explicitly denies that regimes of toleration need tolerance.

Drawing this distinction between "tolerance" and "toleration" is useful in keeping straight whether what is at issue is the object and practice of toleration or the virtues of a person or group. John Locke's *A Letter concerning Toleration,* for instance, centers on what is to be tolerated—namely, diverse Protestant religious beliefs and ceremonies—and practices of toleration but not on cultivating tolerance as a virtue. As we will see, Locke's account suffers partly because there is no sustained defense of tolerance as a virtue. Williams would disagree. That they limit themselves to the practice is all that we can ask.

The larger philosophical point emerging from this discussion is that it draws attention to tolerance as a virtue. In classifying tolerance as a virtue, something is being said about it both taxonomically and evaluatively. Taxonomically, tolerance belongs to the genus of personality or character traits. It is a disposition. We have many such dispositions, tendencies, or traits to believe, feel, and act in certain regular, broadly recurring ways. The credulous, for example, believe too readily, usually based on the flimsiest evidence or no evidence at all; gloomy people feel depressed because they tend to see only the dark side of situations; and the witty among us entertain with their clever remarks and turns of phrase.

Not all personality traits are virtues or vices, as these examples show. It is not vicious to be gloomy, though most of us do not like to be around people who persistently point out the hole in the doughnut. Depending on the context, of course, morally neutral character traits can be deficiencies, even vices. We do not want credulous scientists, boring dinner companions, or gloomy nurses. Similarly, a nonmoral virtue in one context can be a vice in another. Is there anyone who appreciates a witty tax auditor? To make it clear that not every disposition to act is either a moral virtue or a vice, consider the tendency most of us have to put on either our left or our right shoe first or the disposition we are said to have of turning right on entering stores. These are simply habits, neither good nor bad. They tell us nothing about our underlying character. Not all dispositions are habits, of course, for habits exhibit a particularly strong, repetitive, context resistant nature. Other dispositions will have more varied expressions, such as friendliness, gloominess, shyness, absentmindedness, and so on.

This said, it remains true that virtues and vices are among the most important of our character traits. As virtues and vices, they are not merely ways of feeling, believing, or acting. One must also do so in the right circumstances and for the right reasons and from a fixed character. James Wallace (following Aristotle) provides a good working definition: "A virtue is a capacity or tendency to act in ways that meet the three conditions of knowledge, motive, and proceeding from a fixed character.[4]

A virtue—any virtue—is thus conceptually bound up with good actions and good agents. I might do the right thing, but unless I do so for the right reasons or appropriate motives, I will not manifest the corresponding virtue. Further, a virtue—again, any virtue—is to be distinguished from particular acts of virtue and from certain properties, such as rights. And, as already seen, we do not normally withdraw our ascription of a virtue just because, on occasion, someone acts "out of character." This is a bit tricky, however. There may be some occasions of such monumental significance that one incident may lead us to withdraw our previous judgment and to indelibly define one's character. A cowardly person may intentionally and knowingly perform a single act of such enormous bravery, for example, that we completely revise our judgment of his character. We may even think that our hero must have been courageous all along. In making such judgment, we suppose that he did not do the courageous deed inadvertently or for unworthy reasons. We still require that it be done for the right reasons and with the right motives.

Someone who does what a courageous, generous, or tolerant person would do but lacks the appropriate reasons and motives that make him courageous and so on may do the right thing, but we do not conclude from that alone that he is courageous and so on. Often, of course, we do not care. All we care about is whether a person stands firm in battle, gives to charity, or puts up with those whom he detests. There are two reasons, however, why we often care a great deal whether someone has the corresponding virtue. First, one is more likely to act in a generous or courageous way, for example, if one is a generous or courageous person. If an ungenerous man gives to charity solely to enhance his prestige or to curry favor, for example, it might turn out that his charitable giving would stop when it no longer serves his self-interested ends. Second, it often matters why someone does what would be a virtuous act and not merely that he does it. We want our closest friends to care for us out of friendship and for no other reasons, even perfectly good reasons. If a friend visits you in the hospital, you hope that his visits are motivated solely by the following thought: "My friend is ill and in the hospital; I belong at his bedside; there is nowhere else I wish to be."

Virtues are like skills in that they have to be learned. This may seem counterintuitive; are not some people, by nature, caring and generous? The answer is yes and no. Some people may be naturally giving and caring, but one needs to learn how much to give and to care, in what circumstances, and for what reasons. It is not generous (and thus not virtuous), for instance, to give money to addicts or guns to children who want them, nor is it generous to give away what is not yours to give. Part of learning the nature of any virtue is mastering when and how much one should feel as well as behave. Even grief has its appropriate forms, feelings, and objects. We do not admire those who grieve as deeply for the loss of a pet as they would for the loss of a child.

Although virtues are like skills, they differ in an important way. There is no special technique one must master in acquiring a virtue. A violin virtuoso or a cabinetmaker needs to learn techniques and also develop sensitivity to music or wood. To express the inner meaning of a certain musical passage, a violinist must learn to bow in a certain way; to bring out the beauty in wood, one must learn how to cut it properly. There is nothing equivalent in learning a virtue. To find courage in speaking one's mind, it will not be of any help to take lessons in oratory. Mastering oratorical skills might make one a more effective champion for one's cause, but not more courageous.

One final point. Virtues would not be virtues were they easily learned and lived. Speaking up for what one believes might be comparatively easy for one person but difficult for another, and so with all the virtues. Particularly distinctive of virtues is that—at least initially and sometimes always—we have to overcome a strong desire to act otherwise than virtue would have us act. Selfishness is the chief culprit, though not the only one. Virtues require us to sacrifice something important to us, often something of real value. This is clear when we think about courage and generosity. But it is true of all virtues. Loyalty to one's friends or cause can be exceedingly difficult because it necessitates making many sacrifices, as does every virtue. Just because we deeply treasure something, such as loyalty, then, does not mean that it comes easy.

Toleration played an important role in the rise of political liberalism in the seventeenth and eighteenth centuries. Today it remains a core value of political liberalism. Without it, liberalism would be transformed into something unrecognizable. In particular, toleration imposes certain restrictions on state interference in the lives of its citizens. Although indispensable, however, toleration is far from the whole of liberalism. In all its forms, liberalism entails much more, and necessarily so. It must, for instance, define the proper role for freedom, equality, justice, and rights. Further, any variety of liberalism must show how each element relates to the others and how *political* matters relate to *social* matters. How liberals integrate these features and make some more prominent than others give each variety its characteristic coloring. In all, however, toleration figures prominently and indispensably.

So, however central tolerance is to liberalism, it is not the whole of it. Core values are not sole values. Even if we end our examination with a sound and agreed understanding of toleration and tolerance and their place within political liberalism, we would have grasped only one element of a complex picture. Without understanding the place of freedom, equality, justice, and so on, our picture would be impoverished. Worse, it would be unrecognizable. Tolerance itself will take on additional meaning and justification only as embedded in some broader outlook. Even some obviously nonliberal thinkers will find some place for toleration, as we will see when we consider the views of Aquinas. The extent to which they can find a place for tolerance as a virtue is less clear. In any case, tolerance will need to find its own proper place among all the other elements that define the liberal tradition.

CUTTING TOLERANCE DOWN TO SIZE

Some contemporary philosophers reduce tolerance from the mountain it was in classical liberal thought to a rapidly eroding molehill. Williams predicts that tolerance as an attitude will be seen historically as an "interim value" between past "exclusivity" and future commercially based cosmopolitanism. Toleration as a practice will be around until people become suitably blasé. Tolerance as an attitude or virtue seems squeezed between moral indifference, politically expedient compromise, and skeptical pluralism. As those who inhabit contemporary pluralist cultures become increasingly indifferent to religion, sexual orientation, and expression, the argument goes, we will have less and less need to be tolerant and less and less need to practice toleration. Either we ourselves will not care much one way or another about these things or, even if we do, we will not care what others think or do regarding them. The oft-heard remark "That's their business, not mine" captures this nicely.

Further, where people really do disagree deeply about what matters, all we can really hope is that they can hammer out some political compromise that will keep the peace. We would think it a great accomplishment were we able to get the Protestants and Catholics in Northern Ireland, the Tamils and Sinhalese in Sri Lanka, the Hutus and Tutsis in Rwanda, or the Greeks and Turks in Cyprus to live up to an enforced peace.

Finally, however historians may characterize the present, they are unlikely to call it the "age of certainty." Skepticism is no longer merely a philosophical stance to occupy our idle thoughts. With the possible exception of science, skepticism permeates our age. Our skepticism shows itself not merely theoretically but practically. We may be attached to our religious faith, moral beliefs, and way of life, but we doubt that they can be satisfactorily defended, even to ourselves. We will soon replace tolerance by a shoulder shrug as we say, "Who knows?" about nearly everything that once mattered deeply.

One reason tolerance appears so elusive is that it admits of several different shades or degrees from bare tolerance to mere tolerance to full tolerance. Understanding these degrees or gradations will help us see what place tolerance has in moral, social, and political thinking. The lower grades of tolerance are compatible with highly illiberal forms of feeling, thought, and action. Full tolerance, on the other hand, can be found only within political liberalism, broadly conceived. Often it may be necessary to settle for one of the lesser grades of tolerance, even in a liberal society, as Williams makes clear. It is not, however, the ideal—whether or not we agree with Williams that the ideal is impossible.

BARE TOLERATION

Bare toleration acknowledges the grudging desirability of not coming to blows with people who must live together provided that no one needs to pay any attention to their well-being or even their survival. The more they can be ignored, the better. A *New Yorker* cartoon captures the mood perfectly: A religious man walks the pavement of New York City wearing a sandwich board that reads "Put Up with Thy Neighbor." The cartoonist suggests that to ask New Yorkers to love their neighbors is simply out of the question. As long as each of us goes our own separate way without interfering with anyone else, all will be well. "Each" here includes religions, communities, or racial and ethnic groups, not only individuals. Although the barely tolerant know that those whom they tolerate do not live in different, hermetically sealed spheres, they behave as if they do. Were the tolerated to disappear altogether, their loss might be noted, but not regretted and certainly not mourned. It might even be celebrated. Their disappearance would probably bring from the barely tolerant a long sigh of relief. No longer would they have to bear the burden of knowing that they might inadvertently cross paths.

Although starkly drawn, this portrait does not caricature. Throughout history, people have lived this life, exercising this degree of toleration, paying as little attention as possible to those whom they tolerate. As long as others "keep to themselves," all will be well or comparatively well. Because relations between tolerators and tolerated are virtually nonexistent, possibilities of misunderstanding, suspicion, imagined border crossings, and perceived slights are magnified. It then becomes exceedingly easy for tolerators to find themselves behaving intolerantly and doing so with a vengeance. Pogroms were an instance of this. As long as Jews kept to their ghettos, they were largely invisible. Still, the powerful always knew where they were. Because they were held in such sustained yet ignorant contempt, it was easy to imagine them up to all kinds of nefarious activities. It is not surprising, then, that the barely tolerant cease being tolerant at the slightest provocation, real or imagined.

Many great imperial and colonial powers adopted this attitude. While "the natives" kept to themselves and did not disturb any significant economic interests of the rulers, colonialists were, for the most part, barely tolerant. Indigenous people did not merit their attention enough for the colonists to behave intolerantly. Not showing proper deference, however, could be an unforgivable impertinence meriting severe punishment. "India would be delightful," a British colonial once sighed, "if only there weren't so many Indians." Without them, of course, the British East India Company would have had no reason for being.

If the barely tolerated are largely invisible to the barely tolerant, it cannot be assumed that the reverse is true. The barely tolerated must be constantly alert to the moods and policy swings of the barely tolerant, for they know that they avoid serious trouble only at their sufferance. This is why the tolerated often have a finer sense of the psychology of the barely tolerant than the barely tolerant do of themselves. It is an essential survival skill. If those barely tolerated counsel their own to avoid mixing with those who barely tolerate them, it is probably because they know they always run the risk of stimulating their intolerance. To keep to themselves is the best protection.

Sometimes two groups of people will each wish to keep to themselves. This need not be because one is more powerful than the other is or because one is more likely to behave badly to the other. Often it will be because each lives remotely enough from the other that there is neither need nor opportunity to interact and, as far as each can see, nothing much to be gained by doing so. This, however, is not toleration. Each simply leaves the other alone. In today's world, however, this option is increasingly rare.

MERE TOLERATION

We best capture mere toleration by the slogan "Live and let live." The merely tolerant, unlike the barely tolerant, acknowledge the full existence of others. They see that those whom they tolerate have a way of life providing substance and meaning for them, though differing markedly from their own. Yet they do not believe that it is anything like as good. "It's their funeral," the merely tolerant conclude, so they see no reason to oppress or otherwise intervene, provided only that their own way of being is not disturbed. I call this "mere tolerance" because it describes those satisfied with a static, even passive, understanding of their relations with those whom they tolerate—and not only *whom* but *what*. What those whom they tolerate believe or hold dear is not, to the merely tolerant, worth any deep examination. It is enough to see that other ways are different—and inferior—and for each to go their own way.

In many cases, the attitude of the merely tolerant approaches complete indifference: "So they believe this foolish thing or do these stupid things; what is it to me?" Yet there is this difference. The merely tolerant at least make the initial judgment—sound or unsound—that what they tolerate is inferior to what they themselves believe or do. They are not indifferent about that. What seems not to matter is why others believe what they believe or live as they do. As long as nothing disturbs the status quo, the merely tolerant are satisfied. To put the point differently, they will "let live" provided that no greater demands are placed on them.

This stance to tolerance is widespread, summed up in more than one slogan: "You go your way, I'll go mine" and "To each his own." Taken superficially—as slogans should be—each is uncontroversial. But like "Business is business," such truisms can mask deeper attitudes to that which is tolerated. Beneath their innocent, even banal, surfaces lie such thoughts as these: "I'll go my way (and not yours) because yours is inferior; if you wish to travel along your low road, however, that is nothing to me" and "I'll stick to my own because it is superior to yours, but I don't expect that you'd be able to see that." Again, "Let me go my way, and I'll let you go your way because your way is nothing to me."

Earlier I said that this attitude approaches complete indifference. It also, clearly, approaches complete complacency. My way is just fine, thank you. Why should I feel any challenge from another set of attitudes, beliefs, or way of life? If I find mine satisfying, surely that is enough. If you find the same is true of yours—however inferior they may be—that is fine with me, too. This attitude falls just short of complete complacency only because it has made the cursory judgment that my way is better than yours. The fully complacent seldom reach even that level of self-reflection.

FULL TOLERANCE

Full tolerance is captured by John Stuart Mill's thought[5] that each of us has a life to live, individually or collectively, and that this is in itself worth pursuing just because it is one's own (individual or collective) life. Over and beyond the content of one's attitudes, beliefs, and way of life, in other words, the fact that one adopts them as one's own or forges them oneself is a distinct reason to tolerate them. It is not always a sufficient reason, of course, but it is a distinct reason — and a reason particular to a liberal outlook.

In taking this stance, we are neither indifferent nor complacent. We are not indifferent because we believe that living one's own life, to be at least partly the author of that life, is desirable from within our own point of view. Even if we disapprove of the particular way in which others live their lives, we at least recognize that one good thing is that it is one's own. Clearly, that may not be enough, for the particular "experiment in living" on which others have embarked might, in our judgment, be intolerable.

We are not complacent because we believe that living one's own life opens up possibilities for interaction with others. First and foremost, we will not gratuitously hinder others. Since we recognize the worth of living one's own life, we may even have some motivation to help those with different attitudes, beliefs, values, and ways of life realize their goals. Because we believe that it is good that people live their own lives, we will be gratified when the life of an individual or community goes well — again, with the proviso that it meet criteria of acceptability to be discussed in later chapters. And if we can help, we will have reason to do so. Further, we may find that a particular experiment in living is, when we examine it closely, superior to ours. To the extent that we are serious about our own lives (again, individually and collectively), we must confront the possibility that we can learn from others and change our ways.

To be fully tolerant does not entail that we cannot have critical reactions to the content of the attitudes, thoughts, or conduct of those tolerated. All forms of tolerance necessitate having critical reactions to that which we tolerate. Otherwise, we would be either totally indifferent, complacent, world-weary, or fully accepting. Nor should "critical reactions" be limited to private, unexpressed responses. The fully tolerant do not — as do the barely and merely tolerant — deny themselves the opportunity, even the responsibility, of critically engaging those whom they tolerate, for the fully tolerant value more than that one lives one's own life. The content of a life also matters. It would be a strange doctrine that held that being at least partly the author of one's own life matters but that what one "writes" does not. To take the literal analogue, we care both that a novelist's book is truly hers but also that it is a story worth reading. It is enormously important that one's life has value, not merely that it is one's own.

Because those with a liberal temperament value individuals trying to live out their own conceptions of a good life, we might sometimes help individuals and groups pursue their good even when we find it deficient in various ways. An example might help. The fully tolerant will be moved to provide Amish communities with special help, such as paving the shoulders of highways to make it easier and safer for them to travel by horse and buggy. This is so even if they disapprove of certain aspects of the Amish way of life, such as their attitude to higher education, vaccinations, and ostracism as a form of punishment. Full tolerance, therefore, involves a deep respect for the individuals and communities whose life projects are different from one's own, even where one disapproves of elements in it, even thinks that it is a generally inferior way to live. Full tolerance is *not* acceptance. The fully tolerant recognize, however, that it is usually difficult to remove objectionable elements from a system without destroying the whole. They will be acutely aware of what I call the "Sweater Principle": We sometimes pull on an offending bit of thread marring our sweater only to find a shapeless heap of yarn at our feet.

The fully tolerant, finally, recognize that there can be much good—though a different good—in attitudes, beliefs, and ways of life that we ourselves do not find congenial. It is not that we do not see what is regrettable, say, about an Amish way of life. We see that only too clearly. What we may overlook are the incredible strengths in that way of life, the values—again, perhaps markedly different from our own, maybe even in competition with them—that it instills. Their way of life is not ours, but we see that it enables Amish to live rich, constructive lives. This does not mean that the Amish themselves are imbued with a liberal temperament. Having a liberal temperament is neither a necessary nor a sufficient condition for living a worthwhile life. Having a liberal temperament, however, can help one see the value in ways of life and systems of belief that are not, themselves, liberal in any respect.

FULL ACCEPTANCE: BEYOND TOLERANCE

We move beyond tolerance altogether if and when we come fully to accept an alternative way of feeling, thinking, and acting—though it is not ours or one we are tempted to adopt as our own. The latter point is important. Full acceptance does not entail that we deprecate our ways of thinking, feeling, and acting. Further, we might have good reasons for thinking that our way is better in some respects (and worse in others) yet fully accept the other. Most Pennsylvanians, for instance, do not tolerate the Amish. They find an Amish way of life fully acceptable. Preferring a "mainstream" way of life to that of the Amish is not necessarily to judge one superior to the other. We will still undoubtedly find unsatisfactory and unsatisfying elements in both. The consumerism that marks contemporary American life, for example, is an unsatisfactory aspect of it; the active discouragement of higher education among the Amish, however, is something unsatisfying, given our "mainstream" interests and sensibilities.

In fully accepting what we ourselves do not adopt, we are not committed to saying that there is nothing to choose between in adopting one way or another. Sometimes another set of attitudes, beliefs, or entire way of life might be essentially unavailable to someone not raised in it. One reason might be, as we have seen, that the way of life is not open to outsiders. More likely, however, a way of life will be emotionally and intellectually unavailable because of who one has become. Our social identities become fixed early in our lives. A few always seem to be able to make enormous transformations, shedding old social identities like a discarded snakeskin. Such radical transformations, however, are as remarkable and puzzling as they are rare. An American in Paris typically remains an American. He seldom becomes a Parisian.

So, we can find practices, attitudes, and so on fully acceptable and thus move beyond tolerance though we find aspects of them distasteful, unlovely, or unlikable. It is not that we cannot dispute about taste. We do so all the time, often employing good reasons. Some things, however, genuinely repel us, though we cannot put our finger on why (e.g., certain cooking odors and mannerisms). Or we might find something fully acceptable yet find that it leaves us cold (e.g., certain forms of artistic, religious, or sexual expression). It would be wrong, however, to say that we tolerate them, for we accept them as fully worth pursuing. They just are not for us.

What differentiates moving beyond tolerance from full tolerance is this: When we fully tolerate, we still at least mildly disapprove of that which we tolerate overall but stress both its worthwhile aspects and the fact that some person or community authentically adopts it. When we move beyond tolerance, we might disapprove of various aspects of that which we tolerate yet approve of it overall. This does not mean that we think it is as good as it could be or even as good as some others. But we judge that it is more than good enough.

As these latter remarks suggest, we often find alternative ways of feeling, believing, and being as equally valuable to our own though we do not adopt them as our own. When this happens, we find no fault at all, or, if we do, we judge that they are not worse than our own. And sometimes we move even further beyond tolerance, as when we actually adopt what were once alien attitudes, thoughts, or ways of life. This is what happened to Saul on the road to Damascus. Accepting that the content of another way is as good as one's own way, however, is still a long way from actually adopting that other way. Yet, as we have seen, it happens.

TOLERANCE AS A RISKY BUSINESS

The risk that it might happen leads some to resist toleration in the first place. As we come to recognize that alternative ways are as good as our own, we can also come to see that they are better or, if not better in themselves, suit us better than do our own. Some conclude that it is better to arrest the dynamic before it begins. Once we find ourselves in a dynamic situation, the outcome is difficult to control. If one is insecure, then allowing alternatives will be seen as inevitably threatening.

There is also the worry that the specious attractiveness of these other ways will prove irresistible, especially when flowing from a much larger, much stronger society. Such fears are neither wrong nor silly. Traditional societies are not mistaken in worrying that tolerating Western dress, music, and ideas will completely overwhelm them, with a subsequent loss of old ways of life, including age-old religious and family life. The Amish, we know, have grounds to fear that they will vanish if they give in to the dominant, affluent consumerist society around them. To mandate tolerance, therefore, looks like nothing more than an insidious way for a powerful society to dominate, maybe even obliterate, its neighbors. In chapter 8, we will have to confront this genuine worry.

There is, too, the concern that if we tolerate that which we rightly find undesirable, we will gradually become inured to it and ourselves become "corrupted." Again, these fears are not always wrong or silly. As movies become increasingly sexually explicit and violent, we might worry that our own sensibilities will become coarsened. In that case, we would come to accept baseness and violence in our own lives and not merely tolerate depictions of them on the screen. If we begin by disapproving but tolerating, say, conspicuous consumption, sooner rather than later we may find its allure fatally attractive. In these and similar cases, it might be thought that the best policy is not to let the camel's nose under the tent in the first place. These concerns are undoubtedly often overblown, but they cannot be dismissed out of hand. The worry is that a form of Gresham's Law operates: Just as bad money tends to drive out good, so vices drive out virtues. Often, however, these worries mask simple prejudice and bigotry. The *real* worry is that as our children and fellow group members become more familiar with those we do not now tolerate, they will see the genuine attractiveness of what we now reject.

There is, as far as I can see, no a priori solution to this "either/or" conundrum. One must make one's judgments and assess the risks. About some things, of course, we judge that what we are asked to tolerate is so vicious that those things are utterly and completely intolerable. In such cases, we judge that there is nothing to be said for that which we intend to suppress. It is simply intolerable.

One final matter needs stress: The transition from bare toleration to full tolerance to beyond tolerance is neither inevitable nor typically desirable. The transition can be arrested at any moment for good reason. Knowing more about alternative beliefs and ways of life can solidify our judgment that they should be tolerated but not fully accepted. The movement can even reverse. The more we know, the less we may be willing—again for good reasons—to tolerate at all. Familiarity can breed deserved contempt.

In succeeding chapters, we need to examine more closely not only the circumstances in which questions of toleration arise but also the kinds of considerations that justify toleration—and its limits. We will see that the kinds of reasons offered are insufficient if tolerance is to play the important role assigned to it in liberal political thought and practice.

NOTES

1. Bernard Williams, "Toleration: An Impossible Virtue?" in *Toleration: An Elusive Virtue*, ed. David Heyd (Princeton, N.J.: Princeton University Press, 1997), 26–27.

2. Nick Fotion and Gerard Elfstrom, *Toleration* (Tuscaloosa: University of Alabama Press, 1992), 9.

3. Fotion and Elfstrom, *Toleration,* 10.

4. James Wallace, *Virtues and Vices* (Ithaca, N.Y.: Cornell University Press, 1978), 53.

5. John Stuart Mill, *On Liberty* (London, 1859), ed. David Spitz (New York: W. W. Norton, 1975), especially chapter III.

Chapter 4

The Circumstances of Tolerance

Justice, David Hume says, is a jealous virtue.[1] When questions of justice arise, we concern ourselves with what we are *due*. We insist on what is ours *by right*. We jealously, possessively guard what is *ours* and do not willingly accept being deprived of *our fair share*. We demand that no one snatch from us what we justly own and that no one deny what they justly owe us. Although we might give away what is rightfully ours, we cannot be faulted for guarding what is ours. Sometimes we judge those who insist on their rights as behaving ungenerously, even selfishly. We recognize that for everyone to press their rights whenever possible would make civil society unworkable. Still, we maintain that no one can take away what is justly ours without our full and free consent.

A sense of justice does not come either naturally or easily. Some virtues, like generosity, both express our underlying personality and have obvious utility. Hume thinks, in contrast, that justice is like chastity. Neither one initially appeals or strikes us right in all instances. Hume notes that sometimes acting justly can even cause harm. A poor widow might make better use of money than the rich banker to whom she owes a debt. Justice nonetheless requires that she pay back her loan punctually, with interest. We grasp the importance of justice once we understand that promise keeping benefits society in the long run and that we ourselves have an interest in living in a just society.

Although a jealous virtue and therefore less flattering to our nature than generosity or courage, a sense of justice is essential to a good society. Without it, tyrants and governments exploit, oppress, and enslave. Whatever advantages an unjust society might have in terms of economic efficiency or military security, it is not a society fit for free men and women. Justice may not actually be the *first* virtue of political institutions, as John Rawls contends.[2] Surely, however, it is *indispensable,* as a cursory study of unjust regimes everywhere would show. No society is ever thoroughly just. Justice always remains an ideal, an aspiration never fully realized. Even when partially achieved in some limited sphere, moreover, just institutions and conduct are forever endangered. Someone might be tempted to act unjustly hoping to attain some personal good but also to realize some alleged greater good, for example, for God, or country, or some desirable social ends like the eradication of poverty. Champions of justice therefore stress the need for constant vigilance. It is not easy to develop a sense of justice or to act justly because doing so often means forgoing a significant advantage. That an advantage is unfair does not make giving it up easy. To develop the disposition to act justly is to acquire a real, hard-earned virtue.

If justice is a jealous virtue, then tolerance appears to be a *grudging* virtue. We tolerate what we disapprove, what we wish were otherwise, what we think distasteful, disgusting, or morally deplorable. For a variety of reasons, however, we bite our tongues, clench our fists, and barely restrain ourselves from lashing out against those whom we tolerate. This understanding and defense of tolerance is deeply rooted both in history and in how we still think about tolerance. Historically, tolerance was advocated primarily when the costs of intolerance were prohibitive or counterproductive. Thomas Aquinas, as we will see, urges that the Church tolerate prostitution because otherwise "lust would consume the world," and that would put the reputation of the Church in jeopardy. This might indeed have been the wisest course of action for the thirteenth-century Church, but it is also a grudging admission that forbearance is only the lesser of evils.

Again addressing justice, Hume contends that virtue arises only in certain circumstances: specifically, circumstances marked by moderately scarce resources, conflicting desires, and limited altruism. If we find something in abundance, or no one wants it, or people love giving it to others, then questions of justice do not arise. Siblings tend to quarrel over their just desserts, not their fair share of vegetables. Nations fight wars over the just distribution of water rights only when water is in scarce supply. Otherwise, no one cares how much anyone uses.

As there are circumstances of justice, there are similarly circumstances of tolerance:[3] namely, the circumstances in which appeals to tolerance make sense or have a point. It makes no sense, as just mentioned, to tolerate what one already accepts and approves. If we accepted the position some urge that prostitution is best described as "sex work" and if in fact (and not just in language) we came to think of it on the same moral footing as any other freely chosen labor, we would not tolerate prostitution. We would *accept* it, for we would then regard such women (and men) as providing a useful, even needed, service. We would no more tolerate them than we do those who clean septic tanks. We would simply accept them and the unpleasant job they do. Clearly, whether prostitution/sex work is on the same moral footing as most other freely chosen labor is a substantive moral question. We cannot answer it by arbitrary renaming or redescription. But if we do come to see that there is nothing particularly wrong with prostitution—however much it might not be one's own idea of a distinguished or fulfilling occupation—then questions of toleration do not arise. It might not be our "cup of tea," to put it mildly, but then neither is cleaning septic tanks for most people.

Nor, to take a different type of circumstance, does it make sense to talk about toleration to those who lack any understanding of the concept. Here we can only prepare the ground for understanding by appealing to analogues or obliquely related notions. Toleration would then be introduced slowly, even sideways, to someone or into a culture, just as each of us comes to learn and to master a moral vocabulary. This need not be the patronizing instruction of untutored people, though too often we approach it just this way. After all, those introducing us into the vocabulary and methods of science or an appreciation of twentieth-century music need not be patronizing. A particular society might have had little need for toleration or have a set of notions that does much of the same work as tolerance, albeit using a more diverse, less concentrated vocabulary. Analogously, while it is true that the ancient Greeks did not have a concept of rights—and certainly nothing like our notion of *human* rights—clearly they had notions of entitlements and property. These would have provided traction for the introduction of rights had they acknowledged the benefit of including them in their moral vocabulary.

This last point raises a deeper worry that we will confront later. Namely, just as we can imagine the ancient Greeks saying to us that they can say and do everything that needs expressing without appealing to rights, either explicitly or implicitly, so cultures lacking the notion of toleration might say the same. Further, even if tolerance as a virtue is central to *our* way of life, it does not follow that it must be central to every morally decent way of life. Maybe cultures can thrive morally without a well-developed conception of tolerance as virtue or practice. If so, then an articulation and defense of tolerance must be addressed only "to those whom it may concern"—and this might well be far from everybody. Still, it does not follow that tolerance is dispensable for those whom it *does* concern. And those might be the vast majority of contemporary, pluralist societies populating the world. And we need to see the evidence that societies that do not have it in their moral and political vocabulary are not *also and therefore* marked by cruelty, derision, and contempt for the powerless within them.

Knowing the circumstances in which appeals to tolerance have purchase does not, by itself, *justify* anything. Continuing the analogy with justice, we may know both (a) that questions of justice *arise* when resources are scarce and (b) that before us is a case of scarce resources. We would still be no closer to knowing what (b) requires. It does not tell us, for instance, whether to distribute resources on grounds of prior possession, need, utility, equality, fair procedures, entitlement, or some other basis. We might agree about the circumstances of justice, in short, yet disagree about which distributions are just. All the difficult substantive work would remain. This helps explain why theorists disagree about competing conceptions of justice. It also helps explain why we are divided in our political life over the justice of such contentious issues as affirmative action, taxes, wealth redistribution, punishment, and compensation for injury.

The same is true of tolerance. Grasping the circumstances of tolerance picks out the general field, but knowing this alone cannot settle when tolerance is required

or desirable or the particular form it should take, even supposing it is warranted.
Knowing that questions of toleration arise only when divergent attitudes, beliefs,
and practices are not accepted by the powerful, for instance, tells us only that *here*
is where substantive arguments about tolerance and its limits take place. It does
not provide us with the answers. We might agree that the *paparazzi* exceed the
bounds of good taste, but is their behavior intolerable? Speech that vilifies on the
grounds of race clearly causes deep wounds, but does that make it intolerable?
Should we, for instance, expel perpetrators of it from universities?

Certainly we cannot concoct any formula for answering these questions or set-
tling the arguments. We may pride ourselves in thinking that we can at least frame
principles from which we can derive, albeit not deduce, specific injunctions. To
revert to the example of justice, if we could settle on a single, substantive conception of justice as utility, or as need, or as fairness, then we would at least have
a principle from which to proceed. I am inclined to think that even this more modest enterprise is still too ambitious for tolerance, if not for justice—though I think
it is true there, too. In subsequent chapters we will look at *reasons* that bear on
questions of justifiability, though I am under no illusion that they are fully adequate, let alone complete. One advance caution: We tend to look for a single, conclusive justification for this or that. But the world is seldom so tidy. With tolerance (as, I believe, with justice), there are several different justificatory reasons,
some applying with greater force in different sorts of cases.

The circumstances of tolerance do not constitute a set of formal necessary and
sufficient conditions. If a particular circumstance is missing, weak, or deviant in
some way, we cannot automatically dismiss claims of tolerance as resting on simple conceptual error. Moral, political, and social notions are far more complicated
than this suggests. As Aristotle noted, we should not call for greater precision of
a subject matter than it can provide. Moral and social philosophy are not geome-
try and therefore should not have to meet standards required of geometrical
proofs. Instead, the circumstances provide us with a core and focus of understanding. It is a way of saying, "Our quarry is likely to be found here," but only
likely, for sometimes there is simply no quarry. And sometimes quarry appears in
unexpected places. So although I will describe the circumstances that follow as
conditions of tolerance, this should always be understood with "typically," "usually," and "normally" attached.

TOLERANCE: ITS SUBJECTS AND OBJECTS

We must answer two questions whenever issues of tolerance arise: Who, or what,
tolerates? And who, or what, is tolerated? The answer to the first question provides us with the *subject(s)* of tolerance; the answer to the second provides the
object(s) of tolerance. Both subjects and objects of tolerance[4] can be individuals,
groups, or institutions such as church or state—anything, in short, that exhibits

agency, that is capable of *doing* something, of *acting.* Not all groups qualify as *subjects* of tolerance since many lack the requisite structure to *act* as a group, to exhibit *agency.* While American Catholics of Polish descent comprise a distinct group in that they share a characteristic cluster of beliefs, attitudes, practices, and a historical ancestry, they cannot be *subjects* of toleration because they do not, as a group, undertake projects. (To the extent that the Knights of Columbus consist largely of American Catholics of Italian descent, it can be a subject—and object—of toleration.) Similarly, the poor cannot be subjects of toleration. Both, however, can be the *objects* of toleration, for to be the object of toleration the capacity to act is not crucial: It is enough to be identifiable as a group. The powerful might hold American Catholics of Polish descent or the poor in contempt yet still tolerate them. Of groups lacking agency, it will remain true that the *individuals* constituting them can be both subjects and objects of toleration. Only those *groups* with sufficient organization, however, can be proper subjects of toleration, for only of them can we say that they act. Any identifiable group, however, can be an object of toleration.

For many reasons, but often because they are the objects of intolerance, individuals within a group might organize themselves. Once organized, they can become agentive. They will then acquire the status of a (possible) subject of toleration. In the United States, for instance, vibrant Polish-American clubs engage in a variety of charitable and cultural activities. Even homeless people have occasionally been able to organize themselves into effective lobbying associations. And in some countries, prostitutes have organized themselves into unions to protect and advance their interests. Communication has made it possible that far-flung groups that transcend national boundaries can organize themselves into agentive institutions (e.g., opponents of whale hunting and lovers of Macintosh computers). A search of the Internet would uncover agentive associations for nearly any conceivable grouping. Although typically the identified group organizes itself—for instance, Mothers Against Drunk Driving (M.A.D.D.)—this need not always be the case. Agentive organizations exist on behalf of people with severe mental handicaps, for instance, but the beneficiaries of the organization did not organize them.

The last two examples indicate an interesting feature of all institutions. Namely, organizations can be founded on *behalf* of people who are not themselves members of the organization. M.A.D.D. was not founded by those motivated to protect their own lives or, obviously, the lives of their deceased children but to spare other mothers the grief caused by drunk drivers. Organizations that lobby on behalf of the mentally handicapped typically are not led by handicapped people, nor need the members benefit in any obvious way from their efforts. Similarly, animal rights organizations exist to protect the interests of animals, which are unaware of the efforts made on their behalf.

There are distinctive kinds of groups that deserve special attention: those defined by caste or sex (and gender) or those from a particular ethnic, national, racial, linguistic, class, or religious background. As a practical matter, these are groups today that are most often the principal objects of toleration, for these are the groups marked by deep *difference* from those with power, and, as we will see, difference constitutes one of the circumstances of tolerance. Once opinion makers of one group label another group as "other," the possibility of intolerance arises. As social scientists and philosophers have argued, too, those unlike us serve a strategic, not always benign, role in our lives. Their otherness, their strangeness, illuminates our own characteristics, our own virtues—and our own self-ascribed superiority. Such groups are often the objects of tolerance. But they are never its subjects, except indirectly. The fisherman caste, a low caste, cannot act. Its members individually and acting in concert, however, can create economic and political institutions reflecting the interests of the caste, and these institutions do possess agency.

Caste is a particularly distinctive grouping. It denotes an endogamous group with hereditary membership, usually organized around a traditional occupation and marked by various degrees of ritual purity and pollution. Examples include rice farmers and fishermen. While not as rigidly structured as often portrayed, castes are nonetheless highly and complexly structured, fall into well-defined hierarchies, and offer little upward (or downward) mobility. India in particular continues to struggle with the consequences of its caste system, which, despite legal reforms, remains a powerful social force.[5] While caste and class do not coincide, the higher the caste, generally, the greater the status, power, and wealth.

Caste provides us with a paradigm example of *social stratification,* that is, the distribution of valued resources according to social status. This might be marked in terms of ritual purity, aristocratic birth, economic strength, military prowess, or whatever else happens to be highly valued (e.g., nationality or membership in a high-status profession). Those with high (not necessarily the highest) status wield power and find themselves able to extend or deny tolerance to castes lower on the totem pole.

Class difference in some countries has had effects similar to those found where caste dominates, so that one class will have far greater status, power, and wealth than others. Although Karl Marx (1818–1883) overemphasizes the role of class in determining the course of history, he is right to recognize its enormous influence in determining the social stratification found in a country. Importantly, classes create objects of toleration and, if they organize in certain ways, subjects. Although the working class can be only an object of toleration, not a subject, the unions they form can be both. As with castes, class hierarchies make those at the bottom of the structure virtually invisible. However much they are among us, they might as well not exist, except as objects of contempt and ill-treatment.

Race, like caste and class, provides yet another example of salient group differences and social stratification. Just as some countries are more sensitive to caste and class than others, so it is that race matters more in some cultures than in others. In nearly all, however, race makes *some* difference, and in many it makes a significant difference. Similarly, as with castes and classes, desirable and undesirable characteristics become associated with various racial differences: This race is industrious, intelligent, or pure; that race is lazy, stupid, or morally corrupt. Judgments such as this usually lead to regimes of intolerance. Intermarriage, for instance, is not merely frowned on but is sometimes cruelly forbidden. Powerful institutions often deny civil rights to those of the "wrong" race, class, or caste. So, those on the bottom suffer spiritually, politically, and economically. Those who do not conform to the common understandings of race, class, or caste often flee to cosmopolitan areas, where the differences, if not accepted, are more likely to be tolerated.

Ethnic, national, and linguistic differences can be as powerful as those categories just mentioned. Most societies, for instance, tell jokes mocking the alleged stupidity or backwardness of an "inferior" group in their midst. These contemptuous jokes not only purport to illustrate, but also reinforce, the superiority of some groups over others. The English tell "Irish" jokes, the French tell "Belgian" jokes, the Danes tell "Jutland" jokes, and those in lower Michigan tell "Yupper" (Upper Peninsula) jokes.

Linguistic differences, too, create objects of toleration. This can be especially powerful when allied with state power. When governments make one language the official state language, those unable to speak it are severely disadvantaged. Opportunistic politicians in Sri Lanka, for instance, helped create its decades-long ethnic conflict by declaring Sinhala the official language, thus squeezing Tamil-speaking Sri Lankans from prestigious and financially secure positions.

Religious differences continue to be extraordinarily divisive. Adherents of different creeds often live tolerantly, even acceptingly, side by side in many parts of the world. In many other places, however, they most assuredly do not. True believers holding power can be exceedingly intolerant of those who worship the wrong god, or the right god in the wrong way, or who understand their common god's injunctions differently. A salient feature of religious intolerance is that intolerance, even persecution, is usually worse for heretics and apostates than for those subscribing to wholly different faiths. It is as if heretics and apostates should somehow know better. By their heretical beliefs or apostasy, dissidents threaten the very heart of the church. Partly the threat is rooted in the fear that others within the flock will follow a false shepherd. When dissidents challenge the dominant creed, propose a heretical theology, or advocate innovative rituals and practices, defenders of the established church typically feel compelled to repel an attack from within. Although general beliefs and attitudes might be ascribed to races, classes, and castes, none has a dogmatic *creed* or set of *ritualistic practices*. (Habits and customs are not rituals.) In other respects, however, the story is largely the same as it is for caste, class, race, and ethnic background. "True" religions, acting through their institutions, can extend or withhold tolerance to dissidents and outsiders. It is only in their institutionalized forms, however, that religions can be subjects of toleration because only as an institution can a religion act.

Gender differences[6] have existed forever, but only recently have they become recognized for the ways in which they, too, create objects of toleration. What distinguishes gender intolerance is that it obviously cuts across all the lines so far considered. Whatever their emotional, economic, or political invisibility, the actual presence of women is inescapable in every caste, class, religion, and ethnicity. Further, their dominant role in reproducing culture is evident, though plainly not self-evident, to those who treat them intolerantly. Given that women are found everywhere, the possibility of (in)tolerance toward them exists everywhere. Stratification along gender lines can therefore occur everywhere, from the most despised castes, classes, and so on to the most honored. Women of any class/caste/religion, for instance, can feel ill-treated by their same-class/caste/ religion husbands.

This list is hardly exhaustive. Age and tribal identity can be extremely important in fixing one's place in the social order. And each, in different societies, provides objects of toleration and, with tribes, subjects. Physical appearance, too, serves as a powerful marker of social standing. This is true not only of "gross" distinctions between the physically whole and physically scarred but also of far more fine-grained distinctions that grade the relative attractiveness of people. In a society where it is better to be light-skinned than dark-skinned, for instance, the dark-skinned might themselves discriminate on the basis of skin tone. I have said enough to show how groups can easily become the objects of toleration and, sometimes—where it makes sense to speak of agency—the subjects, too.

As used here, *institutions* have a formal structure of rules, roles, and offices or at least a quasi-formal structure with spokespersons or leaders. In its early years, the Palestine Liberation Organization was such an institution, though lacking the type of formal structure it now has. Not surprisingly, this is true of many incipient revolutionary groups. Rarely do they formally constitute themselves until after months or years of underground activity and informal leadership. Because they hover between an amorphous group and a formal institution in their early years, it is not always clear who speaks for revolutionaries or rebels or where authority lies. Institutions need not be legally incorporated, though rules, roles, and offices have to be clearly marked and understood.

Although a narrower characterization than sociologists often use, this stipulation marks out significant subjects, and objects, of toleration. Once a group interested in dog breeding organizes itself into a kennel club with specific rules about what constitutes a separate breed, what counts as a good specimen of its kind, who will enforce rules and how, and what conditions must be met for membership, that group institutionalizes itself. As an institution, the kennel club might exclude applications for dogs lacking a "proper" pedigree.

As with institutionalized churches, the American Kennel Club both shapes and reflects the beliefs, attitudes, and practices of its members. Often, however, there may be significant strains between officeholders and the general membership. In such cases, officeholders, if they have enough power, can become exceedingly intolerant of members who oppose their understandings of the purposes and practices that the institution was designed to foster and to protect. And, as noted previously, officeholders and members can come to have interests that (for better or worse) are not those of the beneficiaries of the institution and are even sharply at odds with it.

We have seen that when, for example, midwestern farmers organize themselves into cooperatives, or factory workers into unions, or a caste, class, or nationality into political parties, what was merely an identifiable group and thus only a possible *object* of toleration becomes a possible *subject* of toleration, for it is through its institutionalized organization that it can act, that it can do things. Here we have to distinguish between a *practice,* such as education, and an *institution,* such as a college or university, that helps carry, shape, and protect the practice. Many practices can exist without institutional support, though a central reason for creating an institution is to provide support and protection for the practice. People can play soccer, or raise dogs, or teach one another without forming a club with a governing authority. Such institutions do, however, offer a wide range of support and regulation.

The interactions between institutions and practices are complex. Institutions always, at least to some extent, take on a life of their own, and this has implications for the practices, too. Soccer players, dog breeders, and educators might even find that their practices are corrupted by institutions intended to support them, as criticisms of "mindless," "bumbling," "turf-conscious," or "corrupt" bureaucrats remind us.

We also need to remind ourselves, for example, that while a particular educator might be intolerant of educating women and while it may be true that, in a particular country, *all* educators are intolerant of educating women, the intolerance expresses itself *distributively.* Once these educators form a university, however, and if, as in the imagined case is likely, the practice of intolerance is built into the criteria for admission, then we can say that the university *itself* is intolerant of women. As time passes, it may be true that a particular university remains intolerant while fewer and fewer of its officers and faculty are. And conversely. Acting through their officers, the university might fight the intolerance of its faculty.

The complexity of relations between institutions, their officers, and their members means that we must move cautiously and discriminatingly in making judgments about the degree of tolerance or intolerance of any particular institution. An institution might be de facto racist, for instance, but not de jure, and conversely. Furthermore, because many institutions are highly complex, some significant elements might be more or less autonomous. They might well become more or less tolerant than the institution as a whole. Finally, we need to distinguish between an institution abstractly conceived and particular concrete instances of it. We must distinguish between a modern banking system, for example, and the many banks that give it life. Only the latter can be said to *do* things by *using* the banking system. Were we to accuse the U.S. banking system of sexism, for instance, we should understand that as shorthand for saying that U.S. banks and financial institutions act in sexist ways, maybe unintentionally and nondeliberately.

Subjects of toleration must be agents; objects of toleration need not. This means that the range of possible objects of toleration is much wider than the range of possible subjects of toleration. So far, however, we have just looked at individuals and groups as possible objects of toleration. Other possible objects of toleration include beliefs, attitudes, practices, commitments, habits, rituals, tastes, and even body language. Here I will emphasize individuals, groups, beliefs, attitudes, and practices since they occasion the most salient cases of (in)tolerance. We may so despise someone's beliefs, attitudes, or practices that we find ourselves responding intolerantly to them individually or as a group. Female genital cutting performed in many African tribes, however, is a prime example of a practice many find intolerable, though not necessarily either the individuals who perform the procedure or those who authorize it.[7] Many vehemently believe that this mutilating practice should stop yet do not despise its practitioners. Unlike a racist acquaintance who should know better, we may be inclined to diminish the degree of responsibility of those who perform clitoridectomies. The principal reasons are not only because of its acceptance over several generations and integration within the culture's traditions but also because we think that many within the culture have not squarely faced and thoughtfully considered objections to it. We might therefore judge the *practice* harshly but not those performing it, though obviously the practice would not exist without agents. A racist acquaintance, however, probably has no such excuse.

So geography, language, race, or ethnicity identifies many groups, but they are not the only markers. Sometimes we identify a group far more by its beliefs, attitudes, economic livelihood, or ways of expressing its spirituality. Think, for instance, of Baptists, civil libertarians, bleeding-heart liberals, homophobes, Buddhist forest monks, and professional wrestlers. Whether we approve of them or not, their beliefs and so on define an important aspect of who they are. This may be self- or other-identification. Baptists and professional wrestlers happily self-identify; neither so-called bleeding-heart liberals nor homophobes would do so, except ironically or defiantly. Further, when we identify a person or group in one way, they are typically something else as well (e.g., a French-speaking Roman Catholic Canadian hockey player).

What distinguishes these kinds of identifications from sex, ethnic, racial, or national identity is that they are *largely* within our control; ethnic, racial, linguistic affiliation, or national identities are largely *not* so. Maybe one can "pass" as a member of another race or ethnic group or transfer one's *political* allegiance. Still, one remains forever a female, Brazilian, or white. I say "largely" because sometimes our attitudes so permeate our being that they might not be much within our control, even over the long run. And occasionally people go to great lengths to change their sexual or national identity—and (more or less) succeed.

We find potential objects of toleration wherever there is difference, especially deep difference, and deep difference exists everywhere. Potential subjects of toleration are fewer only because to be a subject one must be an agent, that is, someone or something that can act.[8] Still, potential subjects are numerous, so the overall field of toleration is extraordinarily broad, even endless.

We can make a good case that the primary objects of intolerance are always people (and animals), for although one might be persecuted for one's beliefs and so on, it is always and primarily people who suffer as a result. Even when intolerance is justifiable—for instance, in reacting vehemently against slavery—it is, in the end, individual human beings who benefit or pay the price.

We must tread carefully here. That individuals eventually benefit or suffer from (in)tolerant responses does not entail that *objects* of intolerance are limited to sentient creatures. To the contrary. It may be precisely because of their race or beliefs, for instance, that individuals suffer. Nor does the fact that individuals, in the end, benefit or suffer because of tolerance mean that we cannot speak sensibly of the flourishing or stunting of attitudes, beliefs, communities, rituals, and so on. We only have to be careful that we do not think of these as having a life of their own without being embodied in living human beings.

DIVERSITY AND DIFFERENCE

Diversity and difference create the field for tolerance. They range over many kinds of things: beliefs and opinions, actions and practices, tastes and sensibilities, whole ways of life, and matters of caste, race, class, and so on. When there is little diversity or when the diversity does not run deep or where power is so one-sided that possible objects of toleration barely seem to exist for possible subjects, the circumstances simply are not ripe for either the practice of toleration or the development of tolerant attitudes.

Now that practices and attitudes of toleration are common, we are inclined to see questions of tolerance arising when differences are, if not inconsequential, less than earthshaking. This is possible only because the ground has been prepared by differences that are deep and deeply troublesome to many. Were all diversity and difference near the surface, it is unlikely that either the practice or the attitude of toleration would have arisen. There simply would have been no pressing need. Surely toleration has its present importance only because differences among us are profound. Once in place, lesser differences ride piggyback, as it were, on an understanding that arises from far greater ones.

Without deep and divisive differences, toleration would not have the important place it does, not only in abstract liberal political theory but also in the lived life of contemporary pluralist, liberal societies. We can make a similar point about natural or human rights. Such rights were created (or recognized?) in the seventeenth century in response to certain deep needs that many felt were unmet by emerging nation-states. Once firmly in place, the language of rights grew like topsy, so that matters for which rights would originally not have been established now seem commonplace. Many believe, with cause, that this expansion has diluted the strength that rights-based claims once had. This is a worry, too, regarding tolerance. Like rights talk, tolerance talk can become a mantra that obscures more than it enlightens.

Diversity sufficient to create grounds for claims of tolerance could be nothing more than a single dissonant belief or act in an otherwise highly homogeneous culture or personal relationship. That is unlikely, however, since even beliefs and acts of great singularity are usually complexly connected with other attitudes, beliefs, and practices. Indeed, a single, jarring belief unconnected to some web of beliefs would be extraordinarily odd, even bizarre. Beliefs are not freestanding in this imagined way.

It is when diversity and difference run deep and wide that the most difficult cases regarding tolerance arise. Whole ways of life often rub up against one another—and rub one another the wrong way—or, if not a whole way of life, a profoundly important aspect of a person's or culture's identity (e.g., an individual's sexual identity or a culture's religion). In such cases it is impossible to imagine that what offends is like a minor blemish that we might surgically remove without changing the patient. It is more like removing the hands of a pianist: While the person continues to exist, she is no longer a pianist. And it is in just these cases that those with power are tempted to act, for so much seems—and is—at stake when diversity and differences are profound and extensive.

DISLIKE, DISGUST, AND DISAPPROVAL

The alliteration not only is a useful mnemonic device; it also brings out the strongly *negative* character of the context or circumstances in which the questions of toleration arise. We could add other "D's" if we wished: distaste, deplore, disdain, and despise. We could also add other responses from elsewhere in the alphabet. But perhaps the "Three D's" are wide enough to encompass the central cases where questions of toleration arise.

It is important to notice that we need not have articulated reasons for our responses, except for (dis)approval. Even here, the reasons need not be moral. They might, for example, be aesthetic, theological, or based in etiquette. Dislike differs from disapproval in that we need not have articulable reasons for what we dislike: "I don't know," we sometimes say, "I just don't like it, that's all." The same is true of what offends or disgusts. We need not have, and typically do not have, reasons to justify our disgust at offensive odors. We will see in chapter 5, however, that liking and disliking implicates reasons far more than we might think. When we disapprove of something, we surely imply that we have defensible reasons for it. Sometimes, however, it is merely bluff. When we find we lack good reasons for what we said we disapprove, we retreat to the more visceral terms "dislike" and "disgust."

Dislike and disapproval resemble belief and knowledge in this respect. If I claim to know something but cannot adequately make my case, I can still believe but not know. This is evident when our knowledge claim turns out to suffer the indignity of being false. The resemblance is this. I may begin by disapproving of something, but when I realize that my reasons are inadequate, I typically retreat to the safety of dislike: "I'm not sure I can any longer give convincing reasons why I disapprove of X, but I still loathe it." To continue to disapprove without reasons invites the criticism "But your disapproval is utterly groundless." That one's likes and dislikes are (sometimes) groundless, however, is not necessarily a criticism. Must people who intensely like or dislike sushi have reasons? Those who disapprove of sushi, however, imply that they have reasons (e.g., that it is wrong to eat animals or that eating raw fish is dangerous).

There is this further difference between knowing/believing on the one hand and disapproving/disliking on the other. While I cannot know without believing, I can approve without liking and disapprove without disliking. This happens surprisingly often. Some people who disapprove of gossip nonetheless find it enjoyable, and some who disapprove of boxing still watch it avidly. Maybe it is not so surprising since guilty pleas are not surprising.

One final caveat. Whereas one must have reasons for disapproving *of* something, one need not have reasons for disapproving something. Only those in authority have the power to disapprove in this sense, and while they *should* have reasons, they might not. In particular, they should disapprove X because they disapprove *of* X. It is enough for them, however, to disapprove X if the disapproval falls within their legitimate authority. It follows from this—though not only this—that one can approve that which one disapproves *of* and conversely. As a political payback, for example, a senator might approve appointing a political hack to his staff, though he disapproves of doing so. That is, he exercises his authority in making the appointment but does not think that he has justifiable reasons for doing so. This is not to say that he has *no* reasons; otherwise, he would not do it. It is to say that his reasons—given the legitimate rationale for appointing people to one's staff—are defective even in his own eyes.

That we have powerful positive and negative responses to attitudes, beliefs, actions, practices, and ways of life for which we cannot give reasons is neither surprising nor intrinsically irrational nor regrettable. It is not surprising because our "gut reactions" initially guide us in making judgments. To be sure, we can explain many of our responses. Giving justificatory reasons for them is another matter, except in the broad sense that, as human animals, our emotional and affective lives are central to what we are. There is often an explanation of why we find this or that disgusting. Sometimes the explanation will not show that we differ fundamentally from those who do not share our disgust. The thought of buying a dog to butcher for dinner, for instance, fills most westerners with revulsion. Most westerners, however, do not feel similarly appalled by the thought of buying lamb chops. Part of the explanation is that, in the West, dogs are pets, part of the family,

while sheep, even baby sheep, are not. Those countries that do not blanch at
butchering dogs also do not regard them as pets. Since pets are simply animals
one includes in the family (whereas dogs are canines, whether in or out of the
family), it is not as though westerners have correctly identified dogs as pets while
others have not. It is just that, through our lens, we cannot but see dogs as pets
and might be stunned that others do not see them the same way. Perhaps we think
that dogs somehow *deserve* to be pets, but it is hard to imagine how this claim
could be convincingly established.

Nor need our affective responses be irrational. There is nothing irrational about
adoring chocolate or abhorring the stench of rotten eggs. In these instances, there
might even be a physiological basis for our responses. Rotting vegetables and
meat, for instance, are usually bad for people and animals, so offensive odors
warn us away. Yet even when there is no physiological basis for our reactions,
there is no reason for thinking that our responses are in any way irrational. Individuals, communities, and cultures need a shared affective life as much as they
need a shared economic life to thrive, maybe even more so, for without a shared
affective life—without, that is, sharing a love of place, foods, home teams, and
patterns of living—it may be impossible to share more "rational" endeavors, such
as economics, science, and philosophy.

If so, then there is nothing regrettable about the fact that we do not always have
articulable reasons for finding things offensive or disgusting. Without these responses, we could not mature as an integrated personality or as a community.
Like our ability to speak the same language, we acquire shared likes and dislikes,
loves and hatreds. Indeed, one such object of love and hatred is language itself.
Just as American English can grate on the ears of the British, so southern American English can grate on the ears of northern Americans. Further, as George
Bernard Shaw wittily depicts in *Pygmalion,* language identifies who is "in" and
"out," so serving as a powerful force for both social cohesion—and exclusion.
There is nothing regrettable about the fact that people love to hear their own language spoken "properly." There might be much to regret, however, when we act
intolerantly to those who do not speak our language. That one loves one's own
language or patch of the world or musical forms just because they are one's own
is neither intrinsically irrational nor regrettable. Because we tend to want others
to value what we value, moreover, we are often tempted to respond intolerantly
when others reject or are indifferent to what we value—or have competing values of their own.

That emotions and affective attitudes are not always reasoned does not show
that they never are. To the contrary, reasons are deeply implicated in our emotional and affective life. They help shape and direct it. Anger, for instance, has targets and has those targets for reasons. Jack might be angry with Jill because he
mistakenly thinks he overhears her insult him. If Jack becomes convinced that he
misheard Jill—that not only was no insult intended but none given—Jack would
be irrational to continue in his anger. He has nothing to be angry *about.* It might

take some time for him to "cool off," but that is simply the physiological consequence of becoming angry in the first place. What would be incoherent is for Jack
to say, "Yes, I agree you didn't say what I thought you said, but I'm still furious
with you"—and so with most emotions and affective responses: love, grief, pity,
shame, embarrassment, and so on. We can, at least to some extent, show that emotions are misplaced by showing that the reasons informing our emotions are mistaken or misguided. "There is nothing to be ashamed of," we say. And if we are
correct and the target of our remark agrees, then to continue to feel ashamed would
be pathological. It might be exceedingly difficult, nonetheless, to accept this ex-
culpatory judgment. That, too, may be pathological. Often, however, our resistance results from nagging doubts that, deep down, we might have done something
shameful, that we have hidden our true motives even from ourselves. Our reasons
might be inadequate, twisted, or defeated by stronger reasons, but that only shows
that we can *argue* with someone that his emotional response is inappropriate—
something we could not do if all emotions were necessarily arational.

POWER AND THE TEMPTATION TO ACT INTOLERANTLY

Only the powerful can establish tolerant practices or exhibit tolerant acts, for only
they are in a position to do so. But we must not exaggerate this point. First, nearly
every person, group, or institution is powerful relative to some other person,
group, or institution, at least occasionally, if not persistently. If Reds are powerful
relative to Blues, Blues may nonetheless wield significant power over Greens.
This is not just an abstract possibility but is typical. One class, for example, might
control the fortunes of another class, but within the latter class, men might control
the fortunes of women, and adults always control the fortunes of young children.

Second, although Reds might be able to exercise power over Blues in one respect, Blues might be able to exercise power over Reds in another respect. Parents and children, for example, often find themselves in this position vis-à-vis
each other. A father can deny his daughter the car; she can make his life miser-
able. Third, we must take care not to exaggerate the power of the powerful. The
exercise of intolerance usually runs some risk of resistance and therefore the possibility of failure. Only rarely are acts of intolerance risk-free.

Fourth, we need to distinguish tolerant *acts, practices,* and *institutions* from
tolerant *attitudes.* Just because someone is not in a position to act intolerantly to
those with greater power, individuals and groups might nonetheless harbor deeply
intolerant attitudes. Not infrequently, those who once were powerless gain power,
and then their intolerant attitudes reveal themselves in intolerant acts, practices,
and institutions. If the comparatively powerless harbor (in)tolerant attitudes, then
there is some reason to believe that if they were to get the upper hand, they, too,
would *act* (in)tolerantly. Individuals and groups locked in relations of subordination often mirror one another.

The distinction between (a) acts and practices and (b) attitudes and dispositions is similar to the distinction between *racism* and *racist, sexism* and *sexist.* The former is an institutionalized form of discrimination, and only those in power can exhibit it. Anyone, however, can harbor racist or sexist attitudes, including those who are themselves victims of racism and sexism. Reds might control the leading institutions of a society and so can express their racist attitudes to Blues in powerful ways. Blues, however, might be just as racially contemptuous of Reds as Reds are of Blues. They just cannot do anything about it for the moment. But they might long for the time when they can.

The comparison with racism and sexism reveals another similarity. Racist or sexist practices and institutions can continue even after most people have ceased to hold racist or sexist attitudes. They can so shape the political, economic, and cultural landscape that it might take decades of concerted effort to rid ourselves of the scars, even supposing that we have the will and intelligence to do so, for in molding how we think and feel, practices and institutions change our very way of perceiving the social world.

If a society wishes to rid itself of, say, racial, sexual, religious, or ethnic intolerance, therefore, it will seldom be enough simply to change attitudes. Institutions are like huge oceangoing tankers that continue their course long after the engines have been shut down. We might need affirmative efforts thrusting engines in reverse to prevent (further) catastrophe. Since the racism and racist pair and the sexism and sexist pair are simply two instances of intolerance as practice and attitude, it is not surprising that the similarity holds.

More needs to be said about this circumstance, however, than that Reds hold power over Blues. The Reds must be seriously tempted to behave intolerantly. If some of the Reds are phlegmatic, jaded, or world-weary, for instance, they might respond to that which they dislike or disapprove of in Blues with a dismissive sigh: "Oh, those silly, disgusting fools; but who cares?" As argued earlier, people do not show themselves to be tolerant simply because they cannot generate enough energy to act on their convictions or tastes. It is not that the Reds are indifferent: They do wish that the Blues were otherwise. It is just that, because they lack sufficient motivation, they are not tempted to intervene in the lives of Blues. They are neither accepting nor indifferent nor forbearing.

Typically, individuals, groups, and institutions holding power are sorely tempted to intervene in the lives of those who think or act in ways they find disagreeable or detestable. We considered previously why diversity and difference affect us so deeply, and we can also understand why we often wish to prevent or curtail that which offends or disgusts. Almost everyone begins life thinking that one's own way is not only *a* desirable way to live but also *the* right way and the *only* right way. Other ways of thinking and acting and organizing social life, therefore, strike us as more than merely strange. Our initial temptation is to think that we should make them conform to *our* way, the *right* way.

UNWELCOME RESPONSE

To these circumstances of toleration we must add that the behaviors contemplated must be unwelcome to the objects of toleration. We might take this for granted, except for some odd cases. Br'er Rabbit begged the devouring fox not to throw him into the briar patch, although Br'er Rabbit was perfectly at home there. However much the fox hoped to torture Br'er Rabbit, he failed miserably. Usually, however, everyone knows perfectly well what responses people detest, so the Br'er Rabbit problem seldom happens. But not never. Some men, for example, seem genuinely puzzled that many women do not welcome their sexual advances since they themselves, so they say, would welcome the sexual advances of women.

The severity of unwelcome responses need not be great, though generally the severer the response, the more unwelcome. One can express one's intolerance in many ways: facial expression, body language, words, laws, economic pressure, imprisonment, torture, mutilation, and death. It is clearly preferable to be called a name than to be lynched, but that should not blind us to the fact that looking past or turning from someone might be not only unwelcome but severely harmful in both the short and long run, for even this display of intolerance—which is mild in comparison with persecution of various other sorts—can adversely affect one's well-being. Individuals, groups, or institutions that are persistently snubbed by the more powerful not only have their sense of self-worth undermined but are cut off from enjoying full access to what the broader culture has to offer.

WILLINGNESS TO ENTERTAIN
THE POSSIBILITY OF TOLERATION

If an individual or culture lacked the concept of tolerance, it would be misleading to describe them as intolerant—or tolerant. Far more frequently, some individuals seem unable, as a psychological fact, to control themselves. Here the concept of intolerance applies, but depending on the explanation, the intolerant might (or might not) be excused for their destructive behavior.

Far more prevalent and serious is that many individuals and groups are *unwilling* to entertain the possibility of toleration. If one is powerful enough, why permit deep differences to coexist? Life for the powerful is made easier if everyone conforms to prescribed ways. With religious persecution, the powerful might also feel God's call demanding that they bring heathens and dissidents to heel. The imperatives of national identity and history have proven to be every bit as demanding. "Ethnic cleansing," for instance, flows not from God but from the demands of identity and history. Even to raise the question of toleration will seem like a betrayal.

What this suggests is that in (too) many contexts, it is *fruitless* to urge toleration. The circumstances do not exist for toleration to gain any foothold. Some lack the capacity for toleration and therefore cannot develop the ability to be tolerant. Far more often, however, toleration is both understood and not beyond anyone's ability. Hostilities, misunderstandings, and imperatives of God, nation, or history are so strong, however, that there is no *room* for toleration to gain a foothold.

Or at least not in the short to medium run. A deep-seated unwillingness to countenance difference forecloses the practical possibility of developing either policies or attitudes of tolerance. At best, other powerful forces can insist that the worst overt actions be stopped. This can range from informal pressures imposed by families to a court order to an international peacekeeping force to forced partition. While this in itself is not enough to change feelings, attitudes, or dispositions, it might be enough to put an end to bigotry and other intolerance. And this might help prepare the ground for tolerance to grow, however slowly. History teaches, however, that there is no guarantee of success.

While the distinction between being unable and being unwilling is clear enough in the abstract, we often cannot tell the difference in a concrete case. This epistemological difficulty does not matter much. Few people or societies literally lack the *capacity* for toleration in the sense that the blind lack the capacity to see or the deaf to hear. It is more likely the case that, because of relative isolation or some other set of circumstances, the capacity has not been developed.

Sometimes a person, group, or nationality capable and generally willing to practice toleration might become so enraged that considerations that would otherwise move them are brushed aside. In the heat of unreasoned anger—which might last until it is finally and cruelly spent—the intolerant are totally unwilling to listen to pleas for toleration. We have seen this recently in the genocide in Rwanda and the ethnic cleansing in Kosovo. The frenzied killings and other atrocities cannot be touched by reasoned arguments. When this happens, the violence either must be stopped or must run its course. Until then, pleas for tolerance are unlikely to be heard.

One final point. Inability and unwillingness are seldom all-or-nothing conditions. Typically, a person, group, or society will find it *difficult,* not *impossible,* to show forbearance. Especially in the contemporary world, it will be rare even for individuals, and certainly for larger social groups and institutions (including society as a whole), to plead inability. Unwillingness remains an obstacle to greater toleration, but not because of any inability. People need to see the benefits of living in a tolerant society and themselves living tolerant lives.

CONCLUSION

The circumstances of toleration provide us with informal conditions specifying the field of tolerance—the circumstances in which questions of toleration arise. By calling them "informal," I mean to draw attention to the fact that each is "typically" or "normally" present and present "more or less." As mentioned at the beginning of this chapter, these circumstances or conditions specify *where* questions of tolerance arise. As with the circumstances of justice, we must keep in mind those robust instances that gave toleration the salience it has. The central case in the West is that of religious toleration. Religious wars of the sixteenth and seventeenth centuries were both devastating and futile, and it was out of that experience that the "modern" notion of toleration was shaped.

Yet toleration is not confined to religious bigotry. In our day, religion is but one divisive difference where questions of toleration arise. National, ethnic, gender, and culture differences of all sorts provide a rich array of instances calling for toleration. The "culture wars" in the United States, for instance, are not fought exclusively or even predominantly over religious questions. The place of women, minorities, and gays in society and the limits of free expression are now central to questions of toleration. In other parts of the world, different divisions come into focus (e.g., class, caste, and ethnic identity).

The farther one gets from robust, core instances, the weaker, the more diluted the claims of toleration. A parent who tolerates a child's messy room by withholding such unwelcome responses as a scolding trails along in the wake created by the robust instances. Comparatively minor instances such as this get their purchase by capitalizing on the logic of the concept, not its significance. That is, we grasp how tolerance is *used* in such cases, but what is missing is the gravity of that which gives tolerance its centrality to contemporary political life and which has proven to be so contentious. Without robust instances, the minor ones would hardly merit our attention.

Yet there remains something missing from this account of the circumstances of tolerance that will be the subject of the next chapter: the relation between the tolerable and the intolerable. I have given the impression that tolerance is, as it were, the "default" position, that refusing to tolerate differences always shows one to be a bigot or, at the very least, imposes on one a heavy burden of proof to show otherwise. Clearly, this cannot be correct. That one does not tolerate racism or pedophilia or cruelty to animals does not warrant the charge of bigotry or intolerance. Quite the contrary. To tolerate racism, for instance, is itself intolerable. But now we might worry that it begins to look as though tolerance and toleration are simply heavily freighted emotive terms used rhetorically to silence those with whom we disagree. Were that true, the language of toleration would be better abandoned. Fortunately, it is not true. But we need to understand how the tolerable and intolerable are connected. As we will see, the relationship is not as straightforward as we might think.

NOTES

1. David Hume, *Enquiry concerning Principles of Morals* (London, 1751), in *Of Justice,* sec. 3, pt. I; P. H. Nidditch, *David Hume: Enquiries concerning Human Understanding and concerning the Principles of Morals* (Oxford: Clarendon Press, 1974).

2. John Rawls, *A Theory of Justice* (Cambridge, Mass.: Harvard University Press, 1971).

3. The specification of the circumstances of tolerance, and the phrase itself, follows in a general way the account offered by Susan Mendus in her *Toleration and the Limits of Liberalism* (Atlantic Highlands, N.J.: Humanities Press International, 1989). Mendus's own list has earned broad, though not universal, acceptance. The characterization provided here, however, differs from hers in various ways, including the addition of the last circumstance or condition: the ability and willingness to entertain the possibility of toleration.

4. And intolerance, of course. But because it is tedious to say so continually, it will usually be left unstated.

5. Roughly one-seventh of the population, or 120 million people, are *untouchables,* and they are not so much the lowest rung on the caste ladder as off the ladder altogether.

6. How sex and gender relate is contentious, though most sociologists regard gender organization as largely social, not biological. For our purposes, sex, gender, and sexual orientation provide objects of toleration because all three serve to mark sharp differences often reflected in social stratification.

7. The *Washington Post* (July 21, 1999, A3) reports that female genital cutting occurs in twenty-one African nations. The frequency, they report, varies between 5 percent in some countries to over 75 percent in others.

8. Methodological individualism holds that *only* individual human beings are agents since only they have beliefs, attitudes, purposes, and the ability to *do* something. While it is true, say, that a legislature cannot do anything unless its members do something, it is not true that, when a legislature acts, only its members act. Legislatures, not members, pass bills, ratify treaties, and declare wars. Similarly, it is Germany that made reparations to Jews for wrongs done to them, not individual Germans, many of whom were not even born in 1945. Of course, if no individual Germans had voted to make reparations, none would have been made. One need not assume that legislatures or nations act in a disembodied way. Methodological individualism and alternatives to it raise deep questions in the philosophy of social science but are largely irrelevant to understanding the difficult questions of toleration.

Chapter 5

The Intolerable

We all have had the experience of biting our tongue and clenching our fists in what proves to be a vain attempt to put up with something we find utterly deplorable. When pushed too far we explode: "That's it! That's too much! That's simply intolerable: I won't put up with it another instant." Parents know this experience, as do their children. Both find the other stretching the limits of toleration beyond the breaking point. The experience is ubiquitous: among colleagues and friends (or former friends), officials, groups, institutions, and nations. We do not always know, in advance, where we will draw the line. Typically, moreover, we do not draw it consciously, and often we cannot articulate the reasons for drawing it where we do. Yet we know — or come to know — when a line is crossed. We then react angrily with words, deeds, violent outbursts, dictates, or laws. These clearly and definitively designate the beliefs, acts, people, groups, or practices intolerable. They are beyond the pale.

It is easiest to imagine interpersonal cases: parents and children, husbands and wives, employers and employees. The same phenomenon, however, arises regarding groups, practices, and institutions. One group becomes "fed up" with another (e.g., employers with laborers). If a group does not already have an organizational structure, being "fed up" provides powerful motivation to formulate one. As certain understandings or tacit agreements that may have fostered forbearance earlier become undone, a heretofore unnoticed line is crossed.

The intolerable is simply that which we will not forbear, that which we fervently believe we rightly refuse to allow. The intolerable is that which lies "beyond the pale." The etymology of this expression refers to stakes demarcating legitimate authority. Anything outside these stakes was said to be "beyond the pale." An expression from sports captures the same notion: "out of bounds." Unlike clearly demarcated boundaries on soccer pitches or basketball courts, we do not typically know the boundaries of toleration in advance. They are like invisible trip wires that we discover only when crossed. The barely tolerable occupies that space equivalent to dusk: that murky, transitional period between twilight and night. While we cannot say precisely when dusk becomes night, we know when it is pitch black and so, too, where something crosses the invisible line between the barely tolerable and the intolerable. Whatever reasons we might have had for tolerating what we now find intolerable, those reasons are finally—and often suddenly and decisively—defeated. It is as if a dam bursts.

Sometimes the dam bursts because those we tolerate insist on pushing us "too far"—though we cannot say in advance how far that is. Sometimes the dam bursts because we might tolerate something occasionally but not continually, or we can tolerate it when done discreetly but not publicly. There are other triggering causes. Those we tolerate might not be appropriately grateful for our forbearance, or abuse the leeway given them, or flaunt what we regard as their appalling beliefs and practices, or demand *acceptance* for what we find barely tolerable in the first place. What is intolerable, therefore, might be tolerable if done occasionally, discretely, and so on. Again, *how* occasionally, discretely, and so on is something we typically do not know until an invisible line is crossed.

Many matters, clearly, are intolerable from the start. Torture, rape, and wanton violence are always and forever out of bounds in any civilized society. These are never eligible for toleration. Different individuals, groups, and cultures will add items to this list, but they are unlikely to be universally shared. Blasphemy, to take one instance, is not everywhere intolerable or even a meaningful category.

We must also remember that different cultures have diverse understandings of what seems, on its face, to be the same. We must not confuse shared *concepts* with shared *conceptions*. Virtually all societies, for instance, forbid incest. Since kinship relations differ cross-culturally, however, what *counts* as incest will differ, too. Most cultures specify that hosts show guests hospitality. Few, however, specify that a husband must offer his wife to a guest for the night. And nearly every culture condemns theft, yet not everyone agrees on what counts as property or whether it is possible to own certain things.

Finally, what cultures regard as intolerably shameful, cruel, or disgusting varies widely. These "moral notions" have already built into them both descriptive and evaluative criteria. A seedy bigamist salesman is (rightly) regarded differently than polygamous marriage in a traditional culture. Problems become acute, however, when those who have one understanding of a practice wish to live among those who do not. Before Utah was permitted to join the union, for example, it had to agree to forbid polygamous marriages.

Even if we confine our attention to single homogeneous cultures we see that attitudes, understandings, and laws about what is tolerable change. Not long ago, forcible sexual intercourse within marriage in most English-speaking jurisdictions was *legally* tolerable and, undoubtedly for many observers, *morally* tolerable.

That the line between the tolerable and intolerable shifts should not be surprising. Nor does it entail any type of vicious relativism. Circumstances *do* alter cases, as the catchphrase has it. A society teetering on the brink of extinction or absorption by another larger society may not be able to budget for as much tolerance as a more flourishing, secure society. Even if tolerance is a virtue, it surely is not the *only* virtue, and toleration may have to give way to other more pressing moral demands.

Altered understandings account for other changes between the tolerable and intolerable. We may think that something is intolerable because of its strangeness. Once we come to see it whole and in its context, however, we bring it within the ambit of the more familiar. We may then judge it to be tolerable, even if it still is not *our* way of believing or acting. Quaker pacifism, for instance, may strike some initially as either shirking one's duty or simple cowardice. A deeper understanding of the beliefs and practices of The Society of Friends will often dissipate that response. We may still believe that one should fight (and kill) to save one's country but recognize in law and sensibility a right to conscientious objection, however much we dislike and even disapprove of those who exercise that civilly sanctioned right. If we do come to this conclusion, we remove conscientious objection from the sphere of the intolerable.

Sometimes our attitude to what is tolerable shifts when we gain more factual knowledge. Fear born out of ignorance is a powerful engine of intolerance. Greater knowledge can remove fear and so intolerance. When AIDS first came to medical attention, some physicians and dentists refused to treat its victims because they feared that the virus might be transmitted like the common cold. Once scientists learned that the transmission of the AIDS virus was far more difficult, medical personnel overcame their fear.

This example, however, is problematic, for we might say, with some truth— given the mistaken factual assumptions—that refusal to treat AIDS victims was not an instance of intolerance at all. That firemen do not rush headlong into a burning building to save victims of a different race does not by itself show that they are intolerant. It only shows that they are not suicidal. We believe that firemen and physicians should take risks, but not foolhardy risks.

We therefore need better examples. Slave owners in the United States defended their peculiar institution on so-called factual grounds. Now one might say, as with the AIDS example, that this simply shows that slave owners were acting on beliefs that, if true, would show them not to be intolerant. The difference, clearly, is that we do not have nearly as much reason to suspect that physicians acted as they did out of prejudice as we do slave owners. In the latter case we have adequate evidence to conclude that bigots manufactured "facts" to defend their antecedent bigotry and privileged way of life.

By dispelling false factual claims about an individual, group, or people, we can nevertheless reach those who, as it were, acquired their intolerance honestly. That is, as children, we are raised with all sorts of conceptions not only about ourselves but especially about others unlike ourselves. Growing up, we have few resources for exploring, let alone critically examining, alleged "facts" used in justification of intolerance. A regime of toleration makes it possible for people to mix, even if not for pleasure, so that misconceptions and outright errors stand a chance of correction. We might learn that what "we all know" about this individual, group, or people is little more than a mask for bigotry.

Where we draw the line often changes as we understand more clearly the implications of attitudes, beliefs, and practices. We may come to realize that intolerant attitudes, laws, and actions directed against gay men and women, for instance, have a devastating effect on their lives and that expressing intolerance simply makes their lives far worse and does so without serving any morally acceptable purpose. The sting is in the last clause: "without serving any morally acceptable purpose." Those who regard living a gay life as intolerable will argue—indeed, must argue—that attempts to suppress living a gay life serve a moral purpose, one mandated by God.

And this is as it should be. That is, whether this or that is intolerable is a *substantive* moral question. We cannot decide it by how we use words, by counting noses, or by appeal to authority. When a disagreement arises about where to draw the line, we have no recourse but to argue the substance of the matter.

As a practical matter, those advocating toleration usually bear the burden of argument. That is, those whose power permits them to place individuals, beliefs, conduct, or groups beyond the pale are unlikely to feel much practical pressure to reexamine the basis of their own beliefs and practices. There is nothing in the nature of the case, however, that privileges one side over another. Neither side alone carries "the burden of proof." Once the question of tolerance arises, there appears to be no recourse but a careful examination of the grounds on which someone or something is held to be intolerable.

Those who argue that their tradition or their religion compels them to hold that this or that is intolerable may obscure this. Their judgments are not up for discussion or reassessment. It is *part* of one's tradition or religion, some argue, that this or that is not to be tolerated. What lies beyond the pale may be something pressed from within the tradition or applied to something outside it. Yet neither traditions nor religions are immune from reasoned criticism since neither makes adherents into unreflective zombies. Traditions and religions recognize this themselves, for throughout history both have been criticized and transformed not merely or even primarily from without, but most effectively and permanently, from within. Traditions and religions respond to reasoned criticism, not always straightaway—who or what does?—but over time and often after long and careful deliberation and after much resistance (reasoned or otherwise).

Further, except for the most traditional societies, neither traditions nor religions are monolithic. We can always find strands in any rich tradition, enduring religion, community, culture, or theory that we can highlight and use to weave an interpretation of its central commitments at odds with the dominant interpretation. No narrative history of Catholicism, the Jewish people, or political liberalism, for instance, could fail to see that they have changed—often radically—in response to internal criticism. A small number of hypertraditional societies do indeed exist. They, however, are more often the victims of intolerance than the perpetrators of it. Occasionally they may act brutally to some in their own small societies, but they offer no larger threat.

Reasoned argument, therefore, helps account for some shifting line between the tolerable and intolerable. There is also, it must be granted, simple weariness that explains some shifts. However much Reds might find the Blues intolerable, exhaustion may lead them to forbearance—especially if Blues keep to themselves. Life is too short, Reds may think, to spend much time and energy trying to suppress the objectionable beliefs and practices of the Blues. Once forbearance becomes a settled stance, it is possible that Reds may one day find that, surprisingly, Blues are not as bad as all that anyway. They may discover that they have more in common than they realized. Still, it was initial weariness, not reasoned argument, that led to a shifting line.

Other explanations include the gathering strength of those who are not tolerated so that it becomes much harder to fence them out, pressures by "outsiders" to ease up on intolerant conduct, and recognition that a policy of intolerance turns out to be politically or economically counterproductive. These all apply more to large racial, ethnic, and national groups than to individuals and to whole ways of life than to individual beliefs, actions, or conduct. Usually it is some combination of these factors that leads to greater toleration. Reds might find Blues growing in strength while, simultaneously, Blues in other nations pressure their own governments to exert influence on Reds to adopt a more tolerant policy. So, Reds might find that their own well-being suffers by continued intolerant practices. Still, in the short run, history seems to show that the initial response of the intolerant to challenges is a redoubling of efforts to suppress. When core values are at stake, those in power may feel that they have no choice but to continue their vehement opposition—or perish in the attempt.

What is the intolerable? It is crucial to recognize that the intolerable does not designate a natural kind. It is a class having nothing in common other than a refusal to put up with items in it. There is, in short, no set of intrinsic properties characterizing it. We may declare something intolerable for many reasons: because it is grossly rude, disgusting, unjust, unfair, abusive, cruel, offensive, sinful, wicked, or vicious. The intolerable, in short, is not a deep moral category but designates items placed there because of *logically prior* judgments and conclusions. Something is not intolerable *and* cruel but is intolerable *because* it is *so* cruel, not intolerable *and* disgusting but intolerable *because* it is *so* disgusting, and so on. To say that something is intolerable, therefore, is only to say that we should not and—subject to a few qualifications—will not tolerate it.

The intolerable is therefore not like gold. There is no analogue to atomic weight possessed by every intolerable thing. Classifying something as intolerable is more like classifying a plant as a *weed,* that is, as a nuisance that should be eradicated. When asked, for instance, why you are destroying a plant, you might naturally respond, "Because it is a weed." You could of course be mistaken; the

plant you are uprooting is a rare orchid. More interesting, however, are controversies about whether a given plant is or is not a weed. These are not disputes
about whether a plant belongs to this or that botanical category but whether it
belongs to an *evaluative* category—namely, the category of plants that are
nuisances—and so desirable to eliminate if one can. One man's weed can be another's flower. If it should turn out that kudzu can cure the common cold, we
would no longer classify it as a weed. We would reclassify it as a medicinal plant.
Like a cold, it might continue to annoy, but because of its curative powers, it is
no longer a weed. Instead, we would cultivate it, not try to stamp it out. Notice
that there is nothing *arbitrary* about classifying a particular plant as a weed,
though weeds do not constitute a basic biological category. Presumably we have
reasons for judging that a particular plant species is a nuisance; for instance, it
takes nutrients from the soil without furthering our purposes, it chokes out plants
we wish to grow, or it is ugly. When we discover the medicinal or economic benefits of a plant, these qualities are enough to lead us to remove its designation as
a weed.

Similarly, we generally have reasons for finding something intolerable—and
for revising our classifications when new knowledge, reshaped attitudes, or improved beliefs take hold. Some regard male homosexuality as intolerable because they believe that it leads to pedastry. As this groundless contention loses
its grip, one powerful reason vanishes for finding homosexual behavior—and
homosexuals themselves—intolerable. Many may now continue to think that homosexuality is sinful or deficient in some important way yet now judge that it is
not intolerable. Still others conclude that, far from being inherently deficient, a
homosexual life is fully acceptable, even if they do not find it personally appealing. This is like moving the classification of a plant from "weed" to
"flower"—even if the flower holds no particular attraction. Once we recognize
its genuine and positive attractiveness to others, we would rightly regard it as a
flower. Some plants do not move from weed to flower or medicinal plant but
simply to a "tolerable" plant—neither particularly attractive nor useful but not
warranting eradication.

Not every slight, abuse, injustice, sin, and the like brings with it questions of
toleration. Many are what lawyers call *de minimis,* beneath notice. Before questions of toleration arise, the wrong or sin must be sufficiently serious. Some judgments seem to carry seriousness with them, for instance, those described as
wicked, vicious, and cruel; others do not. Even those judgments that imply serious wrongdoing, sin, or offense are sometimes used in ways suggesting lesser
wrongs, sins, and offenses. Reds may say that it is a "sin" or a "crime" that Blues
are lazy, pushy, or excessively loud. But we mean this only half seriously or in
jest, as when someone says that "there ought to be a law" against wearing leisure
suits in public. What we need to keep squarely in view is that toleration arises
only once we pass a threshold of seriousness. The abuse, offense, or injustice
must be a *serious* breach. Certain acts may be thoughtless, inconsiderate, or un-

kind yet not amount to cruelty. Only after establishing the seriousness of a breach do we then consider whether it is intolerable. So we might deem seriousness a further circumstance of toleration.

Because viciousness, cruelty, and many other concepts embody evaluative notions, their negative judgments are, so to say, built-in. The physician who jabs a needle into the arm of a three-year-old is, from the child's perspective, cruel. While we recognize the pain, even terror, from the child's perspective, we withhold the judgment of cruelty, unless we conclude that the physician deliberately used harsher methods than necessary or relished his task.

The intolerable (and the tolerable) are highly contextual. That is, what counts as a serious breach in one context may be tolerable, even trivial, in another. Parents may think (correctly) that their teenager's slovenliness is intolerable and intervene in ways their child finds unwelcome. To accept an invitation for a dinner party but not appear is intolerable in societies having formal dinner parties. These instances of intolerable behavior are, however, beneath political notice. Still, what is beneath our notice now might have been deserving of its notice at an earlier time in different circumstances. Some of Jane Austen's women face ruin because of ill-advised dalliances that would not raise an eyebrow today.

All this has at least two implications. First, what counts as a serious breach depends on whether we are thinking of individuals, intimate groups (such as the family), small institutions (such as colleges or professional organizations), or larger institutions (such as religious organizations), including the state. Something beyond the pale at one level may not be so at another. This is not only a matter of size. Because size often entails other factors, however, size often does matter. It is a question of what is regarded as *vital*. Neatness and politeness are not vital to (most) religious ways of life; orthodoxy (usually) is. Religions typically regard heresy, not rudeness, as intolerable.

A second implication is that convention plays a significant part in what counts as tolerable or intolerable. This is obviously true of slovenliness and rudeness, but it is even true regarding such notions as cruelty and honesty. That our standards often embody, reflect, or take account of conventions, however, does not entail that either our standards or our conventions are *arbitrary*. There are often excellent reasons for our conventions and standards of tolerable belief, conduct, and attitudes. Polite behavior, for instance, helps make social relations go more smoothly. In the abstract, what counts as polite, impolite, neat, or slovenly is wide open, but only in the abstract. In the concrete, lived experience of any culture, the range is fixed. Kindness and cruelty are also open if considered abstractly but less so than matters of etiquette. Some cultures, for instance, may inculcate a candor, even bluntness, in interpersonal interaction that others rightly regard as intolerably insensitive if practiced in their own society. Still, nowhere could it be regarded as anything but cruel to inflict intense physical pain to extract confessions. (Maybe we can justify cruelty in certain extreme circumstances; it would not, however, cease to be cruel.)

While conventions need not be arbitrary, sometimes they are—or become so as the justifying reasons no longer apply. We need to tread carefully here. That we have this instead of that convention applicable to, say, expressions of mourning may be a historical accident but not that we have some convention or other. That no one can give good reasons for preferring one set of conventions to another in this instance does not show that our conventions are arbitrary in any deep way. The conventions probably continue a tradition whose origins are completely lost or largely accidental or established for reasons that no longer hold. Still, the set of conventions may continue to have a point and serve a purpose. Although no better than any other set on offer, they are equally good, though different. In truth, sets of conventions are seldom, if ever, "on offer." That we drive on the left or the right side of the road is *conventional* but not really a *convention*. Most of our conventions are customary, and the customs themselves develop as slowly and inadvertently as coral reefs.

It is true, however, that conventions can be, or become, arbitrary. This most often happens when the reasons that justified them no longer hold—and no new justificatory reasons replace them. When deep changes take place, for instance, conventions that helped smooth social interactions can become a terrible bar to them, hindering instead of easing social intercourse. Since conventions are generally embedded in whole ways of life, they seldom make sense when those ways of life undergo a radical change. They nonetheless can sometimes have a life of their own and survive long after they have served any useful purpose. In such instances, the conventions may become quaint reminders of the past. In other instances, they can become intolerable.

We can say the same for conventions and traditional practices that embody evaluative assumptions that were once unchallenged but are now thoroughly discredited. When men simply took for granted that women were inferior to them morally and intellectually (and sometimes spiritually), customary practices arose embodying those beliefs. Women, for instance, were not even considered for leadership positions of public or religious institutions. Although few any longer hold the beliefs on which the habits and customs were based, sexist practices may continue their malign momentum until directly and forcibly challenged as intolerable.

If the intolerable is something of a grab bag, it nonetheless serves as an important marker, for asserting that something is intolerable declares that toleration of it is unthinkable. This judgment is far stronger than finding something undesirable or unjustifiable or even seriously flawed. To judge something to be intolerable is to put everyone on notice that intervention would be fully justified. In declaring that sexual relations between adults and prepubescent children are intolerable, we express our willingness to prevent pedophilia and punish convicted pedophiles.

Holding anything to be intolerable, moreover, implies that we have no doubt whatever that our intervention is morally justified. We firmly believe that our case is open and shut. No one ever thinks, "I'm inclined, on the whole, to find X intolerable," for to make the judgment is to set aside any reservations. That we *feel* absolutely sure about our claims of intolerability does not entail that no one can challenge them. We can make mistakes about this as about most things. As a marker, however, the "intolerable" shows us the line that may not be crossed. We will not consider anything over that line a proper subject for toleration. Nor does it follow that we will tolerate everything not yet found intolerable. We may eventually find that a line has been crossed, for on reflection we may conclude that what we have been tolerating is intolerable (at least if done publicly and so on), and so intervention to stop or prevent it is warranted.

We can now see why, despite being a grab bag, the intolerable is the dog and tolerance the tail. Questions of the degree and limits of toleration arise *only* in the moral space that remains unoccupied by the intolerable. The intolerable is the border that may not be crossed, a border that is often hazy and seldom brightly lit. It is only when crossed that we learn the limits of toleration. We may conclude, for instance, that something is tolerable if done discreetly or rarely or as part of a religious ceremony (e.g., smoking peyote) or privately but not otherwise. Having determined that something is not intolerable in and of itself does not entail that there are not circumstances in which we would judge it to be intolerable.

This is not in any way hypocritical. What we do discreetly, rarely, or privately may well have fewer devastating consequences than if done indiscreetly, often, or publicly. This is not the nonsensical view that anything anyone does discreetly, rarely, as part of a religious ceremony, or privately is permissible. That one discreetly, or rarely, or privately tortures animals "in the privacy of one's own home" does not make it tolerable, only unknown. It is, instead, the eminently sensible view that not all questionable, even lamentable, conduct warrants intervention. The same is true of people with deplorable attitudes and beliefs. A political party might judge that it is tolerable for its members to have certain "deviant" views yet intolerable that the party should nominate those holding such views for public office.

What explains this? The answer, I believe, is that standards of toleration do not address our highest aspirations. Their aim is far lower. In this way they are like the standards found in criminal law. These, generally, provide minimal standards of legally acceptable conduct. Far from reflecting our highest aspirations, they usually require only that we do not sink below standards we can require of bad people. Most jurisdictions, for example, do not legally require anyone to be a Good Samaritan, though we praise those who are and may provide some legal protection for those who cause harm acting as Good Samaritans.[1] Criminal law would make civic life impossible if we made the standards of saints and heroes our minimal threshold for noncriminal behavior. There are many reasons for this, most applicable to toleration. The extensive invasion into the lives of others, the extraordinary power that would have to be given to law enforcement bodies, and the consequent power that would reside in the state are only the most obvious reasons we set modest aspirations for criminal law.

Similarly, social life would be impossible were we to deem intolerable any conduct or attitudes that did not meet the highest standards of moral rectitude, let alone aesthetic or personal sensibility, that we espouse—especially since we ourselves seldom meet these standards. While we disapprove of various attitudes, beliefs, acts, and practices, we may also determine that they are not *so* bad that we cannot permit them, however reluctantly and grudgingly. This is true even when, by our own account, the result of toleration is that third parties suffer harm, provided that, we judge, it is not bad *enough*. Obviously, others might disagree, and such disagreements are the stuff of controversies about concrete cases. We search, individually and collectively, for the line between the tolerable and intolerable.

We have seen that to say that something is intolerable implies that intervention would be justified. To this we must now add "everything else being equal." We need the ceteris paribus clause because sometimes there are good reasons not to intervene even if one has the power and will to do so. Most westerners judged that the Soviet invasion of Czechoslovakia in 1968 was intolerable, yet most did not clamor for their governments to intervene. Suppose that a realistic threat of intervention would likely have caused the Soviet Union to pull back—but only by greatly increasing the risk of a catastrophic thermonuclear war. Given this supposition, would the fact that Western governments did not intervene show that the invasion was tolerable? On its face it would seem to since no one lifted a finger to stop it. The invasion was, at least, *tolerated,* for surely, one might argue, the Western governments *put up with* the invasion.

But this is too quick. Undeniably, they did "put up with" the invasion in that they did not intervene when they could have. The reasons, however, had nothing to do with a judgment about the degree of wickedness of the invasion, *its* intolerability. The reasons were entirely *external* to any judgment about the tolerability of the invasion. Specifically, Western governments judged that the moral and political risks of intervention were far too high. To say that Western governments found the invasion tolerable, therefore, misleads, for it suggests what is not true, that there were good *moral* reasons for the invasion and domination of Czechoslovakia by the Soviet army or at least *tolerable* reasons for the invasion. But there were no such reasons. There were, however, good moral reasons for not risking World War III over the Soviet Union's invasion.

We may feel uneasy about the distinction just drawn because we have yet to examine the possible justifications for toleration. When we do, we will see that not every reason for putting up with something counts as an instance of toleration. We have already seen, for instance, that weariness, laziness, or indifference does not count as toleration, though they are examples of simply putting up with what one disapproves. Such explanations do show something about one's character (or the character of one's nation, church, and so on) but not that one is tolerant. It shows only that one is worn out, lazy, or indifferent.

Similarly, if two ethnic peoples keep themselves from killing each other only because a peacekeeping army credibly threatens to punish either side who acts violently, it does not show that the ethnic groups tolerate each other, that they find the other's existence tolerable. They do not. They simply are not willing to engage in behavior that will bring the roof down on themselves to satisfy their loathing of those whom they find intolerable. Nor does the threat have to be physical. Credible economic threats can suffice, for example.

We need to grasp the normative reasons for that which we disapprove of, not merely the fact that we do not intervene when we could. Unless we look at these reasons, we will not see how tolerance can be a *virtue*. In this, tolerance is like other virtues. Making a clever pun shows no wit if done because one does not fully understand the language. Nor does standing firm in the face of danger show courage if one is unaware of danger or is more terrified of being shot as a traitor is.

We can draw several general lessons from this discussion of the intolerable. In declaring that something is intolerable, one is not claiming that this thing has certain features, nature, or properties that force us to classify it as intolerable. The intolerable is not a category of this sort at all. Instead, one implies that there are sufficient reasons for holding that the conduct, attitude, practice, and so on in question ought not to be tolerated, that all the reasons there may be for tolerating the conduct and so on have been fully and convincingly defeated.

Changing circumstances, we have seen, can transform what was tolerable into the intolerable. Something that might be tolerable under certain conditions may cease to be when these conditions change. "Loose lips" do not normally "sink ships," but in wartime military gossip is intolerable. Conversely, behavior rightly regarded as intolerable in times of crisis may be tolerable in times of normalcy. Circumstances change our thinking in other ways. Changes in scientific knowledge, for instance, can change our understanding of what is and is not tolerable by altering our understanding of causes and consequences. *If* secondhand smoke can cause cancer, then smoking in confined public spaces is intolerable, for it imposes an unwarranted health risk on others. Finally, what were once deep-seated and pervasive views of the world sometimes change over time, so that what was once intolerable no longer is.

Determining where to draw the line between the tolerable and intolerable is often difficult and contentious. Equally important, we need to know why to draw it where we do. The reasons for line drawing are no less difficult or contentious than where to draw the line, as we will see in chapter 6.

NOTE

1. In the United States, some jurisdictions do impose limited legal duties on citizens to come to the aid of those in distress. Such jurisdictions are very much in the minority. Moreover, some (though not all) do provide some protection for physicians and laymen who accidentally or mistakenly cause harm to those they try to help.

Chapter 6

Thomas Aquinas
and John Locke on Toleration

THOMAS AQUINAS: RELIGION
AND THE LIMITS OF TOLERATION

The concept of toleration was around as long ago as the thirteenth century. Thomas Aquinas (1225–1274), for example, did not have to invent the term. It has its roots in the Latin term *tolerantia* and was used by classical writers.[1] Nor is there any indication that Aquinas gave "tolerance" either an idiosyncratic or a technical sense; probably he did not. He used *tolerance* in the central way that we still use it: to bear as a burden, put up with, endure, forbear, allow to exist. *Tolerantia* and its cognates occur only occasionally in Aquinas's work and do not loom large in his philosophical or theological thinking generally. On one occasion, however, he uses it to make clear what the Church should, and should not, tolerate. It is worth quoting in full:

> Human government is derived from the Divine government, and should imitate it. Now although God is all-powerful and supremely good, nevertheless He allows certain evils to take place in the universe, which He might prevent, lest, without them, greater goods might be forfeited, or greater evils ensue. Accordingly in human government also, those who are in authority, rightly tolerate certain evils, lest certain goods be lost, or certain greater evils be incurred: thus Augustine says (*De Ordine* ii, 4): "If you do away with harlots, the world will be convulsed with lust." Hence, though unbelievers sin in their rites, they may be tolerated, either on account of some good that ensues therefrom, or because of some evil avoided. Thus from the fact that the Jews observe their rites, which, of old, foreshadowed the truth of the faith which we hold, there follows this good—that our very enemies bear witness to our faith, and that our faith is represented in a figure, so to speak. For this reason they are tolerated in the observance of their rites.
> On the other hand, the rites of other unbelievers, which are neither truthful nor profitable are by no means to be tolerated, except perchance in order to avoid an evil,

e.g. the scandal or disturbance that might ensue, or some hindrance to the salvation of those who if they were unmolested might gradually be converted to the faith. For this reason the Church, at times, has tolerated the rites even of heretics and pagans, when unbelievers were very numerous.[2]

Here Aquinas considers three applications of tolerance: to Jews, heresy, and prostitution. He takes as given that Christianity (i.e., Roman Catholicism) is superior to Judaism. Before the New Covenant, however, Jews had a special relationship with God, a relationship deserving of respect. Furthermore, Aquinas explains, Jews remind us of our Christian origins. Although we have outgrown these origins, we must continue to tolerate those who remain tied to the Old Covenant, even if they are enemies of Christianity.

It is important to emphasize that Aquinas urges toleration for the sake of Christianity, not for the welfare of Jews. While Jews may survive, indeed flourish, that is only a by-product. The well-being of Jews constitutes no part of Aquinas's argument. Presumably, if Judaism disappeared because all Jews converted to Christianity, Aquinas would have been pleased. Today many would find the thought of tolerating Jews deeply offensive. It strikes us as patronizing at best and disparaging at worst. The inclination of many would be to say that Judaism is Christianity's equal, in the sense that both are fully acceptable forms of religious expression. In the thirteenth century, however, Aquinas's plea for (mere) toleration of Jews was progressive, particularly in the light of more virulent anti-Semitism.

Heresy is a different matter. Unlike Jews, heretics grow up as Christians and so must have once grasped its fundamental truths. Their rejection of orthodoxy leads them from God. As renegades, they deserve toleration that is more limited. The Church, Aquinas states, ought to tolerate heretical deviations twice. This gives the Church opportunities to convince heretics of their errors and to help guide them back into the fold. Presumably, even good people can go astray in grasping difficult, even mysterious, theological doctrines, and conforming to the orthodox doctrines can be personally demanding. If heretics stubbornly refuse to recant after a second relapse, however, Aquinas not only recommends excommunication but that the Church should turn them over to secular authorities to be put to death.[3]

Toleration for heretics is real yet obviously limited. Aquinas recommends that the Church tolerate heretics (but never heresy) partly for the sake of the heretics themselves and not solely for the good of the Church. Toleration gives heretics time to reflect and change their thinking. And subsequent history demonstrates that the Church felt justified in using coercive measures to encourage heretics to think again. This extremely limited tolerance of heretics does not extend to heresy itself, which is intolerable. In this, Aquinas's position differs from the previous application of toleration to Jews. Both Jews and their beliefs (defective because incomplete as he believes them to be) are tolerable. They are tolerable because Aquinas thinks that other considerations override our otherwise worthy aim of stamping out false or misguided religious belief.

Once heretics show themselves to be incorrigible, the Church must concern itself primarily with its own good and that of the faithful and only secondarily with the souls of heretics. Persistent heretics show themselves to be incorrigible, beyond earthly redemption. Whether they know it or not, heretics will be better off dying a cleansing death by fire than continuing in their apostasy. The Church will certainly be better off, Aquinas believes, for unless heretics are eliminated, they easily mislead the gullible into following them down the path to perdition. Aquinas fears not for the Church's institutional survival but for its sacred task: to shepherd Christians to God. It cannot perform this task if it is indifferent to heresy or to heretics who spread false doctrine.

Prostitution is a different matter altogether. Here Aquinas recommends toleration on the grounds that efforts to curtail it would "convulse the world in lust"— and "scandalize" the Church. He does not say how the Church would be scandalized, but presumably he has something like the following in mind. Except for those with a special calling and those with superior interests or unusual self-control, the need for men to satisfy their sexual desires is virtually insatiable. Without the outlet of prostitution, sexual frustration would express itself in even more undesirable ways: obsessive sexual fantasies, masturbation, and sexual misconduct in and out of marriage. It is in this sense that the world would presumably be "convulsed in lust." Further, serious efforts to curtail, let alone stamp out, prostitution will inevitably fail. Futile efforts to eliminate prostitution will only make the Church look ludicrous in the eyes of the faithful, an object of derision. Attempting the impossible only brings into question the Church's reputation for wise leadership. This, in turn, would undermine its sacred task. To avoid the scandal of incompetence and misplaced priorities, therefore, Aquinas recommends that prostitution be tolerated—that we put up with it as a burden to be born.

To put up with prostitution is far from full toleration, let alone acceptance. Aquinas was not in doubt about its sinfulness and thoroughgoing wickedness. Instead, he thinks that the Church must show it what I call "bare toleration" to avoid ridicule and scandal. As with mere toleration of Jews, the argument is made not in terms of promoting prostitution or helping prostitutes live better lives but in terms of protecting the interests of those in authority, the tolerators. Presumably, had Aquinas believed either that prostitution could be extirpated easily or that it was so horrible that Christianity could not flourish in its presence, he would have judged it intolerable.

Aquinas also discusses toleration briefly in his *Commentary on the Nicomachean Ethics* of Aristotle. He remarks there, with apparent approval, that if someone has an "ineffective belief," it deserves tolerance, but tolerance is not to be extended to vice or "to any of the other censurable dispositions."[4] A little later he says, "[A] man apparently deserves more pardon for sins about naturally desirable things, because tolerance is more readily extended to such desires common to all, precisely because they are common."[5] The desire for food in excessive amounts (i.e., gluttony) is given as an example, though, he quickly adds, not the desire for delicate foods. That sin need not be tolerated. All gluttony is sinful, but not so wicked that authorities should try to end it. Desires for luxury foods, however, were not immune from restrictions since gluttony can be satisfied on "common," readily available foods.

HISTORICAL INTERLUDE

As noted, tolerance does not feature prominently in Aquinas's thought or in medieval social, political, and moral thought generally. According to the *Oxford English Dictionary,* the word does not appear in English until the early sixteenth century. And, as an issue, toleration does not emerge until the Protestant Reformation and the consequent European religious wars of the sixteenth and seventeenth centuries. Even then, *philosophers* were not first on the scene. They certainly cannot claim credit for making religious toleration a preoccupation of seventeenth-century politics. Circumstances, as it were, thrust the notion forward. Political and religious leaders (and undoubtedly innumerable ordinary people) concluded that endless killing, strife, and turmoil brought on by religious fanaticism was not worth fleeting victories. Surely many were driven to support religious toleration through exhaustion. They needed no sophisticated arguments to convince them that toleration was sound policy. Others did try to develop arguments to show that religious toleration could be justified as something more than relief from fatigue or an unprincipled compromise between competing groups who could not be assured of getting the upper hand permanently—something more, that is, than a modus vivendi.

Some based their position on the need for social and political stability. Still others sought justification in God's Word or the rights of an Englishman or in the claim that what unites Christians is more important than what divides them. These and other reasons jostled together in the polemics of the day, even if not altogether consistently. This, too, is understandable—any argument in a storm. Before turning to John Locke, we should pause to mention, if only in passing, that other philosophers helped prepare the ground for Locke's own defense of toleration.

Since Aquinas makes it clear that toleration was not unknown in the medieval world, we should not be surprised that thinkers before Locke had something to say about it. While their views are not as well known as Locke's or as influential, they helped prepare the way for greater (if still limited) tolerance. Further, some of their arguments are still in play today. I call this section an "interlude" because its purpose is not to recapitulate the history of tolerance; that is ably done elsewhere.[6] Instead, I wish to indicate that, historically, toleration has been defended from more than one perspective, that Locke is not the only "founding father" of religious toleration.

At this historical distance, it may be hard to grasp how eager members of one religion were to persecute those of another. This is so despite a tradition of toleration in Christian thought, as we have already seen in Aquinas. Some Christians argued that we have to acquire faith freely, so persecution is not justified. Others argued that Christians should love, not persecute those who were weak and misguided. And still others, like St. Paul, Origen, and St. Cyprian, developed the parable of the "tares" (from Matthew 13:24–30, 36–43), cautioning against pulling up weeds for fear of destroying the crop. Other strands in Christianity, however, led to the opposite conclusion. While agreeing that faith cannot be forced, many (like Aquinas) agreed with St. Augustine that no death is worse for the soul than the freedom to err.[7] As religion became a serious *political* issue and not only a personal moral question, these arguments squared off against each other.

Locke's immediate predecessors in Europe also thought long and hard about tolerance.[8] The French philosopher Michel de Montaigne (1533–1592), for example, provides an intriguing case for toleration. He grounds it in a skeptical attack on presumptuous claims to religious and metaphysical knowledge made by philosophers, theologians, and priests, claims far outstripping our feeble capacities: "Presumption is our natural and original malady. The most vulnerable and frail of all creatures is man, and at the same time the most arrogant."[9] Why can we not be more like animals, Montaigne pleads, which "are much more self-controlled than we are, and restrain themselves with more moderation within the limits that nature has prescribed to us?"[10] The culprit is *imagination.* It leads us to pursue superfluous and artificial desires instead of our natural, animal desires. Our tendency to worry about the future, moreover, fills us with fear, desire, and hope. These distract us from the here and now: "We are never at home, we are always beyond."[11] We need to satisfy our animal needs and enjoy mental tranquility. And that entails that we avoid getting caught up in fruitless battles that reach beyond our rootedness in everyday experience. Self-knowledge is possible because it is experiential. I can know that I am hungry now or, more generally, given to losing my temper. No one, however, should take seriously the preposterous claims of philosophers and theologians.

We need not linger here to evaluate Montaigne's own explanations or consider at length his skeptical arguments about propositional knowledge, whether of science, philosophy, or religion. What is important for our purposes is how he helps prepare the ground for tolerance. If we are to be "at home" with ourselves, we need a sphere of privacy in which our sensual self can develop freely and within which we can attain peace of mind. By preserving a sphere of privacy, we concede to the state power over what is public. This does not bother Montaigne, who, like Hobbes, believes that we would be at each other's throats without law and order. If we can establish a sphere of privacy, however, then we will have established a regime of toleration for free political thought and freedom of conscience. It is in our deepest self-interest to establish and maintain such a regime.

Montaigne's defense of toleration rests on his belief that human nature is essentially animal, that we need mental tranquility, and that metaphysical and theological truth-claims are phantasms of human imagination. What is notable about

Montaigne's skeptical arguments is not their philosophical acumen but his own deep humanity, his care for the individual human personality. It is this that the fantasies of philosophers, theologians, priests, and politicians stifle. Montaigne's humanity and deep aversion to cruelty in the name of religion cannot fail to impress. Further, his is a concern directed at the well-being of those affected by intolerance, not the interests of those deciding whether to inflict it. This concern is not reflected in Locke and not much in Aquinas. The modern sensibility Montaigne helps shape resonates in the argument I will develop in chapter 8.

René Descartes (1596–1650) adds that we need benevolent love, a love that seeks the well-being of that which it loves. He names this love *generosity,* and it combines elements of Christian love and Aristotelian magnanimity.[12] Now generosity is not just fuzzy good feeling. It rests on a determinate judgment about the nature of good and evil. Human good is freedom. It is the source of our greatest self-esteem. We only act freely, however, when we put aside our passions in favor of others. Unless we do so, community and friendship are impossible. Christian fanatics lack just this generosity. What motivates them is not Christian charity but vanity and arrogance—the same conclusion Montaigne reaches. By letting their passions run wild, fanatics destroy freedom and thus self-esteem. Further, our beliefs are worthless unless we arrive at them the right way, namely, through reason. But reason can never be coerced. So, we must tolerate—even if *merely* tolerate—those with whom we find ourselves in sharp disagreement. Bits and pieces of Descartes's arguments reappear in Locke and throughout the history of toleration. Unfortunately, Locke does not avail himself of Descartes's central argument that morality demands that we act generously to others.

Baruch Spinoza (1632–1677) takes Hobbes's notion of natural rights and develops it into a powerful argument for democracy and freedom of conscience. Spinoza's general argument is well stated in the subtitle of the *Tractatus:* "A treatise . . . to prove that not only is perfect liberty to philosophize compatible with devout piety and with the peace of the state, but that to take away such liberty is to destroy the public peace and even piety itself."[13] Human diversity is such, Spinoza believes, that we must expect people to disagree not only about matters of taste but about all matters of judgment. We are contrarian by nature and seldom take kindly to those who gratuitously tell us what to do. The mind simply cannot be controlled, Spinoza argues, and it is wrong to try, an argument echoed in Locke.

JOHN LOCKE: TOLERATION
AND THE LIMITS OF RELIGIOUS COERCION

John Locke (1632–1704) was the leading English philosopher who clarified, modified, and justified toleration in his own day. The powerful polemic of his 1689 *A Letter concerning Toleration (Epistola de Tolerentia)* continues to inform our understanding and defense of toleration. Locke's letter—a forty-odd-page essay—has a polemical purpose: namely, to urge Christian magistrates to tolerate religious doctrines and rituals of dissenters, even though they might have the power to suppress them.

The political and philosophical problem facing Locke was to show that freedom of religious conscience need not—if its limits are clearly understood—destabilize authority grounded in consent of the governed in a Christian (i.e., Protestant) political society. Christian officials, Locke argues, need not fear that tolerance of religious dissenters will threaten peace and tranquility. Protestantism raises the worry for two reasons. First, in denying the necessity of a mediator between man and God, it makes everyone an authority on God's Word. Scholars might well be more learned, but their reading of the Bible is no more authoritative than the humblest peasant. No one can force one's understanding of the demands of faith on anyone else. Following on this is a second worry. If my interpretation of God's Word is as binding on me as your interpretation is on you, what happens if you and I find ourselves in fundamental disagreement over a contentious issue? It would seem that, in good conscience, I should not yield to you or you to me. Magistrates— that is, state authorities—rightly see this as a recipe for social unrest and strife. This concern is exacerbated when magistrates, as devout Christians themselves, support one interpretation of God's Word over another.

There was no need for Locke to stimulate an interest in toleration. It was *the* question of the day in England as on the Continent. As William Popple, who first translated Locke's *Epistola* from Latin into English, said of toleration, "I think indeed there is no nation under heaven, in which so much has already been said upon the subject as ours."[14] Locke's primary concern was England, not France, but he knew full well the devastation religious turmoil brought to France and to the colonies in the New World. As Maurice Cranston writes of the time after the revocation of the Edict of Nantes in 1685,

> I think it is not generally remembered today how cruel and barbarous was the repression of the Huguenots in France in 1685. Protestants who refused to convert, under orders of Louis XIV, were beaten, pillaged, dragooned, their children were taken from them; men were sent to the galleys or driven into exile.[15]

In the preface to his translation, Popple claims, "Absolute liberty, just and true liberty, equal and impartial liberty, is the thing that we stand in need of."[16] Locke's own defense of toleration is far more circumspect, and wisely so, for while just, true, equal, and impartial liberty might inspire, it remains insubstantial until its implications are made plain. And the notion of absolute liberty—even supposing that it is not empty rhetoric—would undermine all political authority. Locke is no anarchist. True, unlike Hobbes, he does not believe that life in a state of nature would necessarily be nasty, brutish, and short. It would, nevertheless, be extraordinarily inconvenient—and unjust—for in a state of nature, everyone is judge, juror, and executioner regarding the proper implications of their own inalienable natural rights. So, the upshot of Locke's state of nature probably is not too different from that envisaged by Hobbes. Locke thinks, consequently, that rational people would consent to enter into a social contract ensuring respect for their natural rights under a common, consented to, authority. In doing so, they would give up any antecedent right they might have had to "absolute liberty" yet retain their natural rights to life, liberty, and property. Yet even in a state of nature, Locke would have rejected absolute liberty, if that means liberty without constraints, for men living without political authority in a state of nature are still morally obligated to respect each other's rights to life, liberty, and property.

Locke's arguments for toleration flow from the theory of political authority he lays out in his *Second Treatise on Government* (1689). The conclusion of the argument is stated as well in his brief *Letter concerning Toleration:*

> The commonwealth seems to me to be a society of men constituted only for the procuring, preserving, and advancing their own civil interests. Civil interest I call life, liberty, health, and indolence of body [i.e., freedom from pain]; and the possession of outward things, such as money, land, houses, furniture, and the like.[17]

Throughout both the *Second Treatise* and the *Letter* Locke stresses that justified political authority is limited to *civil interests* and *outward things.* Every living person has many interests, most especially the inward interest in the care of his own soul. But this is no affair of any "magistrate"—including parliamentarian, judge, or the king himself. Inward concerns are beyond the legitimate interest of the state: "the whole jurisdiction of the magistrate reaches only to these civil concernments . . . and . . . it neither can nor ought in any manner to be extended to the salvation of souls."[18]

That the magistrate *ought not* concern himself with the salvation of souls seems clear to us today. But why *cannot*? Locke gives two reasons. First, faith is such that it simply cannot be compelled by outward force. The powerful may compel me to *do* objectionable things, such as recant, or torment me for what I believe, but they cannot, Locke believes, force me to alter what I believe. Magistrates therefore attempt the impossible if they try: "Confiscation of estate, imprisonment, torments, nothing of that nature can have any such efficacy as to make men change the inward judgment that they have framed of things."[19]

Locke may have been too optimistic even in his own day. Just as facing a noose "wonderfully concentrates the mind," as Samuel Johnson declared, so the rack may well lead a person to reconsider the cogency and strength of his convictions. It is not that victims of torture simply say whatever pleases their tormentors. They might actually come to believe what their tormentors wish them to believe. Torture need not even come into the equation. Those today who honestly believe that blood transfusions are contrary to God's Word sometimes reevaluate their beliefs when their child's life hangs on the strength and depth of their conviction.

Today we have even more evidence that beliefs can be changed through persuasion, especially using subtle, manipulative techniques. Magistrates (and others) need not be so naive as to believe that they can change *every* dissenter's beliefs. They might, however, entertain reasonable hopes of altering the convictions of most dissenters, thus isolating and rendering ineffectual those who continue to resist. Among the time-honored methods are suppression of the written word, preventing dissenters from entering satisfying careers and professions, subjecting them to public ridicule and humiliation, and providing massive rewards for those with "congenial" beliefs and attitudes. Again, the aim of the sensible magistrate is not to extinguish dissent altogether. It is enough to isolate and contain dissent to a tiny, manageable minority who might then appear to be irresponsible zealots. While Locke was surely familiar with such methods, he does not show why magistrates attempt the impossible in employing them. He simply asserts that this is so.

Locke's second argument for maintaining that the care of souls cannot belong to magistrates rests on his claim that there is but "one way to heaven." Now, once we are in a civil society, we are morally bound to obey legitimate authority. Since different princes have radically different ideas about where the narrow road to salvation lies, ordinary subjects might find themselves in an impossible position, for what if a prince orders that everyone follow a path that some subjects believe leads straight to Hell? As freely consenting members of a political state, subjects are under a political obligation to obey; as freethinking creatures of God, however, they are bound to exercise their own judgment about the path to salvation. No matter what subjects do, they will be violating one obligation or the other. If they honor their fundamental duty to find and follow their own path to God, moreover, they will necessarily have to take up arms against their prince. Locke believes that magistrates can easily, and rightly, avoid such conflicts if only they limit their religious concerns to the state of their own souls and their own souls *alone.*

Were Locke's arguments sound, he would have a defense of toleration similar to Aquinas's regarding prostitution: namely, that authorities act irrationally in attempting the impossible and thereby court derision and contempt. Yet an important difference remains. Locke's arguments point to the impossibility of changing *beliefs;* Aquinas's arguments point to the impossibility of eliminating *conduct*, in particular, a profitable line of work for which (he believes) there is an insatiable demand. Aquinas's approach appears superior, for at most Locke shows only that suppressing undesirable beliefs is *difficult.* No committed inquisitor would disagree. It shows only that efforts must be redoubled using any means necessary.

"Irrationality" plays a central role in Locke's criticism of religious intolerance, but it is irrationality narrowly understood as "attempting the impossible." Once it is conceded that (indirectly) manipulating belief and faith is not impossible but merely difficult, Locke's argument loses much of its force. He would have been better served by showing how religious tolerance leads to human misery and immorality, as argued by Montaigne, Descartes, and Spinoza, or that religious intolerance leads to social instability and contempt for authority, as does Aquinas.

Without accepting the evidence on which Aquinas bases his opposition, we can endorse the general grounds on which he makes his case. Mere toleration is sometimes the best policy, all things considered, and that includes moral considerations. Probably because of his narrow, polemical purpose, Locke never considers toleration except as it relates to religion. Unlike Aquinas, he does not evince any tolerance to the incontinent and concupiscent.

Locke's own position, fortunately, is not exhausted by the impossibility argument. He also argues that, even if magistrates *could* suppress dissenting beliefs, expressions of faith, and rituals, they *should* not. The care of a soul, Locke insists, belongs to no one but the individual whose soul it is. God has not authorized anyone to have that kind of authority over anyone else. Even if bolstered by consent of the people, "no man can so far abandon the care of his own salvation as blindly to leave it to the choice of any other."[20] This follows from Locke's generally Protestant understanding of faith: "All the life and power of true religion consists in the inward and full persuasion of the mind; and faith is not faith without believing."[21] Insincere confessions of faith are simply worthless. This argument is not confined to Protestants, of course; we find it in both Descartes and Spinoza.

Locke does draw a further distinction that is not limited to a purely Christian context: that between matters that are "necessary" and those that are "indifferent." Magistrates must do what they can to prohibit force, fraud, and abuse if the state is to meet the ends for which civil society is established. Montaigne, Descartes, and Spinoza would certainly agree. Most things, however, are "indifferent" to this end. Magistrates may not generally forbid these *unless* they do so for everyone, without regard to religious context, and for good reason. In Locke's day, for instance, Quaker men wore hats in church, an aspect of Quaker worship that the majority of Englishmen found highly objectionable. Yet unless magistrates can find some (nonreligious) reasons to prohibit *anyone* from wearing a hat indoors, they may not prohibit Quakers from doing so. Dissenters may not be singled out *arbitrarily*.

Locke mentions one apparent exception: Magistrates may intervene to preserve public order. This is not quite the exception it seems, for although there may be nothing intrinsically different about two cases, the fact that one endangers public order and the other does not distinguishes them. There is a parallel "exception" sometimes invoked in American law. Generally, Americans have a constitutional right to assemble and present their grievances to the government. Sometimes this right is temporarily curtailed if authorities fear that riots will erupt—riots caused not by the petitioners but by an unruly mob attacking the petitioners. Such considerations would have loomed even larger in Locke's day, when the reach and power of the state was significantly less than it is today. With this exception, however, indifferent things, then, are not generally subject to magisterial suppression. Locke states explicitly,

> Whatsoever is lawful in the commonwealth, cannot be prohibited by the magistrate in the church. Whatsoever is permitted unto any of his subjects for their ordinary use,

neither can nor ought to be forbidden by him to any sect of people for their religious uses.[22]

At the same time,

> those things that are prejudicial to the commonweal of a people in their ordinary use, and are therefore forbidden by laws, those things ought not to be permitted to churches in their sacred rites. Only the magistrate ought always to be very careful that they do not misuse his authority, to the oppression of any church, under pretence of public good.[23]

Locke's division between matters that are necessary and those that are indifferent is not as unproblematic as he makes out, for the *meaning* and, therefore, the religious, moral, and political *significance* of something can change fundamentally depending on its context, whether secular or religious. The same physical object can be transformed depending on the web of understanding in which it is embedded. For Christians, for example, wafer and wine served in Holy Communion are not *merely* so. And coins might be money in one social setting but only jewelry in another. So, too, the seemingly innocuous act of wearing a hat in church can mean humility and respect to Quakers but insulting arrogance to Anglicans.

No small part of the practice of toleration is learning how to understand behavior and practices from within a web of meanings not one's own. Locke seems oblivious to this, perhaps deliberately so. There is not even a hint that he recognizes that seemingly "indifferent" matters take on charged meanings and significance that may be regarded as "necessary" in various religious and social settings.

Locke's plea for religious toleration has clearly defined limits. We have already seen that magistrates may forbid activities close to the nerve of a religion, provided they do so for general policy reasons and not merely to show disapproval. But their authority extends far beyond this. Religionists who, because of their faith, owe their allegiance to a foreign power are not entitled to any religious toleration:

> It is ridiculous for any one to profess himself to be a Mahometan only in religion, but in every thing else a faithful subject to a Christian magistrate, whilst at the same time he acknowledges himself bound to yield blind obedience to the mufti of Constantinople; who himself is entirely obedient to the Ottoman emperor.[24]

Closer to home, Locke had deep reservations about extending religious toleration to "papists" for two reasons. First, like Muslims, they (allegedly) owe their allegiance to a foreign power. Not only this, but some Catholics claim that kings lose their crowns if excommunicated. Second, Roman Catholics, Locke maintains, are taught that they need not keep faith with heretics:

> Their meaning, forsooth, is, that the privilege of breaking faith belongs unto themselves; for they declare all that are not of their communion to be heretics, or at least may declare them so whensoever they think fit.[25]

The fundamental reason for withdrawing toleration from Muslims and Roman Catholics is not the falsity of their doctrines or their objectionable rituals. It is instead Locke's judgment that their commitments might well lead to public instability.

For similar reasons, Locke does not extend toleration to atheists:

> Those are not at all to be tolerated who deny the being of God. Promises, covenants, and oaths, which are the bonds of human society, can have no hold upon an atheist. The taking away of God, though but even in thought, dissolves all.[26]

Like Catholics, who exempt themselves from keeping faith with heretics, so atheists—because they deny God's existence—cannot be trusted to keep faith with anyone. Unless we fear God's wrath, Locke thinks, any oaths, promises, contracts, or covenants will be worthless. This is certainly his view about laws, which "are of no force at all without penalties."[27] Atheists believe (falsely, Locke thinks) that they can escape divine punishment if they behave badly. But we cannot rely on magistrates alone to punish those who break their covenants. Since atheists may think that they can "get away with it," they cannot be trusted to honor the social contract they freely enter. Because atheists are inherently unreliable, they necessarily threaten public order. This is so even if atheists do not *actually* cause disorder. Although Locke does not share Hobbes's bleak picture of mankind, he does believe that human nature is weak and venal. Without fear of divine sanction, civil society would be under constant threat of dissolution.

There are, then, several exceptions to Locke's stout defense of religious toleration. Further, Locke's words are subject to expansive interpretations. Throughout history, magistrates have declared that various sects threaten public stability. Contemporary experience, moreover, provides ample evidence that there are indeed religious sects who court self-destruction—and the destruction of everyone around them.

Despite his genuine defense of religious toleration, then, Locke gives magistrates significant leeway in restricting religious practice or participation in public life. That he does so shows that, in the end, Locke favors the *perceived* need for stability over *actual* religious toleration, for if, in the judgment of lawmakers and judges, a religious practice is deemed prejudicial to social order, it may be prohibited, despite its seeming "indifference." Provided that magistrates do not forbid practices for purely religious reasons, Locke offers a bitter brew to those whose conscience enjoins them to follow paths magistrates find threatening:

> [A] private person is to abstain from the actions that he judges unlawful; and he is to undergo the punishment, which is not unlawful for him to bear; for the private judgment of any person concerning a law enacted in political matters, for the public good, does not take away the obligation of that law, nor deserve a dispensation.[28]

Even if the magistrate unjustifiably forbids something on religious grounds, there is no earthly recourse. God will exact His punishment in due course. Until then, better to keep the law and enjoy peace than plunge into war. In the *Second Treatise,* Locke notes that if magistrates become increasingly arbitrary and systematically violate the natural rights of the people, the government and—in extreme cases—political society itself dissolves.

Locke's advocacy of toleration, qualified though it may be, did not go unchallenged in his own day. His most trenchant critic led Locke to three further letters on toleration. Although they add little that is not found, at least implicitly, in the first *Letter,* they do make Locke's position clearer.

The critic was Jonas Proast, an Anglican clergyman. He agrees with Locke that civil authorities may not use torture to bring about religious conformity and that punishment cannot *directly* lead to a change of heart. Proast nonetheless defends a position of religious intolerance that would, in Locke's opinion, seriously undermine the fragile Toleration Act of 1689. Just as Locke's original *Letter* was published anonymously, so, too, was Proast's first reply. Subsequently, each adopted pseudonyms: Locke became "Philanthropus" (Friend of Man) to Proast's "Philochristus" (Friend of Christ). Their choice of pseudonyms nicely captures the difference between them, though Proast might better have styled himself "Friend of the Established Church." Locke and Proast agree that there is one true religion and that it is Christianity. A major difference between them, however, lies in the identification of true religion with a particular *church.* Locke takes Williams's "broad church" view, holding that Christianity lives in many (though not all) churches. Proast, to the contrary, maintains that the true religion is found in the Church of England alone.

Although the dispute between Locke and Proast is narrow, the chasm separating them runs deep. Proast directly challenges Locke's "impossibility" argument on the same grounds as I did earlier, though with a different orientation. Conceding that faith in the true religion cannot be directly caused by force does not preclude the possibility that coercion, fear of punishment, and punishment itself may lead a nonconformist to reassess both his reservations against the Established Church and the reasons underlying his own dissenting faith. Locke disagrees with the dissenters, so he cannot defend them on the grounds of truth. He does, however, complain that Proast confuses the true religion with a particular church. Yet since Locke himself does not believe that *every* church that calls itself Christian is true to Christianity's core belief, Proast undermines part of Locke's argument.

Locke must argue, therefore, that coercion and fear of punishment simply cannot succeed in bringing someone to faith in the true religion, except by happenstance. History shows that most people do not change their beliefs because of religious persecution, though it may affect their conduct. Further, even supposing that some souls might be saved, many more will be lost in reaction to persecution. Finally, since Proast cannot specify what constitutes "moderate force," it will be all too tempting for magistrates to conclude that with just a *bit* more force dissidents would see the light. We simply lack any independent criterion of how much force is needed either in general or in a specific case to lead one to reflect on one's religious beliefs. Locke thus fears that Proast's defense of "moderate force" is an open invitation to zealous magistrates to use heavy-handed methods that Locke and his contemporaries knew well.

Locke has a further reason for rejecting any suggestion that magistrates should even lean one way or another. According to his general political philosophy, individuals enter a social contract to protect their God-given, inalienable natural rights. Given that magistrates cannot exceed their writ, they may not—even if they can—use either force or manipulation to bring stubborn, conscientious dissenters back to the true religion. Locke's argument is simple and straightforward:

> Violating any natural right is an injury; the aim of the commonwealth is to protect us from injury; in a state of nature, everyone would regard having religion forced down one's throat as a severe injury; therefore, the magistrate has no right to do what may not be done in a state of nature.[29]

Locke clearly wins on this point, if one accepts (a) that political obligation and authority rest on consent and (b) Locke's particular views concerning natural rights, their number, and what they imply. This is only to say that Locke's defense of religious toleration cannot be divorced from his general political philosophy. Nor is this surprising. Neither tolerance nor any other significant political virtue is freestanding. Locke initially makes it appear as though toleration is an exception because of his labored use of the impossibility argument. Once Proast threatens that defense, Locke must dig more deeply into his political philosophy to show not the impossibility but the *illegitimacy* of religious intolerance.

Proast forces Locke's hand in yet another way. Locke concedes not only that Christianity is the true religion but that the Church of England embodies it. If this is so, Proast argues, why should magistrates, at least in England, not use moderate force in leading nonconformists to reconsider their (false) beliefs? After repeating objections we have already considered, Locke resorts to a fresh argument. He does so by denying that Proast, or anyone else, can *know* that Christianity is the true religion. Since we cannot *know* that the Church of England is the only true embodiment of the only true religion, any magistrate would be abusing his authority (setting aside other objections) were he to force people to reconsider their contrary beliefs. One's belief in the resurrection of Christ—at the indispensable bedrock of Christianity—is a matter of reasoned faith. It is neither self-evident, demonstrable, nor empirically verifiable. It should not, therefore, be legitimately imposed on anyone:

> To you and me the Christian religion is the true, and that is built . . . on this, that Jesus Christ was put to death at Jerusalem, and rose again from the dead. Now do you or I know this? I do not ask with what assurance we believe it, for that in the highest degree not being knowledge, is not what we now inquire after. . . . For whatever is not capable of demonstration, as such remote matters of fact are not, is not, unless it be self-evident, capable to produce knowledge, how well grounded and great soever the

assurance of faith may be wherewith it is received; but faith it is still, and not knowledge; persuasion, and not certainty.[30]

Locke repeats this argument in his *Fourth Letter* but never defends the grounds on which it is based. Those familiar with Locke's *An Essay concerning Human Understanding*[31] will know, however, that he there develops not only his distinction between faith and reason but his measured empiricist epistemology that culminates in the more thoroughgoing empiricism of David Hume decades later.

Maurice Cranston argues that Proast successfully forces Locke "to acknowledge a more sceptical attitude to religion as such than he had previously admitted."[32] If religious beliefs can never amount to knowledge, then—since beliefs, but not knowledge, can be false—we must hold our religious beliefs at a certain skeptical distance. Locke does argue that magistrates may not use force to inculcate religious beliefs (partly) because we cannot know them to be true. But this does not entail that Locke thinks we ought to be less wholehearted in our religious commitments. To concede that we lack religious *knowledge* is not to adopt a "sceptical attitude" to them. It is only to acknowledge that religion is a matter of faith, not knowledge.

Peter Nicholson,[33] whose lucid essay on the dispute between Locke and Proast I have followed, notes that in *An Essay concerning Human Understanding* Locke argues that we can indeed demonstrate God's existence and that his existence is therefore a matter of knowledge. Because God is no deceiver, we can also know that which God reveals in Scripture must be true. What we cannot know, however, is whether our *interpretation* of Scripture is always correct. Where Scripture is silent we can be assured that God has not spoken. Since Scripture is silent on both the authority of magistrates to force religious belief and the specific institutional embodiment Christianity must take, magistrates may not enforce particular rituals or institutions.

There are other, more general, reasons for rejecting Cranston's claim that Locke adopts a skeptical attitude to religious belief. Skepticism, rightly understood, is an epistemological claim that we lack certain knowledge about something or other. Few will argue that we are not entitled to believe something unless we know it to be true with certainty. Knowledge, Locke rightly points out, does not exhaust our grounds for *trust*. We can be *assured* of something without *knowing* that it is true. We cannot have proof or incontestable evidence that our friends will not betray us, but this fact should not lead us to skepticism about our friendships. I can be fully assured in my trust without it being based on incorrigible knowledge. That I cannot *prove* the loyalty of my friends, therefore, does not introduce any skeptical distancing from them.

Yet does Locke not concede that where magistrates *can* know, then religious enforcement is justified? And since we can know that God exists (according to Locke), why can magistrates not use force to convince atheists of *at least* this? Although Locke does not extend toleration to atheists, he nowhere argues in favor of their persecution. The reason, I think, is that he falls back on both his "impossibility" argument and his general justification for political authority. If, however misguided, a man denies the existence of God, then force is (almost) certainly not going to lead him to think otherwise. Further, our natural rights preclude authorities from enforcing anything that would injure us in a state of nature, as religious persecution would do. Of course, as Locke says repeatedly, religious toleration does not preclude anyone, including magistrates, from using rational methods of persuasion to get men to see the error of their ways and recognize true religion.

Locke's four *Letters* on toleration show how much religious toleration matters to him. They also show how much Proast forces Locke more deeply into his general political philosophy and his deepest epistemological views. Most commentators think Locke satisfactorily answered Proast's criticisms. I am not so sure. In any case, we can see that Locke's defense of toleration cannot rest complacently on foundations initially set down in his original *Letter.*

This points to one general lesson we can learn from Locke: No defense of toleration can be freestanding. The case for toleration, and its limits, must be situated in a more general political philosophy, perhaps even a general philosophical outlook. The grounds for toleration, as Proast forces us to see through his criticisms of Locke, are not self-evident. Locke's impossibility argument is relatively freestanding, as is the defense of toleration on the grounds that it is less exhausting to be tolerant than intolerant. Both, however, are hostages to empirical fortune. If persecutors become more subtle and sophisticated or if intolerant warring parties find renewed energy, neither argument will have provided toleration with a principled defense. Locke sees this, and arguments that remain undeveloped in his first *Letter* receive greater elaboration in his subsequent replies to Proast. While he never abandons the argument from impossibility, he relies much more heavily on arguments that show the *unjustifiability,* not the *impossibility,* of religious intolerance.

There is more we can learn about toleration from Locke's four *Letters.* Toleration, Locke makes clear, does not mean either that we must approve of what we tolerate or that we cannot criticize what we tolerate. Locke himself urges each of us, including magistrates, to engage in rational discussion with those they must tolerate. Therefore, criticism, even vehement criticism, is not itself a manifestation of intolerance, unless it is hectoring or harassing. Yet Locke leaves something out. He speaks not of rational discussion but of persuasion and instruction. But engagement should be a two-way street. There is not the slightest hint in Locke that magistrates might learn something from those they tolerate. To do so would move magistrates beyond *mere* tolerance *toward* full tolerance. It would create the possibility that *either* side might find its beliefs shifting. Because of Locke's polemical purpose, he would not have wanted to alarm his opponents more than he clearly did. His concern is primarily solely to state authorities, urging them not to force the beliefs and rituals of the Church of England on everyone. Still, a principled defense of tolerance should do more than this. It should recognize that a practice of toleration that goes beyond bare or mere tolerance places one's own convictions at risk.

A Letter concerning Toleration brings out other aspects of the logic of toleration. We tolerate that which we disapprove. Further, in tolerating that which we disapprove, we do not deny ourselves the right to criticize or remonstrate. Locke also makes clear that the argument for toleration is always directed at those who have the power and inclination to act intolerantly. That magistrates are the subjects of toleration makes sense because they have the power to act intolerantly. And because Locke assumes his magistrates to be devout Christians, they will presumably have the temptation to suppress what they believe to be false and, to the extent that they can, force (or at least lead) people to affirm the principles of the Christian faith. This is only natural. When something, such as religion, matters enormously, there is a standing wish to see others embrace it as well.

We need to consider one more matter before leaving Locke. His defense of toleration is severely limited—too limited for matters concerning us today. Problems of religious toleration remain, but even they are broader than Locke considers. Even when limited to religion, we are asked to tolerate much more than Locke envisaged. Now, moreover, many extend arguments for toleration to matters Locke himself probably would have found utterly intolerable (e.g., gay relationships, gender equality, universal suffrage, and sharing as equals one's society with members of other cultures and races). To many, Locke's interests and arguments seem remote from today's acute problems to provide much insight. Yet, I hope we have seen that we can learn much from Locke—negatively and positively—about the defense, and limits, of toleration generally. And as we will see in chapter 7, Michael Walzer makes a case for toleration that is not far from Locke's.

NOTES

1. Joseph Lecler, *Toleration and the Reformation,* vol. 1 (London: Longmans, Green and Co., 1960), x.

2. Thomas Aquinas, *Summa Theologiae,* "Utrum ritus infidelium sint tolerandi?" SS Q 10 A 11, trans. English Dominicans (London: Burns, Oates, and Washbourne, 1912–36; reprint, New York: Benziger, 1947–48; reprint, New York: Christian Classics, 1981).

3. Aquinas, *Summa Theologiae,* "Utrum ritus infidelium sint tolerandi?" SS Q 11 A 3.

4. Thomas Aquinas, *Commentary on the Nicomachean Ethics,* vol. 2, Aristotle Book 7, Lecture 2, 1316.

5. Aquinas, *Commentary on the Nicomachean Ethics,* 1390.

6. See Lecler, *Toleration and Reformation;* Henry Kamen, *The Rise of Toleration* (London: Weidenfeld, 1967); Cary Nederman and John Christain Laursen, eds., *Beyond the Persecuting Society: Religious Toleration before the Enlightenment* (Philadelphia: University of Pennsylvania Press, 1998); and Levine (1990).

7. Augustine, *Ad Donatistas,* 10.

8. For a superb collection of essays on early moderns and their relationship to skepticism, see Alan Levine, ed., *Early Modern Skepticism and the Origins of Toleration* (Lanham, Md.: Lexington Books, 1999). What follows in the next few paragraphs is drawn from Levine's own essay on Montaigne, "Skepticism, Self, and Toleration in Montaigne's Political Thought."

9. Donald Frame, *The Complete Works of Montaigne* (Stanford, Calif.: Stanford University Press, 1957), Book II, Essay 12, 330.

10. Frame, *The Complete Works of Montaigne,* Book I, Essay 12, 346.

11. Frame, *The Complete Works of Montaigne,* Book I, Essay 3, 8.

12. For a detailed exploration of Descartes's argument for toleration, especially as found in *The Passions of the Soul* (1649), see Elizabeth S. Haldane and G. R. T. Ross, trans., *The Philosophical Works of Descartes,* 2 vols. (Cambridge: Cambridge University Press, 1968), vol. 1, 329–427. See also Michael Allen Gillespie, "Descartes and the Question of Toleration," in *Early Modern Skepticism and the Origins of Toleration,* ed. Levine.

13. Baruch Spinoza, *Tractatus Theologico-Politicus* (The Hague, 1670; first translated into English in 1689). For a more extensive discussion, see Steven B. Smith, "Toleration and Skepticism of Religion in Spinoza's *Tractatus Theologico-Politicus*," in *Early Modern Skepticism and the Origins of Toleration*, ed. Levine.

14. John Horton and Susan Mendus, eds., *John Locke: A Letter concerning Toleration in Focus* (London: Routledge, 1991), 12.

15. Maurice Cranston, "John Locke and the Case for Toleration," in *John Locke,* ed. Horton and Mendus, 82.

16. Horton and Mendus, eds., *John Locke,* 12.

17. Locke, *A Letter concerning Toleration,* 17.

18. Locke, *A Letter concerning Toleration,* 17–18.

19. Locke, *A Letter concerning Toleration,* 18.

20. Locke, *A Letter concerning Toleration,* 18.

21. Locke, *A Letter concerning Toleration,* 18.

22. Locke, *A Letter concerning Toleration,* 37.

23. Locke, *A Letter concerning Toleration,* 37.

24. Locke, *A Letter concerning Toleration,* 47.

25. Locke, *A Letter concerning Toleration,* 45.

26. Locke, *A Letter concerning Toleration,* 47.

27. Locke, *A Letter concerning Toleration,* 19. Compare this with Thomas Hobbes, who says that "Covenants without the Sword are but words, and cannot bind any man" (*Leviathan,* pt. II, chapter 17). Locke no less than Hobbes worries about social order and stability in a post-Reformation world. The distance between them is not as great as frequently thought.

28. Locke, *A Letter concerning Toleration,* 47.

29. John Locke, *A Second Letter concerning Toleration* (London, 1692), in *The Works of John Locke: A New Edition* (corrected), vol. VI (London, 1823), 212.

30. John Locke, *A Third Letter for Toleration* (London, 1692), in *The Works of John Locke,* 144.

31. John Locke, *An Essay concerning Human Understanding* (London, 1689), ed. Peter Nidditch (Oxford: Clarendon, 1975).

32. Maurice Cranston, *John Locke: A Biography* (London, 1975), 367.

33. Peter Nicholson, *John Locke's Later Letters on Toleration,* in *John Locke,* ed. Horton and Mendus, 163–187.

Chapter 7

Regimes of Toleration

History shows that regimes that advocate toleration on grounds of policy have been around for over two millennia. But what are "policy considerations"? They are interests that relate only tangentially, if at all, to our deepest moral and value concerns. Instead, they appeal to enlightened self-interest. When shopkeepers take to heart the admonition that "Honesty is the best policy," for instance, they are not motivated by a concern that they do what is morally right—namely, not to cheat customers because it is wrong. Instead, shopkeepers adopting this maxim believe that dishonesty, though sometimes profitable in the short run, is bad for business in the long run. Considerations of policy do not always refer to what is good or bad for business. They also commonly refer to reasons of church or state or, indeed, those of any organized body.

It is not, however, easy to distinguish policy concerns from other reasons. In preserving its cultural heritage, for example, a nation will be protecting a variety of deep values, moral and otherwise. This is also true of voluntary associations. They stand for something, and that "something" typically has moral and value concerns at its heart. When OXFAM pursues its interests, for instance, moral purposes guide it. Nor are charitable organizations a special case. The same is true of the American Kennel Club. Most states, too, are guided by ends that they regard as worthy of pursuit (e.g., spreading a religious doctrine or making the world safe for democracy). That they are so regarded does not guarantee that they are genuinely worthwhile. Yet we have to understand their pursuits in terms of ends beyond narrow personal or group self-interest or political convenience. Some regimes, it is true, have no other ends than ruthless and narrow self-interest. They are often little more than organizations to perpetuate the power and wealth of a family or clan. Yet these are rather the exception than the rule. Defending constitutional rights of individuals or groups, protecting the vulnerable from exploitation, or pursuing a religious ideal are more the norm. The latter should make clear, if it is not already obvious, that nonliberal—even illiberal and undemocratic—states can also pursue what they take to be moral ideals. An autocratic state can take on itself the sacred duty of defending—and spreading—the faith of its people.

Although often amoral in themselves, policy considerations provide essential support for worthy aims. Debates in the United States whether to grant China "most favored nation status," for example, were motivated by both policy and moral considerations, and the policy considerations are often cited to support the moral goals. Nor is it only governments that find moral and policy considerations thoroughly mixed. Voluntary associations, too, rely on amoral policy considerations to forward what they regard as valuable ends, such as deciding which strategies are most effective in raising needed money. Demands for moral purity can lead to moral disaster. Treaties, to take a prominent example, normally contain fuzzy language. Purists object that fuzzy language permits malign interpretations. And so it does. But in itself, vague, general, or hortatory language is neither good nor bad. Diplomats may include unclear language precisely to avoid having to solve vexatious problems immediately. The hope is that solutions can be deferred indefinitely or addressed much later. Sometimes, of course, fuzzy language (or some other policy considerations) can be morally suspect. In such cases we are tempted to speak of them as dishonest, pandering, cowardly, or even treasonous. But there is no reason to suppose that this is the norm.

The upshot is that moral and policy considerations are not always finely discriminable. Nonetheless, the fact that they cannot always be sharply distinguished does not entail that we cannot pick out—always roughly and mostly—where one begins and the other leaves off. Private American universities, for example, must raise money to support valuable educational ends. This why they name buildings, scholarships, and professorial chairs after wealthy donors, whose egos they flatter and wallets they tap. Not all cases are so clear-cut. Alumni weekends continue bonds with the alma mater and so give the university a needed sense of continuity— but also raise funds. Without a sense of continuity, universities could not survive, let alone flourish. That financial support must be derived in this way, however, is an artifact of American culture and its tradition of higher education. Prudential ends, intertwined with ideals served by higher education, clearly drive fundraising practices. Some are acceptable; others are morally dubious. Again, that we cannot always disentangle moral from policy considerations does not mean that we seldom can.

Finally, we need to recognize, indeed stress, that policy considerations can *also* be moral considerations. We need not think of them as always or even usually in competition—or even as distinguishable in many cases. Too much contemporary moral philosophy portrays morality as locked in an adversarial relationship with prudence and interest, ignoring the fact that prudence and interest are themselves objects of moral concern.

Here, however, we will concentrate on regimes that developed, as much as possible, amoral policy-based defenses of toleration. Their diversity speaks to the circumstances that make toleration attractive to political orders that might otherwise be tempted to act with oppressive intolerance—or so argues Michael Walzer in *On Toleration*.[1]

His close-to-the-ground study distinguishes it from typical philosophical theorizing. Philosophers generally, Walzer mischievously observes,[2]

> follow Plato, who spins a tale about philosophers exiting the cave of everyday life, so that they can see how things really are in the bright sunlight of Truth. Most contemporary philosophers reject Plato's theory of Forms—those unchanging, eternal, and perfect exemplars, grasped only by the mind, and which give whatever degree of reality the objects of ordinary experience possess. Yet, they accept the essence of the Platonic tale, for, like Plato, they seek a birds-eye or, better, a God's-eye of the world—a view from Nowhere.[3]

From that exalted, perspectiveless vantage point, philosophers believe that they can see the world, including the world of value, as it really is, free from myopia, ambiguity, confusions, and shadows in the cave. They can aspire to certainty or, if not that, then at least objectivity.

Walzer firmly rejects this aspiration. It is doomed to failure, irrelevancy, and— far worse—the possibility that the aspiration will degenerate into a rigid, oppressive ideology. Walzer prefers to stay in the cave, in the half-light, among the shadows, trying to understand and come to terms with the same things as everyone else in the cave; namely, his fellow citizens. Cave-dwelling philosophers will seek to learn from nonphilosophical denizens. They will not regard their hard-earned efforts to shed light and make the cave slightly more commodious with contempt. Cave-dwelling philosophers may be more reflective than their less curiosity-minded fellows, slightly distancing themselves a bit from their immediate concerns. They will not, however, ever lose touch altogether, as those who leave the cave tend to do. We need reflection and social criticism desperately— but tied to concrete practices found all around us. Besides, philosophers only think they leave the cave; they never do, for there is no place to escape to. Nowhere is not a destination. In shunning the "high priori" way, Walzer sticks close to lived history, life as it is found in the flickering shadows of the cave. He intends his reflections to bring familiar objects out of the shadows, not import new objects from a philosopher's heaven. Walzer modestly aspires to improve our understanding, not perfect it. He knows that, even if he succeeds, much in the cave will remain obscure, cloaked in confusing shadows.

Toleration is no exception. Not only does the concept have a history, but so does the practice. The practice, indeed, has a much longer history than the articulated concept, a history that reveals itself as an example of toleration only at dusk—when, as Hegel says, the owl of Minerva spreads its wings. As we saw earlier, whether as concept, attitude, or practice, tolerance was not an invention of philosophers. They did not have to leave the cave to find it. Toleration arises out of need; it solves, or at least ameliorates, concrete difficulties. Philosophical reflection refines and extends but can never replace—or stray far from—lived

experience. Philosophy, Walzer maintains, must be "historically informed and sociologically competent if it is to avoid bad utopianism and acknowledge the hard
choices that must often be made in political life."[4]

On Toleration is a slim volume consisting of expanded lectures. In it, Walzer
paints with a broad brush, sometimes covering up qualifications he would make
in a more scholarly study. For example, "Toleration makes difference possible;
difference makes toleration necessary."[5] He surely knows that this is too quick.
Difference occurs despite intolerance, and difference does not always make toleration necessary or desirable. When not using a broad brush, Walzer sketches,
alluding to more thorough historical studies that would bring the sketch to life. I
mention these as cautionary alerts since we need to be on guard for what Walzer
paints over or merely sketches.

Walzer does not limit toleration to mere forbearance. As a state of mind, he
says, tolerance describes a range of possibilities from (a) resigned acceptance for
the sake of peace; and to (b) benign indifference; (c) recognition that others have
rights they may exercise in objectionable ways; (d) openness to others; and (e)
various kinds of endorsement.[6] Sometimes he characterizes it not as an attitude
but as a result: "the peaceful coexistence of groups of people with different his-
tories, cultures, and identities, which is what toleration makes possible."[7] But this
does not seem quite right. Such groups can peacefully coexist outside the range
Walzer mentions. This happens, for example, when third parties force them to coexist or when, at the other extreme, they relish each other's differences. In the former case, questions of toleration do not arise; in the latter, there is no need. Toleration, moreover, does not make peaceful existence possible in general, though
it sometimes does. It is true, however, that it helps sustain peaceful existence, especially when fear and suspicion arise. Anyone who exemplifies any of the states
of mind Walzer mentions will be said to possess the virtue of tolerance.[8]

This, I think, distorts what we mean by possessing a virtue. Not only is resigned acceptance not a *moral* virtue, it is not a virtue at all. Both resigned acceptance and benign indifference are attitudes, to be sure. What disqualifies them
as virtues is not that they do not involve attitudes but that they do not involve anything more. Resigned acceptance and benign indifference lack the structure typical of virtues. Compare these two attitudes with Walzer's third possibility: recognition of the rights of others that might be exercised in objectionable ways.
People who allow others to exercise their rights have more than a certain attitude
or state of mind. They have, as it were, a rational disposition, a disposition
grounded in "right reason." That is, underlying their disposition is a recognition
of justifying reasons. Resigned acceptance and benign indifference, on the other
hand, are grounded in little more than emotional responses. There probably is an
explanation why some individuals or groups are resigned or indifferent, but whatever the explanation, it will not be a justification. Throughout, Walzer slurs over
this difference, so that it sometimes is not clear whether he is explaining how a
regime of toleration works or how it is justified.

Walzer is less interested in tolerance as attitude or virtue than he is in toleration as practice. It is not that he dismisses the importance of tolerant attitudes; far from it. When people have tolerant attitudes, he rightly argues, it can make tolerant practices stronger. But not always, and we would be unwise, he thinks, to count on them, not always because toleration may be more secure *without* tolerant attitudes. When everyone acknowledges clear hierarchies of authority and power, he says, a regime of toleration might better survive than if it depends on mutual respect or some other amiable disposition.

We would be unwise to count on tolerant attitudes, Walzer holds, because we would be wildly optimistic if we thought that more than a handful of people will ever develop them. Nor do more than a few *have* to develop them. Diplomats and international businessmen might find tolerant attitudes useful, but others may find it either unnecessary or beyond their reach. Individuals, after all, can engage in common practices without all sharing the same attitudes or virtues. Practices of courtesy and civility typically require no more than that participants follow specified forms; there is, for instance, an etiquette of accepting or declining a dinner engagement. Not to adhere to the formalities is rude. No one, however, much cares about anyone's state of mind. What matters is only that the "formalities" are honored. Someone might be extremely courteous in scrupulously observing all formalities yet feel cold and indifferent to those to whom he is courteous.

Practices of toleration, taken in isolation from states of mind, are like this. A regime—really, a regimen—of toleration can be laid down, even followed to the letter, without anyone feeling tolerant or acting out of tolerant attitudes. People may see that a regime of toleration holds many advantages. So, they may ensure that it is faithfully upheld, severely reprimanding or punishing those who behave intolerantly. By itself, however, this does not show that anyone possesses tolerant attitudes. Toleration, like honesty, may simply be the best policy. It need be nothing more than bare tolerance, scrupulously observed.

Sticking, as he does, close to the ground, Walzer is reluctant to assign any great role to tolerance as a virtue. The reason is that he does not find it, except at the margins, in most historically successful regimes of toleration. If the Roman and Ottoman Empires could do without it, who are we to say that it is necessary? In this Walzer is right. If successful regimes of toleration have more or less dispensed with tolerant attitudes, we cannot deny that they did not have effective practices of toleration. Yet, while remaining in the cave, we might be able to show that such regimes are impoverished in certain specific ways. If successful, we might then provide the virtue of tolerance with a greater role in contemporary social and political arrangements than Walzer (or Bernard Williams before him) is prepared to give.

Walzer astutely observes that regimes of toleration are political or cultural wholes in that their advantages and disadvantages are closely connected. Often, he says, "the things we admire in a particular historical arrangement are functionally related to the things we fear or dislike."[9] They are not, however, organic wholes. That is, the internal connections are not so tightly knit that if one (or a few) are broken, the regime would die. They are far more resilient than that. Still, we need constantly to keep before us that the bad comes with the good; they are functionally related. The hubris of the British Empire at its zenith, for example, is connected with its managerial competence. What Walzer overlooks, however, is that we can seldom be sure that in trying to remove a disagreeable bit of a cultural whole, we may set in train a chain reaction that will cause far more damage to the cultural whole than Walzer seems prepared to admit. Connections among aspects of a culture are not marked "loose," "tight," or "indispensable." Often it is only after an intervention that we find out.

Walzer's five regimes of toleration are presented not as ideal types but as historically grounded realities. Yet in recognizing numerous "complicated cases"—France, Israel, Canada, and the European Community—Walzer simultaneously acknowledges that his fivefold classification may be too neat, at least to fit comfortably the complexities of today's world. And his brief remarks on "postmodern toleration" point to further complications, still nascent.

MULTINATIONAL EMPIRES

These are the oldest, typified by the ancient empires of Persia, Ptolemaic Egypt, and Rome. Groups—usually conquered groups—under the rule of the great multinational empires enjoy substantial internal autonomy, including political, cultural, and religious self-management. That is, groups are allowed to organize their own internal lives without much state interference. However much groups detest one another, they have little choice but to coexist peacefully: The imperial center will see to that. All live under the thumb of imperial bureaucrats who apply the same rigid imperial code universally. This code maintains some minimal fairness, at least as understood by the imperial center. Provided that no group violates this minimal code, bureaucrats seldom interfere directly in the internal life of the (semi-) autonomous communities. They are too busy pursuing the larger ambitions of the empire.

When Pontius Pilate asked, "What is truth?" and washed his hands of an internal Jewish controversy potentially disruptive to the empire, he was acting very much in keeping with his position as an imperial bureaucrat. As long as taxes were paid and peace kept, how the Jews managed troublemakers mattered little. "Hands off" was a useful policy. Roman rule counts as a regime of toleration, Walzer argues, because different groups under its autocratic rule had to tolerate—that is, merely put up with—one another; they had no choice. There is obviously nothing democratic about imperial rule. If anything, it owes its success to its evenhanded, autocratic rule. Not being bound to the parochial interests of any conquered group and remaining aloof from them all, toleration serves imperial ends.

Not only is imperial autonomy autocratic, it is unconcerned with liberal values. As Walzer notes,

> Imperial autonomy tends to lock individuals into their communities and therefore into a singular ethnic or religious identity. It tolerates groups and their authority structures and customary practices, not (except in a few cosmopolitan centers and capital cities) free-floating men and women. . . . [T]he communities are mostly closed, enforcing one or another version of religious orthodoxy and sustaining a traditional way of life. . . . [C]ommunities of this sort have extraordinary staying power. But they can be very severe toward deviant individuals, who are conceived as threats to their cohesiveness and sometimes to their very survival.[10]

Nowhere is this more notable than in the millet (i.e., religious community) system of the Ottoman Empire, which Walzer takes as paradigmatic. This Turkish Empire dominated by Muslims allowed Jews and Christians great latitude in how they governed themselves. Individual Jews and Christians had no rights of conscience or of association against their own communities, however, unless the community itself happened to acknowledge liberal values (as, late in the empire's history, some Protestant groups did).

Walzer, however, appears to be too sanguine about the degree of toleration practiced by the Ottomans. We need to look beyond, and behind, the simple fact that individuals, minorities, or beliefs and practices are not suppressed. For instance, early on, Murad I (1326–1389) began the system of impressing young men from the Christian communities to become Janissaries, or "recruits," to the standing Ottoman Turkish army, an army loyal only to the sultan. Not only were these youths taken from their communities, the empire required them to convert to Islam. Although enjoying high status as elite warriors—and even making or breaking emperors—Janissaries were largely excluded from civil society, forbidden even to marry. This is not the mark of a regime of toleration. The practice lasted for centuries, existing side by side with the millet system. Nor is there anything in the history of the empire to lead us to think that sultans would have sustained the millet system had it stood in the way of exploitation.

To call the Ottoman Empire a regime of toleration misleads and distorts, for it fails to look beyond the fact of bare or mere tolerance to the justifying reasons. True, the Ottoman Empire did not actively suppress non-Muslim religions and cultures, provided that they did not interfere with the hegemony of the Turkish Islamic culture. As we have seen, however, it did not scruple at impressing minorities into its army. Behind both practices lie utterly self-interested policy considerations. The empire was chiefly concerned to exploit the wealth of its subjects. The real, but limited, autonomy the millet system provided—welcome as it may have been given the alternatives—not only did not interfere with that aim but helped achieve it.

Is the mere fact of nonsuppression based on self-interested policy considerations sufficient to warrant calling the Ottoman Empire tolerant of religious minorities? We can call it a regime of toleration if we like, but only because it satisfies one criterion of tolerance, namely, not intervening where one could in that which one does not approve. Yet this, by itself, permits almost every regime to qualify as tolerant, for only an utterly irrational regime would expend energy on interventions that would knowingly frustrate its own self-interest. To the degree that the great empires of the past practiced toleration, it is only as we reflect back and find in them a few elements of toleration. They are, at best, degenerate forms. They do not show that Rawls was wrong to think that tolerance comes into prominence only much later as a consequence of religious conflicts in the sixteenth and seventeenth centuries.

INTERNATIONAL SOCIETY

The degree to which Walzer stretches the notion of toleration can be seen in his declaration that international society also constitutes a regime of toleration, albeit a weak one. Within certain limits, Walzer claims, "[a]ll the groups that achieve statehood and all the practices that they permit . . . are tolerated by the society of states."[11] He adds—whether as further inference or separate point is not clear— that "[t]oleration is an essential feature of sovereignty and an important reason for its desirability."[12]

These are sweeping claims, wholly unsupported. And there is massive evidence contrary to both assertions. Sovereign states have gone to war against each other since arising in the sixteenth century. They may "tolerate" the internal practices of enemy states, but they frequently have not "tolerated" political or economic claims of their enemies. In Europe alone, most states have found themselves embroiled in a war with one or more other states. Nor is this merely a European phenomenon, as wars between India and Pakistan and between Japan and China attest. These wars, as those in Europe, may have had as their immediate cause certain material interests, but clearly ethnic, religious, and cultural forces were also at work. Often wars brought in their aftermath—if not their purpose—annexations or absorptions of portions of other states. Toleration has not proved to be an essential feature of sovereignty. It cannot, therefore, be an important reason for the desirability of sovereignty.

Walzer argues that toleration marks international society for all the reasons he has given earlier: resignation, indifference, curiosity, reciprocity, and costliness. But, again, nonintervention for most of these reasons provides only a simulacrum of toleration. If a state is indifferent to what goes on in another state, how is its nonintervention an act of toleration? This, again, confuses the fact of nonintervention with reasons why. Or take Walzer's "costliness" argument. He points out, realistically enough, that, "[g]iven the nature of international society, the costs [of intervention in the affairs of another sovereign state] are likely to be high: they involve raising an army, crossing a border, killing and being killed."[13] This makes for caution. But toleration? A cost–benefit analysis of interference in the affairs of another state may well militate against interference, but if that is the sole or even the principal reason for refraining from it, then it is a pale imitation of toleration. Cowards, after all, also refrain from intervening, and we do not call them tolerant.

Diplomats, Walzer says, accept the logic of sovereignty—that is, "no one on that side of the border can interfere with what is done on this side"[14]—but cannot simply look away from persons and practices that they find intolerable. They must negotiate with tyrants and murderers. He then makes the astonishing claim that "[w]hen diplomats shake hands or break bread with tyrants, they are, as it were, wearing gloves; the actions have no moral significance."[15] Surely not. If they have no moral significance, then it is surprising that so many feel deep moral outrage when their diplomats shake hands and break bread with representatives of hated enemies. True, sometimes the outrage is misplaced, but far from always. Again, Walzer is driven to this conclusion because—although he gives lip service to the virtue of tolerance—he stresses outward acts of forbearance almost exclusively.

Walzer further argues that, although the breaking of bread has no moral significance, the bargains diplomats strike do. They are, he says, "acts of toleration." This seems wrong on two counts. The bargains struck normally have legal significance. But that is only to say that the bargain struck becomes part of a normative legal system, so that if asked whether such and such a treaty were legally valid, the correct answer would be affirmative. This in no way, however, guarantees that the treaty will not be thoroughly wicked. Walzer here elides the distinction between moral and legal significance. Further, his claim that such bargains are acts of toleration is merely stipulative. Again, they are acts of toleration for Walzer only because nonintervention for any reason whatsoever constitutes an act of toleration. Such bargains also have political significance in that they make it more difficult politically for a disgruntled party to violate the agreement. A current government, for instance, may feel compelled to adhere to an accord negotiated, perhaps in bad faith, by a previous government. The current government cannot violate the accord with impunity because of political fallout. But in what sense does this make it an "act of toleration"?

Sovereignty, Walzer emphasizes, has its limits. Actions and practices that "shock the conscience of mankind" are not, in principle, tolerated. This is true. But this also points out what Walzer overlooks: the role that the intolerable generally plays in our understanding of tolerance, for the reverse is also true. When one state determines that what goes on in another state is undesirable, deplorable, and disgusting yet concludes that it is tolerable, it is using and relying on a distinction between the tolerable and the intolerable. Here is one place where we do find tolerance in international society. Sometimes it is misplaced to be sure, but if the reasons are of the right sort, it counts as an act of toleration. Merely refraining from intervention is not enough. In particular, international society today recognizes a limited right to self-determination. That is, within certain limits—often spelled out in international law—as long as one state does not harm another, other states must tolerate what they regard as errant ways. It is not merely a matter of "live and let live," as Walzer states, but a recognition that it is a good thing that each state determine its own destiny according to its own lights. To recognize this reason is to move closer to full tolerance. That a state's conduct not "shock the conscience of mankind" specifies one of the limits of that self-determination.

Even here there are generally good reasons behind that which shocks conscience. Conscience, after all, is not an arational, emotional shockometer or disgustometer. When conscience is shocked, an implicit reference is made to the deep immorality of what shocks. And, like any moral claim, we must support it with good reasons if it is not to be merely an oppressive response.

CONSOCIATIONS

Consociations are fast fading from the international scene. There are a few multinational states that have stood the test of time, such as Switzerland and Belgium. Others have not been so fortunate: Cyprus, Lebanon, and Bosnia. Walzer points out that consociationalism is a "heroic program because it aims to maintain imperial coexistence without the imperial bureaucrats and without the distance that made those bureaucrats more or less impartial rulers."[16] Heroic programs, like heroic people, tend to have admirable but short lives. Instead of an imperial center, two or more communities separated by such deeply divisive characteristics as language, ethnicity, religion, or history nonetheless freely negotiate a constitutional arrangement designed to protect their mutual interests. They are most likely to succeed, Walzer observes, when the communities that constitute them pre-date the appearance of strong nationalist movements.

What undermines and destroys consociations is the fear that one side or another is gaining the upper hand. If, for instance, demographics or economic prowess changes noticeably, the more numerous or more powerful will want the shift recognized in political arrangements. Further complicating matters, one group may increase in numbers but another in economic power. For any consociation to survive, Walzer says, trust is absolutely essential. He does not mean trust in the sense of goodwill but trust in institutional arrangements. Toleration, he asserts, depends only on that (minimal) degree of trust.

But does it? It may be that in consociations toleration depends on trust, but not only trust in institutional arrangements. Without tolerant attitudes, without cultivating tolerance as a virtue, it is hard to see how consociations can endure, and maybe that is one reason they tend to fail. Institutional arrangements, though indispensable, need to be suffused with people governed by tolerant attitudes. Otherwise, they are likely to become moribund. This observation is not limited to consociations. Walzer overestimates, I think, the self-sustaining power of institutions. No institution can survive for long unless most participants look at the institution as engendering and protecting practices that justify the institution in the first place. If dog breeders did not in the main and on the whole trust one another as individuals devoted to the good of the enterprise, they would not get far in establishing and policing standards by placing their trust in the arrangements of the American Kennel Club.

A few institutions, it is true, can survive if only officials take an internal point of view. A legal system, for instance, can function for a long time that way. But then coercion and effective threats will be necessary to keep those to whom the law applies in line. Even then, however, at least most of the law creators and law appliers will have to see the law as an enterprise that they, collectively, pursue. And that means, collectively and distributively, that they need to trust one another's goodwill and judgment, even if the legal system itself is generally vicious. Otherwise, it is unlikely to have the integrity to count as a legal system.

Consociations would appear to need more. If they are to work—and Walzer is right to stress how attractive yet subject to instability they are—attempts will be necessary to instill in as many consociational citizens as possible the attitude or, better, virtue of tolerance. Only in that way can members of consociational groups fully rely on institutions preserving their consociation, for even if they cannot rely on the unbounded goodwill of their fellow citizens, they can rely on their tolerance.

NATION-STATES

A frequently heard criticism of the notion of "nation-states" is that most states are comprised not of a single, homogenous nation but of a collection of nations. Walzer accepts this but makes the telling point that

> [Nation-state] means only that a single dominant group organizes the common life in a way that reflects its own history and culture and, if things go as intended, carries the history forward and sustains the culture. [In fact,] national groups seek statehood precisely in order to control the means of reproduction.[17]

If these states are liberal, democratic states, then despite the fact that dominant groups organize them, they typically tolerate minority groups. In the United Kingdom, for example, the nation that has, at least until recently, shaped the state was white, Anglo-Saxon, and Protestant with strong roots in English (as opposed to Scottish or Welsh) culture. That, however, does not preclude the state from tolerating a wide variety of distinct groups—distinct in religion, ethnicity, and country of origin.

This requires qualification, for, as Walzer points out, a key feature of contemporary liberal democratic states is not that they tolerate groups as such but that they tolerate *individuals*. This stands in sharp contrast to imperial, international, and even consociational regimes, for they, by and large, take groups as their objects of toleration. Groups in nation-states may form voluntary associations but, normally, neither organizes autonomously nor exercises legal jurisdiction over their fellows. There are exceptions, but, as Walzer says, the exceptions make the majority nervous: "Any claim to act out minority culture in public is likely to produce anxiety among the majority (hence the controversy in France over the wearing of Muslim headdress in state schools)."[18] He acutely adds, "When nineteenth-century German Jews described themselves as 'German in the street, Jewish at home,' they were aspiring to a nation-state norm that made privacy a condition of toleration."[19]

When we relegate toleration to the home, however, the result tends to be greater assimilation, for the group has less power over its members to enforce conformity, let alone obedience. As a further consequence, there tends to be less difference in nation-states than previously considered regimes, as more and more members drift away from their original culture and are drawn into the mainstream. However much Americans think of themselves as members in one of many unique subcultures, for instance, what seems most prominent to an outsider—at least until recently—is how *American* everyone seems.

Effacement of differences in nation-states has a double, interconnected effect. First, just because nation-states are less tolerant of groups than, say, multinational empires, groups have to be more tolerant of individuals in them. One reason is that the state will enforce the individual rights of its citizens, so that a group can be called to task if it is seen to violate those rights. Second, as groups become transformed into voluntary associations, they must become attractive to their members. Not only can they not violate their participant's rights, but they must, also, persuade them not to leave for greener pastures. These twin effects weaken groups in nation-states.

Not all groups, however. Experience shows that religious differences have had more resilience and resistance than other differences. While individuals migrate from one religion or denomination to another, the overall totals remain roughly constant over long periods of time. Walzer contends that national groups are most at risk, especially if they are widely dispersed in a state. And if they are concentrated, they will be suspected of wishing to form their own nation-state and so be subject to state pressure.

The latter raises a possibility that contemporary liberal theorists have, until recently, stopped exploring. Walzer, following on work by Kymlicka,[20] notes,

> After World War I efforts were made to guarantee the toleration of national minorities in the new (and radically heterogeneous) "nation states" of Eastern Europe. The guarantor was the League of Nations, and the guarantee was written into a series of minority or nationality treaties. Appropriately, these treaties ascribed rights to stereotypical individuals rather than to groups. Thus the Polish Minority Treaty deals with "Polish nationals who belong to racial, religious, or linguistic minorities." Nothing follows from such a designation about group autonomy or regional devolution or mi-

nority control of schools. Indeed, the guarantee of individual rights was itself chimerical: most of the new states asserted their sovereignty by ignoring (or annulling) the treaties, and the League was unable to enforce them.[21]

There was another reason these arrangements fell by the wayside. Namely, the Nazis used them as a pretext to invade other countries to protect the German nationals living there. What was conceived as a guarantee against majority suppression became a license to invade.

Should we revive these arrangements? Walzer thinks it is worth trying, provided that group autonomy is coupled with a more explicit recognition of what the members of the group have in common with other members of the nation-state. Walzer would not recognize minority groups as corporate bodies. Instead, he would follow the lead of the United Nations Covenant on Civil and Political Rights (1966): Minority individuals "shall not be denied the right, in community with other members of their group, to enjoy their own culture, to possess and practice their own religion, or to use their own language."[22] Does this go far enough? For is there not a real danger that a minority's culture will disappear unless the group itself is granted some limited rights? We will need to consider the importance of cultural context in the next chapter.

IMMIGRANT SOCIETIES

Curiously, the United States does not fully meet Walzer's characterization of a nation-state. His reason is that American majorities are temporary and, depending on the issue, differently constituted. A crucial feature of nation-states, by contrast, is that their majorities are permanent. Consequently, Walzer says, "[t]oleration in nation-states has only one source [i.e., the permanent majority] and it moves or doesn't move in only one direction [i.e., toward allowing minorities to survive]."[23]

What then of the United States? As an immigrant society, members of different groups have left their respective homelands to make a new life. They can claim no patch of land as their own, for they have left that behind. Partly as a consequence, members of immigrant groups tend to fan out across the country, though there may be concentrations in various regions (e.g., Chinese in California, Scandinavians in Minnesota, Puerto Ricans in New York City). Obviously, continents were not empty when immigrants arrived. So, in the United States, for example, Native Americans were driven from their original homelands. Immigrant societies have a distinctive history that creates new possibilities for tolerance and intolerance.

If immigrant ethnic and religious groups are to sustain themselves, Walzer writes, they must do so as purely voluntary associations, for immigrants arrive as individuals or in individual families. The bonds holding them together may be largely sentimental, of no great binding power. Because of indifference, individuals may drift away from their ethnic or religious origins, assimilating into mainstream culture. A permanent majority, however, will not shape mainstream culture because there is none. Instead, like the Mississippi River, it is shaped and colored by the many rivers that flow into it, each contributing its own distinctive hue.

Because no permanent majority controls the state or is the source of toleration, the role of the state differs from the paradigmatic nation-state. In particular, the state is not committed to any of the immigrant groups constituting it (even if it once was). It cannot, for instance, initiate or defend an established church. It must remain strictly neutral among all constituent groups, not intentionally favoring one over another. An immigrant state, Walzer concludes, typically tolerates all groups and pursues its own autonomous purposes. Furthermore, the objects of toleration are not, strictly speaking, groups (e.g., Mormons, Polish Americans) but choices and actions of individual men and women.

This has enormous implications for toleration, for individuals are now encouraged to tolerate each other both *as individuals* and as each interprets one's own respective subcultures. No longer—though this is a slight exaggeration—is there a single authoritative voice with powers of enforcement defining what is and what is not acceptable. To hold onto members, groups need to exercise toleration. Individuals, too, must act tolerantly to fellow group members if the group is to flourish, for escaping the group has become easy—so easy, in fact, that "escape" seems too strong a term. One can simply drift away, either by moving—or simply by changing one's mind. Coercive efforts to enforce group solidarity, therefore, are likely to fail disastrously.

Many members of immigrant societies do prefer a dual identity (e.g., Jewish American, African American, Asian American, Latino/a American, and so on). However, "[n]o group in an immigrant society is allowed to organize itself coercively, to seize control of public space, or to monopolize public resources."[24] Consequently, "American" specifies a political identity without a cultural one: "Asian" or "Italian" as part of a hyphenated identity, on the other hand, specifies a cultural identity without a political one. Hyphenated Americans can therefore sustain their cultural identities only if they make only the most minimal demands on the state. There is, in Walzer's mind, a real question whether groups can sustain themselves over the long haul. Immigrant states are, after all, comparatively young, so over time—and with fits and starts—dual identities may largely disappear. In its place we might have little more than a weakly normative pedigree, as we do already for many (e.g., Americans of Scottish descent).

The toleration Walzer describes here is real. While still motivated in part by strong amoral policy considerations, it is also motivated by principled reasons at all levels: state, group, and individual. To the extent that states deliberately pursue neutral policies, they deliberately act on the principle that it would violate their legitimate charter were they to favor one group over another. To the extent that groups pursue tolerant policies, it is in part because they recognize, in an immigrant state, that they must respond to criticisms, needs, and fashions of their members if they are to survive and flourish. Individuals, too, have similar grounds for toleration. To the extent that individual members of a group wish to see it flourish, they must strive to understand each other, listen to each other's reasons for shaping the nature of the group. Their tolerance is outwardly directed with the good of the group firmly in mind. They have moved from mere tolerance to full tolerance.

COMPLEX CASES

Objects of toleration vary in the five regimes: (a) groups in multinational empires; (b) groups supplemented by stronger notions of citizenship in consociations; (c) citizenship and individual rights in nation-states with minorities recognized, but only under generic names; and (d) citizenship and individual rights with no special recognition of one's status as a minority. As the individual rights increase in strength, the state becomes increasingly intolerant of exercises of control by groups, and the groups themselves must, if they are to survive, become increasingly accommodating to individual interests.

Walzer not only recognizes but also stresses that this schema is too tidy. Few states conform exactly to type. Most do not fit neatly into any single category. France, for instance, has been a nation of immigrants yet until recently not a pluralist society, for everyone was expected to become a Frenchman in language, patterns of thought, and culture. Walzer quotes a French deputy, Clermont-Tonnerre, speaking on behalf of the emancipation of Jews in 1791: "One must refuse everything to the Jews as a nation, and give everything to the Jews as individuals."[25] Republican assimilationists are now threatened by new immigrant groups who seek to keep their own identities—and not only in private. Walzer judges that their demands teeter between American multiculturalism and something like the millet system.

If France has clear elements of both the nation-state and the immigrant state, Israel has elements of all but consociationalism (and even that was once proposed, Walzer notes). Contemporary Israel, Walzer writes, is a nation-state founded on a nationalist movement with a significant national minority (namely, Palestinian Arabs) who, though citizens, do not find their history or culture mirrored in Israel's public life. It is also a successor of the Ottoman Empire and retains a form of the millet system for its diverse religious communities. Finally, Israel's Jewish majority is itself formed by immigrants from the Diaspora, who vary markedly.

Who is to be tolerated in such a regime: individuals, groups, and, if groups, religious, national, or ethnic? Walzer's promiscuous suggestion is all of the above. The state may multiply religious courts, authorize local autonomy for Arab towns, and yet provide a unified civics curriculum stressing liberal values. While Walzer generally avoids tidy answers to complex political situations, this seems far too messy, for he does not explain how any of this would or could work in practice. How much autonomy, for example, would Arab towns have over the educational curriculum, including their understanding of their own history?

Canada is its own case: partly populated by aboriginals and partly by the French-speaking Québecois—and both conquered as a result of the French–British wars. Can Canada tolerate a special status for Quebec? Can Canada continue to allow, for instance, Quebec to require French-speaking parents to send their children to French-speaking schools but exempt English-speaking parents from this requirement? Walzer suggests that toleration, when extended to groups as different as those found in Canada, "probably" requires some kind of legal and political differentiation. Can special arrangements coexist with liberal democratic requirements? Walzer thinks so but neither shows it nor provides a justification for his suggestion.

The same is true of Walzer's comments about aboriginal peoples. He recognizes that they have not, historically, led a liberal way of life. Of them he says,

> Internally intolerant and illiberal groups (like most churches, say) can be tolerated in a liberal society insofar as they take the form of voluntary associations. But can they be tolerated as autonomous communities with coercive authority over their members?[26]

Unlike members of a millet, aboriginals are also citizens. That may not be their primary cultural identity, but it is their central political identity. And their rights as citizens necessarily curb collective authority. Since the purpose of constitutional rights is to empower individuals, the collective way of life of aboriginals is at risk. Further, aboriginals—such as the Inuit—have a homeland. Because of their conquest and long subordination, Walzer believes that they should be given legal and political room to enact their culture—provided that the state enforces a right of exit for anyone who wishes to leave.[27]

But Walzer is again vague on why legal and political room must be maintained. From what he says, it would appear to be compensation for unjust conquest and long subordination. There is something to that, but I believe the reasons lie at a deeper level. I will explore this possibility in the next chapter.

Because the European Community is in its infancy, Walzer's comments are even more abstract and tentative than about other complicated cases. The powers of member states, for instance, will likely remain more than merely autonomous for a long time to come. Further, it is not a consociation because members will remain nation-states. And yet it is more than simply an elaborate treaty, for treaties do not usually require parties to them to conform to anything like the European Union's "Social Charter." Although still weak, the Charter is already having an effect in the internal social and economic lives of member states. Walzer sees two further major effects of the European Union as it develops. First, it already recognizes regions within states as legitimate objects of social and economic policy—and, he believes, there is likely to be pressure to recognize them as political subjects, too (e.g., the Basque region). Second, as people can move freely from one member state to another, immigration may become much more prevalent. Consequently, states that are now nation-states (e.g., Denmark) may become somewhat more like immigrant states. If the European Union survives and flourishes, it is likely, Walzer believes, to have all the advantages and strains of multiculturalism.

PRACTICAL ISSUES

I contend that tolerance occupies the moral space between mere forbearance and full acceptance. This tempts Walzer, but in the end he regards it as too ambitious. I think, however, this is because he is not sensitive enough to the shades of tolerance. "To tolerate someone else," Walzer says, "is an act of power; to be tolerated is an acceptance of weakness."[28] He cites Stephen L. Carter, who states that "the language of tolerance is the language of power."[29] The mistake is not that tolerance does not involve power; it does. The mistake, and it is a common one, lies in reducing it to nothing more than power. Assuming the mistaken view, however, Walzer argues that it is often asking too much to think we can move beyond toleration to mutual respect.

This is certainly true if we think of multinational empires. Greeks and Turks, for instance, lived peacefully side by side under the Ottoman Empire, but why suppose that their relations were marked by mutual respect? For "mutual respect" can be understood in one of two ways: as mutual *fear* or as mutual appreciation of the *value* of the other. It seems probable that mutual fear marks many international relations. The same is true of illiberal nation-states, which adopt toleration as "the best policy." But why accept this model of tolerance? The reason Walzer gives is that any other model necessarily omits successful regimes of toleration. This is correct only to a degree, namely, to the degree that tolerance is reduced to toleration and toleration, in turn, is reduced to nothing more than an act of power with a reciprocal act of weak submission. He concedes that mutual respect is an attitude, even an attractive attitude that can lead to toleration. But—and this is what Walzer stresses—mutual respect is neither the most likely to develop nor the most likely to be the most stable over time. He therefore places his stress on toleration as forbearance. Walzer, then, pictures toleration as best grounded in practical politics. On this understanding, toleration does indeed seem like a grudging virtue.

Throughout his study, Walzer accents explanation, not justification. That is, what interests him is how his five regimes and complex variations need and foster policies of toleration—and where they break down. Philosophers, he rightly thinks, often move too quickly to justification, ignoring the concrete circumstances in which justification is more than an academic exercise. His accent on explanation, however, too often comes at the expense of any serious attempt at justification. He does, from time to time, make passing judgments of approval, but they are tied firmly to his overriding value: peaceful coexistence.

Walzer traces the many ways toleration breaks down. Class is one cause, especially when it coincides with differences of culture, ethnicity, race, and religion. This happens in all regimes. Those tolerated in the minimal sense of being allowed freedom of worship, for example, nonetheless get the worst of everything that society has to offer. Conquered indigenous people suffer most, along with despised racial groups. Toleration is compatible with class inequality, but "this compatibility disappears when the groups are also classes. An ethnic or religious group that constitutes society's lumpen proletariat or underclass is virtually certain to be the focus of extreme intolerance."[30] Affirmative action is designed to break the link between class and group, not to improve the comparative lot of individual members of a downtrodden class within it. Those hierarchies remain intact as individuals move up and down them.

Gender is deeply implicated in other causes leading to intolerance. Traditionally, imperial states have left gender matters to millets. Other regimes, too, typically wash their hands of gender discrimination, even when extraordinarily brutal. Western nations tolerate cliterodectomies in the sense that there is no serious effort to prevent them in African countries. This is often done on the grounds that it would be intolerant to intervene in the folkways of minority cultures. Yet surely it depends on how we describe the practice. As Walzer notes, for men, at least, the attitude will change the less it is compared to circumcision or the more it is compared to amputation. In general, however, although toleration implies a right to communal reproduction, this right can conflict with the rights of individual citizens, and over the long haul, equal citizenship is likely to triumph.

Besides power, class, and gender, religion can pose a threat to any regime of toleration. First, religions often demand that they be recognized in political structures, not merely that individuals should be able to associate and worship as they please. Further, demands are often made to extend religious toleration to other social practices and concerns. In the United States, for instance, the Amish, as a group, long enjoyed exemptions from certain laws regarding education. The exception was allowed, Walzer suggests, because of the marginality of the Amish, their own wish to live outside the mainstream culture, and their willingness not to flaunt their exceptional status. Still, such arrangements are generally intolerable in immigrant states, though not in consociational states or even nation-states, where there is an established church.

Demands that the state, in the name of religious toleration, enforces the moral/religious values of a specific religion, however, cannot be tolerated. It violates state neutrality. Walzer does not go into much detail, but presumably it is acceptable, in an immigrant state, for individuals to press for laws that generally sail under a religious banner, but not under that description. This is frequently (and often disastrously) done. Prohibition laws, for instance, were marketed under a public health label when the real impetus behind them was rooted in high-church Protestantism that saw that it was in danger of losing its political and cultural hegemony. Walzer sees this same danger in some of the groups within the

Christian majority in the United States today. Fearing loss of social control, they are prepared to tolerate minority religions (e.g., Judaism) but have no tolerance for agnostics and atheists. Their efforts to push "family values" and their own certainties about right and wrong, Walzer says, are examples of religious intolerance.

And so they are. Yet Walzer never explains why. Perhaps the answer is obvious, but I think more needs to be said. Walzer cannot be opposed to moral certainties as such, for he, too, has no doubt about the barbarity of slavery, genital cutting, and widow immolation. He needs to give reasons why partial-birth abortion, for instance, does not "shock the conscience of mankind"—other than the fact that many people are not shocked. But clearly this is not sufficient, for if we stay at the level of emotional responses, countless millions are far from shocked by what seems shocking to Walzer. Again, we are back to sorting out the tolerable from the intolerable. We need to find and justify the basis of our distinctions.

Tolerance and its limits are determined, in part, on the battlefield of state education. Different regimes of toleration, Walzer argues, teach different things. Liberalism, in the sense of requiring children to tolerate existing social identities and the further choices of their fellow students, for example, is the only justifiable policy of an immigrant country like the United States. If it is to educate young from all cultures and not permit rival centers of coercive power, then it must remain strictly neutral among groups. Republican states like France, though also heavily populated with immigrants, requires a strong cultural base to sustain civic participation. Consequently, republican regimes stress how "we are all French"; liberalism leaves much more of culture to private life. Still, we cannot draw the lines too sharply, as Walzer stresses. After all, American schools emphasize the cultural history of English origins, the stories of the Pilgrims, religious freedom and tolerance, and so on.

It is here that Walzer draws a fruitful distinction between pluralism and multiculturalism. The former stresses America as melting pot: All the cultural ingredients are tossed in the pot, but after boiling for a generation or so, the final taste is entirely American. The thought is that immigrants will, without any help from the state except teaching the fundamentals of liberal democracy, eventually cast off their particular origins and simply become Americans. Multiculturalism, on the other hand, teaches children about each other's culture. It therefore brings diverse cultures into the classroom. It does not ignore them as pluralism allegedly does. Walzer would add "allegedly" because a sanitized version of English Protestantism was in fact taught. Walzer applauds this understanding of multiculturalism.

Walzer opposes multiculturalism, however, understood as calling on the state to teach children how to be different in prescribed ways. Although he does not use the term, he is referring to "political correctness"—or worse. If Catholics or African Americans wish to support their own parochial schools, that is one thing. Walzer objects, however, if they demand that the state do it for them because that is designed to reinforce "established or presumed identities and has nothing to do with mutuality or individual choice."[31] Since pluralism exists only at the level of the system, not each and every child, the state, Walzer says, "must step in to compel the various schools to teach, whatever else they teach, the values of American liberalism."[32]

Unfortunately, Walzer does little more than make this strong, controversial pronouncement. And more needs to be said, for its truth is not obvious. While no general argument can be made that would appeal to advocates of all the regimes he considers, in the next chapter I will develop an argument Walzer should accept, at least from within a liberal democratic political arrangement.

Walzer is keenly aware that all political regimes do what they can to reproduce themselves. Even in nonreligious nation-states and states formed largely by immigrants, however, a civil religion comes to be taught: "Civil religion consists of the full set of political doctrines, historical narratives, exemplary figures, celebratory occasions, and memorial rituals through which the state impresses itself on the minds of its members, especially its youngest or newest members."[33]

Civil religion—especially as it is less "religious" and more "civil"—is generally benign within a state but can erupt into intolerance internationally, for the historical narratives of one state can portray a neighboring state as a permanent enemy or elevate a historical battle or site to mythical status. One reason Serbs were adamant about keeping Kosovo is that they lost a heroically fought battle against the Ottoman Turks there in 1389. The battle figures prominently in Serbian poetry, history, and national identity.

Walzer is certainly correct that civil religion can breed international intolerance. But so can it breed resentment at home, for despite Walzer's assurances, particular groups within a state may not recognize themselves in the national stories the state propagates. Nor need they. In the next chapter, I will stress that states can compel all groups to enforce the fundamental rights and duties of a liberal democracy. What it need not do, and should not do, is compel anyone to accept its civil religion as Walzer describes it. No one need accept a state's self-image, even if the state generally supports all that is good. What needs to be accepted are the constitutional underpinnings of a liberal democracy, not the stories it tells itself about them, its exemplary figures, or its celebrations.

Nor does anyone have to accept a "full set of political doctrines." This might seem more problematic, for how can a state, even a liberal democratic state, survive and flourish if citizens ignore or reject its doctrines? It can because it is not a set of doctrines that must be accepted but a set of practices. The state, as such, should avoid, as much as possible, teaching any set of doctrines. It can compel its citizens, for example, to be tolerant of others—but not to accept its account of why. There will be competing accounts, accounts that will in turn shape the practices. To take another example, there is no single, agreed set of doctrines pertaining to freedom of expression that all Americans must accept. Supreme Court judges, political theorists, commentators, and ordinary citizens will each have their say, but none is privileged, and none becomes the doctrine of the state, at least in a liberal democratic state.

Walzer concludes his examination of practical issues by asking, rhetorically, whether states should tolerate the intolerant, for as Walzer notes, most of the groups tolerated by the various regimes he examines are themselves intolerant. His answer is that intolerant groups can be tolerated to the extent that they do not harass their neighbors or persecute their own members. If they wish to excommunicate or ostracize, that is up to them—again, provided that it does not amount to persecution.

I answer Walzer's question in a slightly different way, though not in a way that conflicts with his. I do, however, limit my answer to liberal states: Can *they* tolerate the intolerant? The answer depends on what the intolerant refuse to tolerate and how they express their intolerance. Clearly, intolerant groups cannot be allowed to pursue antidemocratic means to rearrange the constitutional order. They can, as individuals and pressure groups, hope to alter some provisions more to their liking. Would they be entitled to alter basic liberties that define a liberal democracy? The short answer is no. If one does not accept that the liberties enjoyed in a liberal democracy are basic or, though basic, desirable, then one will not see the matter this way. But the question is asked of liberal democracies. And liberal democracies are not being hypocritical in defending themselves from revolutionary attacks on their fundamental principles and practices. This said, it does not follow that groups themselves cannot arrange their own internal lives intolerantly, as some already do. Again, however, there are certain liberal provisos. Walzer stresses some. Intolerant groups, for example, cannot force anyone to join or prevent anyone from leaving them. Forcing and preventing, moreover, include more than the use of force: Intimidation, browbeating, harassment, and other coercive forms of control are also proscribed. Just where to draw the line, however, between permissible and impermissible manipulation cannot be settled in the abstract but only after careful attention to details and context.

Nor can intolerant groups so intellectually or emotionally cripple their members that they have no real chance of leaving. Children, for instance, must reach a minimum level of educational competence in the society at large so that leaving is not a de facto impossibility. Children are a particularly sensitive case. Every group depends for its continued survival primarily on reproducing itself through children of members.[34] Failing to provide an education that would enable a mature adult to survive outside the group is intolerable. So, too, is any group that sexually, emotionally, and physically abused its members, even if the members themselves do not complain. It is no embarrassment to liberalism to say that what counts as abuse will be determined by its standards of guaranteed rights and sense of minimal levels of well-being. To say otherwise—to say that each group may determine its own standards—would be to abandon political authority altogether. This is a possible, though unattractive, position that I will not explore further.

CONCLUSION

Walzer's brief but sweeping examination of regimes of toleration qualifies Rawls's claim that the European religious wars gave rise to toleration. But we have already seen that arguments for toleration extend at least to Aquinas in the thirteenth century. Nor does this rebut Rawls's contention that tolerance only comes into its own only because of the wars of religion. Walzer shows that the great empires of the past were led to adopt policies of toleration but—so far as he argues—for no other reason than political expediency. The boundaries of the concept of toleration are not so tight that this can be dismissed out of hand as a misuse of terms. Imperial arguments based solely on political (or economic) expediency, however, derive their claim to arguments for toleration largely because—from later perspectives—we see them as providing a bare platform on which richer understandings of toleration have been built.

In the comparatively few places where Walzer discusses tolerant attitudes—in contrast to policies of toleration—he tends to elide strikingly different attitudes: resignation, indifference, stoicism, curiosity, and enthusiasm. None of these, I will argue in chapter 8, captures central cases of tolerance. And Walzer barely alludes to tolerance as a virtue. Finally, Walzer holds that the best hope for regimes of toleration lies not in any attitude or virtue (however we might wish that to be) but in institutionalized practices. I suggested earlier that this itself might be wishful thinking, and I will have more to say about the role of the virtue of tolerance shortly.

Despite a variety of reservations and criticisms of his analysis, Walzer's *On Toleration* contains numerous insights. He shows that cave-dwelling philosophers—if their eyes become attuned to flickering shadows on the wall and they pay careful attention—can do far more than simply trade unfounded opinions with their fellows. In short, he makes good his claim that sound social and political philosophy must be historically informed and sociologically competent.

NOTES

1. Michael Walzer, *On Toleration* (New Haven, Conn.: Yale University Press, 1997).
2. See Michael Walzer, "Introduction," in *Spheres of Justice* (New York: Basic Books, 1983).
3. Walzer alludes here to the title of Thomas Nagel's *The View from Nowhere* (Oxford: Oxford University Press, 1989).
4. Walzer, *On Toleration,* 5.
5. Walzer, *On Toleration,* xii.
6. Walzer, *On Toleration,* 10–11.
7. Walzer, *On Toleration,* 2.
8. Walzer, *On Toleration,* 12.
9. Walzer, *On Toleration,* 15.

10. Walzer, *On Toleration*, 16.

11. Walzer, *On Toleration*, 19.

12. Walzer, *On Toleration*, 19.

13. Walzer, *On Toleration*, 20.

14. Walzer, *On Toleration*, 19.

15. Walzer, *On Toleration*, 20.

16. Walzer, *On Toleration*, 20.

17. Walzer, *On Toleration*, 25.

18. Walzer, *On Toleration*, 26.

19. Walzer, *On Toleration*, 26.

20. Will Kymlicka, "Two Models of Pluralism and Tolerance," in *Toleration: An Elusive Virtue*, ed. David Heyd (Princeton, N.J.: Princeton University Press, 1996).

21. Walzer, *On Toleration*, 29.

22. Walzer takes the quotation from Patrick Thornberry, *International Law and the Rights of Minorities* (Oxford: Oxford University Press, 1991).

23. Walzer, *On Toleration*, 30.

24. Walzer, *On Toleration*, 32.

25. Walzer quotes from Gary Kates, "Jews into Frenchmen: Nationality and Representation in Revolutionary France," *Social Research* 56 (spring 1989): 229.

26. Walzer, *On Toleration*, 46.

27. On April 1, 1999, Nunavut separated from the Northwest Territories to become the newest Canadian territory. The Inuit, who comprise over 80 percent of 24,730 residents, are among the first, if not the first, indigenous peoples in the Americas to achieve self-government. The Inuit have gained title to 136,000 square miles of land plus over a billion dollars in compensation, a share in mineral development, and substantial water and wildlife rights. Nunavuts now have significant control over their economic, political, and cultural future. They remain full Canadian citizens.

28. Walzer, *On Toleration*, 52.

29. Stephen L. Carter, *The Culture of Disbelief* (New York: Basic Books, 1993), 96.

30. Walzer, *On Toleration*, 58–59.

31. Walzer, *On Toleration*, 75.

32. Walzer, *On Toleration*, 75.

33. Walzer, *On Toleration*, 76.

34. There are rare exceptions. The Shakers, for instance, took members only through proselytization. Not surprisingly, they died out.

Chapter 8

A Liberal Argument for Tolerance

INTRODUCTION

We have yet to see tolerance as anything more than a grudging virtue, one that is good to cultivate — to the extent that it is good — simply and solely because it conduces to peace and tranquility. Toleration, like honesty, proves to be a wise policy. Why interfere in the lives of others when, with less effort and aggravation, individuals or groups can better pursue their ends by putting up with what they find repellent? "Let them wallow in their own ignorance and barbarism" can happily take its place alongside "Honesty is the best policy." Walzer argues that regimes of toleration, ancient and modern, can thrive without anyone needing to develop tolerant attitudes, let alone acquire the virtue of tolerance. Regimes of toleration neither demand nor urge that anyone care one way or another about those whom they tolerate, their beliefs, or ways of life. In putting up with those whom we tolerate, we might not have done all that we could, but we do all that anyone can demand of us, either as individuals or as groups. Some individuals and groups will cultivate tolerant attitudes, and that is all to the good. Walzer believes, however, that as a society we should not depend on anything as fragile and inconstant as subjective states of mind to sustain a regime of toleration.

In developing his argument for toleration, Walzer follows Locke. Both appeal to the enlightened self-interest of the powerful. Defending toleration by pitching arguments to the interests of the powerful is widespread. The logic behind it seems persuasive. After all, who needs convincing to stay their hand other than the powerful? If we can show that intolerance is generally counterproductive, what better argument could anyone want? Maybe more to the point, what better argument for tolerance is available?

I believe that there is a better argument for tolerance than this. Without a better argument, moreover, regimes of toleration in today's multicultural world are precarious. First, many tolerant policies will be temporary, lasting only as long as it takes one group to acquire dominant power over others. Once a dominant group can oppress another with impunity, why should it not? Is the best defense of a tolerant pluralist or multicultural society merely that it is unlikely that any one group has the power to make it monocultural? Second, it will be difficult for many to attain the type of indifference Montaigne recommends that would allow us to put up with many different ways of life with equanimity. Religion, ethnicity, language, culture, sexual orientation, family organization, and tradition matter too much for this attitude to be widespread. Nor, contrary to Montaigne, is this necessarily bad. Religion, language, and so on provide many with indispensable horizons of meaning. Third, even longlasting tolerance of despised groups amounts to little more than a grudging concession to the ineradicability of evil. It is not a humane response to difference.

To establish a better argument for tolerance necessarily takes us more deeply into contemporary social and political theory. We can do this while still staying inside Walzer's "cave," reflecting on our contemporary social and political circumstances. If the argument succeeds, we will see that (a) tolerance as attitude and virtue is central in establishing regimes of toleration; (b) tolerance helps make multiculturalism something positive, not merely a brute fact; and (c) tolerance, if thoughtfully cultivated, is more than a grudging virtue.

For the argument to succeed, we must restrict its range. It does not apply to every type of regime. Specifically, it will not apply to autocratic or dictatorial regimes, regimes that are utterly single-minded or close-minded, or regimes that refuse to recognize constraints built into constitutional democracies. And it will not apply even where it could apply when civil life has completely broken down through war or other catastrophe. Admittedly, this means that the argument will not have much bite in chaotic, strife-riven, or despotic parts of today's world (e.g., in Somalia, Kosovo, and Iraq). Furthermore, the argument will not move some citizens of generally tolerant constitutional democracies (e.g., members of various hate groups, apocalyptic religious cults, and remote, isolated, and closed communities). These are important exceptions. I believe, however, that the argument has wide application, including in all the great constitutional democracies. Increasingly, it applies to newly emerging constitutional democracies. And it might one day again find applicability in parts of the world that once knew a measure of tolerance but no longer do (e.g., the Balkans and Sri Lanka). Nor is the argument limited to democracies, for it applies to constitutional monarchies, such as Jordan, and to religions that have long preached tolerance, such as Buddhism, and those that did not always but do now, such as Catholicism. So, the argument's applicability, while far from universal, is broad—and enticing.

VARIETIES OF LIBERALISM

Liberalism comes in nearly as many varieties as Christianity. There is no single value, or its priority, on which all liberals agree. Most liberals, however, accept an overlapping cluster of values. Still, their disagreements are many and deep. Some place equality at its heart,[1] others justice,[2] and others freedom.[3] Some hold that liberalism depends on rights (Locke, Kant, and Dworkin), others on utility (Bentham and Mill). Critics contend that liberalism must embrace "hyperindividualism,"[4] while others argue that liberalism can recognize communities and social groups as proper subjects of moral and political concern.[5] Liberalism, moreover, can take both an antistatist libertarian form[6] and a socialist form (English Fabian socialists). Some liberals, furthermore, confine their liberalism to *political,* not broader *social* questions;[7] others see their liberalism in more *comprehensive* terms.[8] Finally, many contemporary liberal theorists maintain that the state must maintain strict neutrality among competing conceptions of the good.[9] By intention, this severely limits the reasons for which people can move to establish, change, or abolish political arrangements.[10] A few, however, argue for a *perfectionist* form of liberalism. They advocate that states should lend their support to desirable practices, character development, and forms of life and to curb undesirable ones.[11]

The connections among these varying positions are not so tight that they constrain advocates from interweaving different strands. And this is what we find. Rawls and Dworkin are "neutralists," for example, but disagree about the relative centrality of justice, equality, and rights. They disagree as well about the foundations of their neutralism. Perfectionists, in turn, are "weak" or "strong" and take opposed positions on the importance of autonomous against more perfectionist outcomes. And at least one advocate of political neutrality (Kymlicka) argues for group rights, a position that would seem to refute the charge that he, at least, could favor hyperindividualism. Nor could Raz, who explicitly rejects individualism, hyper or otherwise, for what some call "weak" perfectionism. Robert Nozick, in turn, is a rights-based, libertarian neutralist strongly opposed to utility-based political principles—as is his justice-loving, antilibertarian but neutralist colleague John Rawls. The imaginative, ingenious ways philosophers have woven the various strands of liberalism into distinctive doctrines and principles therefore makes it difficult to generalize about liberalism.

Yet even among the strikingly diverse set of liberal doctrines there are strong affinities. While not all find individuals the sole source of moral value, all regard particular individual men, women, and children as the basic object of moral and political concern. If anything unites all liberals, it would be this. Rawls's preoccupation with justice, Dworkin's with rights, and Raz's with freedom all have, at their heart, a deep moral and political concern for the lives of individual human beings as lived in this world.

The latter needs stressing. There is a this-worldly preoccupation found in all liberals. Religious nonliberals obviously care deeply about how people live their lives, too. But there is typically a preoccupation about how individuals will fare in a world to come or, if not in a world to come, in another life to be lived on earth. Buddhists and Hindus, for example, care about more than present life;

specifically, they wish to escape the samsaric circle of birth and rebirth, suffering and yet more suffering. There is no reason that they cannot develop liberal institutions based on liberal social and political principles. Sri Lanka began developing such a political order, but the lengthy civil strife between the Sinhalese, predominantly Buddhists, and Tamils, predominantly Hindu, has taken its toll. Nor is there any reason that political liberals cannot *also* be deeply religious. Yet even those who are concern themselves as liberals with the rights and welfare of individual human beings and communities as lived here and now. (Where their moral convictions are religiously based, they might divide with nonreligious liberals.) I thus disagree with Ronald Dworkin, who holds that every plausible political theory has the same basic value, namely, treating people "as equals."[12] He and others think that what principally divides plausible political theories, however, is the specific type of equality called for.[13] Treating people as equals surely matters. But why? The conclusion is inescapable that it matters (to the extent that it matters) because without it our lives go worse here and now. *That* is the foundational idea underlying liberalism. Contemporary liberal theorists try to give the best interpretation of this concern.

There are other affinities among liberals. All are wary of some holding power over others, especially when power is concentrated in coercive institutions, such as the state and dominant economic institutions. Historically, liberalism arose partly as a response to unfettered state domination. The concern of liberals with the proper limits of state authority and power continues. It is this that leads many liberals to maintain that the state must remain neutral among competing conceptions of the good life. More broadly, liberals tend to be suspicious of authority generally, including that found in tightly knit communities or traditions. Most contemporary liberals—though not libertarians—are equally wary of powerful corporate domination. Liberalism therefore has its own traditions, characteristic worries, and general arguments.

Is it, therefore, just another tradition with its own orthodoxy?[14] If so, it is a more relaxed, open tradition than most—and one that finds a valued place for many traditions that conflict with it, at least at the level of moral and political norms. We need to distinguish between "first-order" norms, judgments, and beliefs and "second-order" justificatory positions. People might agree (or disagree) about the first—for instance, that baby selling is wrong—yet disagree about *why.* Answers to *that* question can implicate deep philosophical questions, religious and metaphysical views, and whole ways of life. Liberalism tends to be far more relaxed about what necessarily follows from its orthodox justificatory premises than are many other orthodoxies.

Again reflecting their origins, liberals typically find an important role for rights. Not all think that rights—surely not natural rights—are basic. Utilitarian liberals, for example, accord pride of place to happiness, not rights. We might also find a common, but hardly unique, cluster of values most liberals share. Chief among them will be tolerance. But this is not the only widely shared value.

Liberals also pride themselves on being progressive and broad-minded, though these values (as tolerance) might be honored as much in the breach as in actuality. And one contemporary liberal, Richard Rorty, argues for a minimalist liberalism that consists of one imperative: Avoid thinking "that there is some social goal more important than avoiding cruelty."[15]

Liberals also place great value on lives lived autonomously. Just what this means and why it is valuable will become clearer shortly. Proponents can develop this aspect in many ways. Some develop it romantically or existentially, with the lone individual imagined as bravely, often tragically, making and taking responsibility for everything he (it is usually "he" for romantics) does. Some develop it in a Hobbesian way, imagining individuals competing selfishly for power to get what they desire. Indeed, it is this interpretation that often leads to the charge of "hyperindividualism," an obsessive preoccupation with self not only morally but in every other way. I suggest in this chapter a less romantic, less Hobbesian way to develop the underlying insight.

Since this is not a full-scale inquiry into the varieties of liberalism, I need to say no more about its varied and complex forms. This much had to be said, however, as a cautionary note. Because liberalism takes many different forms, the argument for tolerance that I develop in the pages that follow will not fit comfortably with all versions. Just as significantly, my defense might fit comfortably with views that are not thought of as liberal at all. Specifically, I have in mind communitarian and republican developments in contemporary political thought—developments thought to compete with liberalism. Without more than some fine-tuning, some communitarians and republicans might adapt and adopt the argument developed here. I say "some" because communitarians and republicans, too, come in more than one variety.[16]

SUBSTANTIVE LIBERALISM

The version of liberalism elaborated here regarding tolerance often goes under the title of "weak perfectionism." The name misleads in at least three respects. First, the adjective "weak" suggests that a stronger version would be preferable, when just the opposite is true. We should reject strong perfectionism because it is *too* strong. Strong perfectionists are too easily tempted to call on the coercive powers of the state to intrude into the lives of individuals, communities, and even whole cultures. Anything that can be improved but is not stands as an affront to strong perfectionists. Second, the notion of perfectionism itself misleads. It suggests that human nature is somehow perfectible. We can hope to curb the worst excesses of humanity and encourage the best, but attempting more takes one down the road to intolerance and oppression. At least in this, Kant was right: "Out of the crooked timber of humanity no straight thing was ever made."[17] Third, strong perfectionism suggests that individuals are little more than particular instances of whatever the theory deems perfect, much as a particular isosceles triangle is simply an instance of the perfect isosceles triangle. Strong perfectionists strive to arrange institutions that produce, as far as humanly possible, the Perfect Person, even if it that entails treating particular people roughly.

Because of its misleading connotations, I will refer to the position I elaborate as "*substantive* liberalism." It is substantive in three respects. First, it abandons political neutrality as a constituent feature of liberalism. In particular, it does not demand that the institutions of the state adhere to norms of strict neutrality or indifference between competing claims of value. There are good reasons why the state should be genuinely neutral between competing visions of the good life only when they are all good, that is, only when each is worth pursuing. That some might be better or that all will have defects will not lead substantive liberals to favor any one of them, for substantive liberalism will not use the coercive powers of the state to enforce finer distinctions between good, better, and best. A *good* social and political order is good enough. Even when it seems justified, moreover, there are often excellent reasons why substantive liberals will not use state power, for attempts to make things better often run a high risk of making a bad situation even worse. Still, substantive liberalism does not restrict the state from making evaluative judgments of good and bad, and especially between good and evil, and doing what it can to encourage one and discourage the other.

Second and relatedly, substantive liberalism rejects the sufficiency of *procedural* liberalism. Fair procedures are essential to liberalism because they generally lead to just outcomes. But fair procedures do not exhaust what we rightfully expect in a good society. For that we need to make substantive, concrete arguments about what is desirable and undesirable and do what we can—without causing more harm than good—to bring about a society that is both well-ordered and *good.*

Third, substantive liberalism does not restrict itself to constitutional matters but defends liberalism as a *comprehensive* social philosophy. That is, substantive liberals advocate not only liberal constitutional forms of government, including the legal system but also liberal social institutions, attitudes, and ways of life. These are marked by liberality of spirit, openness to change, appreciation of alternative ways of life, and tolerance. Substantive liberals have an abiding faith that Mill articulates in *On Liberty* that ordinary men and women, if provided with an adequate education, peace, economic security, and supportive political and social communities, can direct their own lives. It is, therefore, a "fighting creed" that competes with other comprehensive social philosophies.

Substantive liberals do not regard their conception of the good life as the *only* good way to live. It is not. They do argue, however, that it is an especially attractive way to live for those living in advanced industrial or postindustrial societies. Even then, it will not be the *sole* way to live a good life for everyone. Substantive liberals will be mindful not to make it impossible for those in their midst who choose nonliberal ways of life.

So, substantive liberalism offers a *comprehensive* social and political philosophy, not a purely *political, procedural,* or *neutral* form of liberalism. Just what substantive liberalism adds (or subtracts) from liberalism with respect to tolerance emerges in two steps. I first develop the arguments for the place of tolerance within substantive liberalism in this chapter and then, in chapter 9, consider objections from various nonliberal quarters. What follows is not a full defense of substantive liberalism. That would take a full-length study of its own. Here I am interested solely in the place and importance of tolerance with substantive liberalism.

WHAT IT MEANS TO LIVE AUTONOMOUSLY

Liberals generally endorse autonomy but disagree about its precise meaning, worth, or implications. All regard it as closely connected with freedom, and doubly so. In living autonomously, not only do we express our freedom, but freedom is also a condition of autonomy. That is, living self-directed lives necessitates that we are unfree in various ways. Clearly, we cannot live fully autonomous lives if we are locked up, coerced, brainwashed, or intimidated. Our autonomy is also seriously compromised by persisting life-threatening dangers (e.g., starvation or murderous warlords). Freedom also depends on having sufficient knowledge and sufficient reasoning ability to use it. Someone suffering severe mental retardation or serious psychological disorders cannot live a fully autonomous life.

We can be unfree in other ways. Some are burdened with a past so oppressive or confining that they cannot live autonomously even if they gain their freedom from prison, torturers, or mistreatment. Think, for instance, of those who have spent most of their adult lives in prisons. Exceptions such as Nelson Mandela only support the generalization. We would not think he was extraordinary if most survived prison as well as he did. Autonomy can be curtailed in still other ways. If available options are few or interchangeable, it is difficult to see how anyone could live autonomously. If all our choices were like those found in the breakfast cereal section of supermarkets, autonomy would be impossibly thin. Insignificant choice distracts us from realizing how trivial many of our choices are, how little autonomy we really have. Finally, the absence of educational or employment opportunities, especially in technologically complex societies, makes it nearly impossible to live autonomously. Exceptions, again, only prove the rule.

The notion of freedom underlying this conception of autonomy is not Kant's austere and rigorous moral autonomy but what Raz calls *personal autonomy.*[18] The difference is critical. For Kant, autonomy entails that our moral principles must be both rational and self-legislated. Because rationality entails universality and necessity, Kant argues that there can be but one moral law for everyone, whatever the circumstances.[19] Self-legislation, therefore, leads not to a multiplicity of moral principles but to one principle—the categorical imperative: *Act only*

on that maxim through which you can will that it should become a universal law.
This is not as rigid or flattening as it might sound, for one brings maxims—
particular specifications—to the categorical imperative, and maxims take circumstances into account, thus concretizing particular applications.[20] Still, Kant's
ambition is to provide us with the one and only account of morality and a strin-
gent set of universally binding moral principles.

The account of personal autonomy explored here is less metaphysical and less
universal. It specifies only one moral ideal among others. Being free—that is, not
unfree in the various ways earlier specified—is only a necessary condition for living autonomously. More is needed, for we can be free from internal and external
pressure yet drift through life without aim or purpose. This is not to say, as Aristotle implies in *Nicomachean Ethics,* that a good life demands a settled, lifelong
plan.[21] It is to argue, however, that a life of sloth or flitting from one thing to another is not living autonomously.

Although an autonomous life might not be strongly unified, there will be a variety of "nested goals" one pursues for a significant part of one's life.[22] Careers
and human relations, clearly, involve not only means/ends connections but also
part/whole relationships. Disciplined practice is a means to becoming a musician;
to learn how to interpret music, however, is part of becoming and being a musician, not a means to it. And so with almost everything humans find significant.
Communal and family life, careers, and playing games, for example, involve
part/whole relationships. Parents who think of their children as entertainment or
as means of securing social insurance for old age will be disappointed. What parents "get out of" raising children cannot be captured by means/end logic. Similarly, friendship cannot be reduced to a means/ends relationship—and still count
as friendship.

It is tempting to add that we are autonomous only if we critically examine the
careers, ends, relations, and so on that we freely choose. William E. Connolly
adopts a strong version of this requirement. He contends, for example, that someone who follows a particular career path simply because his parents and friends
expect him to do so is less autonomous than someone who critically explores "the
contours of the profession under consideration in the light of his own capacities,
strengths, and weaknesses, and compar[es] the career in question to other alternatives that might be open to a person with his interests, capacities, and opportunities."[23] This places a heroic burden on the autonomous person, a burden that
leads us into excesses of romanticism and existentialism.

Connolly seems insufficiently sensitive to the vast middle ground between his
ideal and being part of a herd. Those who enter a career because of the expectation of others, for example, might nonetheless live autonomously once fully embarked on and engaged in it. Surely there are many physicians, clergymen, and
military officers who came to their careers in ways that Connolly disapproves yet
who embraced them wholeheartedly and thus lived fully autonomous lives. Still,
Connolly is correct that one cannot live autonomously without reflection on

means and ends, parts and wholes, significant alternatives, possibilities, and risks, for self-direction is not self-propulsion. It must involve a considerable degree of reflection on what one is about. This said, however, the degree of reflection about what matters remains indeterminate.

Finally, autonomously lived lives are those lived on the basis of good reasons. This connects to both freedom and critical reflection. Freedom and reason are not contraries, let alone contradictories. An old *New Yorker* cartoon explains why. Two jurors are talking, and one says to the other, "I never listen to the evidence; I want to be free to make up my own mind." The juror, obviously, is neither free nor autonomous but licentious—that is, free from reasoned constraint. Arriving at a judgment because it is supported by good reasons does not compromise our freedom; it enhances it. Critical examination or reflection is just bringing reason to bear on whatever is under consideration.

As with critical examination of ends, we need to be careful that we do not demand too much of "good reasons" as a condition for living autonomously. If the notion of living life autonomously makes sense at all, it cannot require that everyone always act for the *best* reasons. Frequently we do not know what the best possible reasons are. Nor is it sensible for a social and political philosophy to demand that one always act on what we think are the best possible reasons, for no one does consistently. Autonomy would be an ideal no one ever meets. The same is true of individual deliberations, choices, and acts. Just because we act for less than the strongest reason does not compromise our autonomy. We compromise our autonomy, however, if we act without any good reasons or, perversely, against reasons we ourselves regard as good.

While this makes obvious intuitive sense, we need to explain why living autonomously requires that we make judgments and choices based on good reasons. Why is it not enough that we simply *choose,* even if for no reasons at all? The answer lies in what it means to be *self-directed.* The phrase itself seems to leave open the possibility that we could act for no reason at all, that we simply direct ourselves to do this or that. When we release an inflated child's balloon, for instance, its own propulsion takes it wherever it happens to go, zooming this way and that until finally running out of air. Self-direction is not like that. It is defined partly by what it is not; specifically, not living one's life by taking directions from others or being pushed and pulled by forces one does not understand. It should not be understood as acting either without or against reasons. We are self-directed when we respond appropriately to reasons provided by our goals, relations, and situation. As Sher puts it, self-directed activity "is motivated by an agent's appreciation of reasons provided by his situation."[24] It is hard to see how it could be otherwise. It is hard to see, that is, why self-direction would be valuable if not reason-dependent.

Understanding autonomy as responsiveness to reasons also explains why the various unfreedoms we have considered count against autonomy. In one way or another, all block responsiveness to reasons. If we are intimidated, psychologically crippled, brainwashed, or harried, we cannot respond as we would without these unfreedoms. When circumstances or powerful individuals and groups present us with too few alternatives or alternatives in name only, they deprive us of opportunities to act in a sufficiently reasoned way. We also cannot respond to reasons if they are beyond us, if we cannot understand or appreciate them, either because of natural or social deprivations.

Sher, following Raz, also argues that making choices uninformed by reasons has little worth. Infants have no trouble giving vent to their raw feelings, and young children make many choices. Neither qualifies them as autonomous. Personal autonomy is an achievement, not something given. It takes attention and diligence. We rightly describe adults who act like children as infantile. An inability (or unwillingness) to shape conduct by responding to good reasons reveals the absence of maturity and leads them to act irresponsibly, as it concerns both their own lives and the lives of others, for mature adults control themselves because they understand why it is good to do so. They also strive to make decisions, choices, and judgments because they regard them as reasoned.[25]

Autonomy, freedom, and reason fit together into a coherent whole. How tight the fit depends on how demanding we are that critical examination is thorough and how good the reasons for which we choose and act must be. The more relaxed the demands, the easier it will be to live an autonomous life. Too tight, and autonomy becomes an impossible aspiration; too relaxed, and we cannot help but succeed. We can still distinguish between more or less autonomous choices and more or less autonomous lives. And it is important to resist the pull of the idea that one can make a fully autonomous choice or live a fully autonomous life only if one always acts for the best or complete reasons. It is not primarily that it sets the bar too high but that there is no "high" at which to set the bar. We should be wary of such notions as "the best reasons" or "complete reasons" not only because we do not *know* what they are but, more profoundly, because there might be no such reasons to know, for terms like "best" and "complete" imply that we can give them sense when used in a moral, social, and political context. If not all values are *commensurable,* as I believe, this will be possible even theoretically, for we will not have a single metric with which to measure.[26]

An autonomous life, then, is one in which individual men and women freely make reasoned judgments about how best to live their lives. It is a self-directed life. An autonomous individual, in Raz's felicitous phrase, "is (part) author of his life."[27] Raz's metaphor expresses two thoughts. First, our lives are like books that we ourselves write. We do not merely appear in our life stories as principal character; we (partly) write them ourselves. How our story goes depends in large measure on authorial freedom, on how we write our story. The second thought qualifies the first, for we are only part or *partial* authors. The background story of everyone's life has already been set. Everyone is born into a particular community with a particular history, everyone has a (largely) unchangeable physical and genetic makeup, and everyone's life is subject to good and bad luck. We do not have the luxury of waiting until our twenty-first birthday to choose our sex, ethnicity, parents, national history, religion, and emotional or physical makeup. (*Who* would do the choosing?) At least to some extent we can alter background features, though seldom without enormous struggle and never wholesale. If changes occur, they will feature prominently in our life story. Can we imagine a life story where someone consigned one's religious conversion, sex-change operation, becoming a parent of triplets, loss of reputation, or immigration to another country to a series of footnotes? Can we imagine a life story where the fact that one lived through a plague, revolution, or civil war or survived an earthquake was merely "background"? We simply do not have the leeway novelists have in fashioning a setting to our liking or having lightning strike when and where we desire. And unlike novelists, we cannot discard rough drafts or write out of our lives misfortunes, mistakes, and wrongs we commit and suffer. Our first draft is our final draft. Or, as I expressed this thought in the preface, although a few lives have a second act, none is a dress rehearsal.

THE WORTH OF LIVING AUTONOMOUSLY

The value in autonomous choices and lives derives from its contribution to one's well-being. It consists, in Raz's words, "in the successful pursuits of self-chosen goals and relationships."[28] Our lives go better just because we live them autonomously. It cannot be overemphasized, however, that living an autonomous life is living a life governed by choices based on good reasons. If we choose arbitrarily, it is extremely unlikely that what we choose will be worth much.[29] To the extent that one makes choices for feeble or corrupt reasons, such choices are not autonomous. And that, in turn, means that they are choices that are unlikely to contribute to our well-being. Raz's debt to John Stuart Mill's characterization of individuality in chapter III of *On Liberty* is evident. It differs, however, in its stress on the centrality of good reasons. We can reveal the difference by quoting Skorupski's sympathetic précis of Mill's view:

> Moral freedom requires that one's desires and impulses are one's own in two ways: they are outgrowths of one's own nature and not imposed from without, and they are not heteronomous. That is, they are integrated into a developed character whose fixed "purposes" or "habits of willing" are fruits of self-cultivation and have sufficient strength to subordinate desires when there is good reason to do so. But these firm habits of will can themselves arise only from the raw material of strong natural impulses and desires.[30]

There is much to admire in Mill's account. Mill is no Hegelian, but he uses Hegelian metaphors to support his position: "Human nature is not a machine to be built after a model, and set to do exactly the work prescribed for it, but a tree, which requires to grow and develop itself on all sides, according to the tendency of the inward forces which make it a living thing."[31] What Mill overlooks, however, is the real possibility that one can have a developed character that is utterly wrongheaded or evil. We can overcome this objection only if we falsely suppose that the "fruits of self-cultivation" naturally produce good character and action. But we do not develop into men and women of decent character if only permitted to breathe the air of freedom. We are not like acorns that will grow into mighty oaks if only given enough good soil, sun, and water. So Mill's account needs to be importantly qualified. Only developments of character that conform to good reasons are valuable.

Further, we should not confuse well-being with happiness or even as, necessarily, a part of happiness, at least not if we think of happiness as consisting in a hedonic state of mind. An autonomous life might well be a constitutive part of happiness, however, if happiness is understood more along the lines of living a well-ordered life filled with worthwhile projects, good friends, and vibrant, healthy communities. The pursuit of autonomously chosen goals and relationships is often arduous. Nor is success guaranteed. Our pursuits might come to nothing. Even then, however, we seldom lose everything. Because our goals are nested in part/whole relations, part of any complex pursuit will entail a variety of challenges and achievements. Had Andrew Wiles not solved Fermat's Last Theorem, his well-being would not have been destroyed, though he surely would have been deeply disappointed, for even had he failed, he would have successfully mastered an enormous range of mathematics, shown why certain strategies do not work, and developed new techniques for approaching other mathematical puzzles. In doing so, he would have still lived autonomously, despite not attaining his boyhood dream.

Something like this is probably what people mean when they say that one's journey is as important as arriving at the destination. The adage is true to the extent that the journey itself involves worthwhile, autonomously chosen subprojects marked by achievement. A journey that we noted only for its failure at every turn would hardly have been worth taking. The adage is also what lies behind Mill's claim that it is better to be Socrates dissatisfied than a fool satisfied.[32] If we understand "happiness" along Aristotelian lines as "a rational activity in accord with virtue," then it might not elude those who seek well-being by living autonomous lives, even if they are dissatisfied.

Autonomous choice and autonomous lives are not for everyone. Autonomy is one, and only one, moral ideal. There are other worthy ways to live. Living one's life in a monastic order might meet the conditions of autonomy but probably does not. Nor is this a criticism. Monastic life provides sources of real value for people living in certain historical circumstances, whether their lives are lived autonomously or not. So, too, the lives of nomadic tribesmen are worth living, though personal autonomy is hardly prized. It is not that such lives have value *despite* lacking autonomy, for that would assume that autonomy is, as it were, the "default" position. It is not. Living a life autonomously, or as part of a disciplined monastic order, or as a forest monk ridding oneself of attachments, or in a tightly knit traditional community can all have value in the right circumstances for the right people at the right time, for all can provide deep sources of value for those who live them out. None is right for everyone, everywhere, always.

How is this possible? How, for instance, can a substantive liberal grant that life in a monastic order can be valuable—if he also rejects the metaphysical underpinnings of religion? The answer is clear. Many genuine values—friendship, self-knowledge, sacrifice, helping others, and communal life—are not exhausted by the metaphysics on which they are ostensibly based. Monks themselves will see these values as subordinate to the supreme value of serving God. But we do not have to accept *their* self-image to see that the way of life they live provides deep sources of value. Naturally, if a substantive liberal agrees with, say, Christianity, then he might find even *more* value in it—or less, for such a person might think that monastery life (at least in today's world) is too pinched to provide any great source of value. So, too, we need not accept the myths and fables nomadic tribesmen tell themselves to see that the lives they lead provide values of friendship, community, self-sacrifice, altruism, loyalty, courage, and so on.

Autonomy, however, will seem attractive to many today, for despite profound and unique differences that mark societies around the world—for example, caste, customs, culture, economic system, and religion—many share common features that make living autonomously valuable. We can sort these features into external and internal. Externally, the world we live in is marked by rapid technological change, sophisticated markets, instant communication, culturally diverse societies, a need to become highly educated, a need to adjust to a rapidly changing social and political landscape, and the expectation of mobility, both social and geographic. Internally (and chiefly because of the previous considerations), our parents raise us to recognize that we must equip ourselves to survive and flourish without the type of extensive cultural support system found among aboriginal tribesmen, to "make something of ourselves," to take responsibility not only for what we do but who we are and will become, to see the world as a realm of free choice and not of necessity, and to accept that our major life choices are principally "up to us." Not everyone will recognize or appreciate the values inherent in contemporary forms of life, however, because not everyone will have the opportunity or desire to grasp their significance.

These external and internal factors conspire so that even those who now choose, say, to become contemplative forest monks might be acutely aware— unlike monks two or three centuries ago—that their decision is itself *another* autonomous choice among many good choices. Features of the modern world have so permeated cultures everywhere that what looks like an embrace of another way of *finding* meaning in life is, in effect, another autonomously chosen way of *giving* life meaning by setting out on a path to find the meaning it offers. Of course this is an exaggeration. In many parts of the world, including in parts of an otherwise thoroughly modern world, there are groups and whole communities that remain insulated from modern intrusions. Such lives are often rich and diverse and provide deep sources of value that overflow with profound meaning and fulfillment.

This might fill us with nostalgia about past ways of life. I do not think, however, that conditions that make living autonomously attractive need to be lamented. This is not because our contemporary conceptions of autonomy are ideal for everyone. They are not. As stated earlier, no moral ideals are ideal for everyone in all circumstances. There are two reasons, however, to keep regrets in check. The first is that the external and internal features I have mentioned are here to stay. Short of autonomously choosing to enter a neo-Benedictine order until the new barbarism passes, as Alasdair MacIntyre once (half in jest?) suggested, we need to make our home in today's world.[33] And second, the recognition that one is part author of one's own life—that well-being consists in successful pursuit of desirable ends and relationships—can stand on its own as a moral ideal rivaling, even surpassing, many past ideals.

THE IMPLICATIONS OF LIVING AUTONOMOUSLY

Critics of autonomy often contend that it is hyperindividualist. This indictment embraces many charges. Autonomy, critics claim, glorifies choice for its own sake and fails to acknowledge that freedom entails responsibility. In particular, critics hold that autonomy stresses humanity's selfish, acquisitive side at the expense of its other-directed, generous side. Stressing autonomy conceives of society in atomistic, reductionist terms and so regards individuals as essentially rootless and "unencumbered" by anything other than by what they freely choose. In portraying individuals as creating their own values, advocates of autonomy vastly underestimate the place of tradition, community, and culture in providing us with sources of value and moral guidance. And, finally, critics accuse proponents of autonomy of failing to acknowledge the value of civic virtues and of overemphasizing reason at the expense of emotional commitments. Not every critic levels every charge, but the list is representative.[34]

Are advocates of autonomy guilty as charged? The previous discussion should forestall many of these criticisms. Autonomy as defended here, for example, does not glorify choice for its own sake or imply that we are essentially selfish, or maintain that individuals are the source of all value. We should not, in short, confuse a defense of autonomy with a defense of individualism, hyper or otherwise. Yet even if we can dismiss this part of the indictment, what about the other charges, especially charges of atomism, rootlessness, and failure to recognize the value of tradition, culture, and community as sources of value?

These are serious accusations. Fortunately, we can meet them. Autonomy calls for, and so implies, the centrality of strong cultures and communities to give it substance. Individuals desiring to live autonomously need them as raptors need air currents to soar. Autonomous individuals, as the authorial metaphor suggests, live their lives against a backdrop and in the midst of a history not primarily of their own making. The backdrop and history supply that without which autonomy would make little sense. An analogy illustrates this. However original and touched by genius each was, neither Einstein nor Mozart appeared out of nowhere fully equipped to generate theories or operas. Without their grounding in what went before, without their understanding of and participation in their scientific and musical traditions, without grasping from the inside what problems and possibilities their pasts presented, they would have accomplished nothing. To say, as we sometimes do, that they stood on the shoulders of their predecessors is not quite right. Their engagement with the past was far less segmented than this suggests. We need to shift the metaphor. They did not so much stand on anyone's shoulders as find themselves immersed in the scientific and musical life around them. This rich life was the sea in which they swam, providing them with the very sustenance needed to make their own distinctive contributions. However much they changed what was in it, however much they even pushed their noses out of it, they could not have done so without thorough familiarity and appreciation of what their sea offered them.

The same is true of everyone, however humble. Everyone is born into a community and culture with its own language and history, distinctive practices and values, and shared forms of art, religion, social organization, and political life. These nearly always supply deep sources of value providing us with worthy ends, projects, relationships, and commitments, so that in choosing and living autonomously, we are bounded by shared understandings. These understandings are both all-encompassing and fine-grained. They tell us, for instance, not only which games are important but how to play them, not only what matters in one's religion but how to show it, and not only which laws and customs to keep but how to interpret them. Or at least initially, for communities, traditions, and so on are not static but vibrant and always in flux. Individually and collectively, we incessantly reshape, even revolutionize, these sources—just as Einstein and Mozart transformed physics and opera, just as our collective political experience in the last 300 years has shaped and reshaped our collective understanding of democracy's possibilities and limits—and continues to do so.

It follows that, if we value autonomy, we must tend to whatever makes it possible and enables it to flourish. Without the nurture traditions, cultures, and communities provide, living autonomously would be impossible; without the goals, careers, and practices they provide, autonomy would be empty. The conclusion is irresistible, if ironic, that a concern for autonomy demands concern for the very things that autonomous individuals sometimes strive to escape, for traditions and communities, though sources of value, are also sources of *dis*-value. And even when they are not, some will find them intolerably suffocating, something that is not *for them*. Without traditions and communities, autonomy would lose its traction and become nothing more than an empty, abstract gesture. One common and richly rewarding way to live can be to tend to one's own culture, community, art, and traditions, even working to transform them into something better. Such a life can be at least as rewarding as one devoted to more self-interested concerns. We need to be careful, however, about what cultures and so on do provide and license and what they do not.

CULTURES AS CONTEXTS OF CHOICE[35]

Many things comprise a cultural community. Typically, a cultural community includes a unique history, a recognized set of heroes and villains, shared social understandings, a common language, accepted religious ways of life, familiar art forms, a set of acceptable careers, distinctive social norms, its own social and political structure, a specific way of organizing family life and gender relations, and often its own beloved (and jealously protected) geographical location. Features salient in one culture might be less so in another. Sometimes it will be difficult to tell where one cultural community begins and another leaves off. And some individuals will find themselves, willy-nilly, members of several cultural communities— or only partial members of more than one. A Native American, for example, who leaves tribal lands to earn a university degree and learn a profession before returning home might find himself having one foot gingerly planted in two cultures, neither of which fits him easily. Combinatorial possibilities are extraordinarily rich and varied. For our purposes, fortunately, an intuitive understanding suffices since nothing in what follows depends on cataloging various cultural communities.

Our question is why cultural communities matter for autonomy. Kymlicka provides an answer:

> Our language and history are the media through which we come to an awareness of the options available to us, and their significance; and this is a precondition of making intelligent judgements about how to lead our lives. . . . Liberals should be concerned with the fate of cultural structures, not because they have some moral status of their own, but because it's only through having a rich and secure cultural structure that people can become aware, in a vivid way, of the options available to them, and intelligently examine their value.[36]

Without a rich and secure culture, one cannot develop self-respect. As Rawls articulates self-respect, it has two aspects:

> a person's sense of his own value, his secure conviction that his conception of his good, his plan of life, is worth carrying out. And, second, self-respect implies a confidence in one's ability, so far as it is within one's power, to fulfill one's intentions.[37]

And we should accept Rawls's further point that self-respect is not so much a part of any rational plan of life as a precondition of it.

Equally important, however, is something Rawls fails to acknowledge adequately, namely, that growing up in a vibrant, self-confident cultural community is a further condition of self-respect, for without this, it will be practically impossible to formulate, let alone pursue, coherent goals, engage in significant forms of life, enter significant relationships with others, or understand one's social world. Individuals deprived of a robust cultural community will lack necessary resources to live autonomously.

This is not conjecture. It is amply confirmed when whole groups of people find themselves cut off from what once gave them a context and resources to live flourishing lives because of war, natural disaster, or breakdown in civility. They find themselves cut adrift, often filled with anxiety and hopelessness leading to lethargy and destruction of self and others. If this condition persists, a cycle of hopelessness develops that experience shows can be exceedingly difficult to break.

Liberals, Kymlicka says, should be particularly concerned with the fate of cultural communities. But this concern is not limited to liberals. It should matter to anyone, though too often we pass over it in ignorance or silence. Too often we take for granted the richness and stability of cultural communities. We should not do so if they are necessary for self-respect and autonomy, any more than we can take for granted the purity of the air we breathe or the water we drink.

We need not, and should not, extract from this culturally conservative conclusions. In particular, it does not follow that we must make every effort to maintain the fundamental structures, norms, practices, and so on of a cultural community just as we inherited them or, alternatively, restore them to what (at least in memory or myth) they once were. Even isolated, highly traditional cultural communities change. Those that do not stagnate, especially when, for the sake of tradition, change is deliberately and forcefully halted. The analogy with music—which plays an important role in most cultural communities—is again apt, for although composers, musicians, and listeners must grow up in a musical culture, music changes continually, commenting on and criticizing itself, responding to technological innovations and other art forms, and changing religious sensibilities, social practices, and foreign influences. Think, for instance, of such innovations in Western music as Gregorian chant, the invention of the pianoforte, eighteenth-century chamber music, and the development of jazz, with its African roots. Attempts to freeze any artistic form is doubly doomed. They cannot succeed, and, to the limited extent that they do, art becomes enfeebled and moribund.

The same is true of cultural communities generally. They are constituted by elements in flux, dynamically responding to each other, to influences outside the community, to their own internal demands, and to contingencies created by man and nature. Cultural communities are differently resilient. None can withstand every type of blow, let alone all blows. Isolated, highly traditional communities sensitively attuned to nature and tightly tied to ancient ways provide deep sources of value to their members. They do, however, find it difficult to withstand foreign cultural assaults or natural setbacks (e.g., the importation of television or persistent droughts). To survive, they must change, and typically they do. Old Amish communities, for example, have developed subtle and complex ways of interacting with, yet keeping at arms length, the dominant society surrounding them. They changed in response to their surroundings and their own internal requirements. It is one reason Amish life continues to flourish despite challenging obstacles.

Dominant or large mainstream cultures also change over time in response to challenges. The salient difference is this: Old Amish, Inuit, Navaho, Welsh, Quebecois, Hassidim, and so on must expend far more energy and devote themselves more strenuously to keeping their cultural communities vital than do those that dominate and surround them.[38] This is not because they are intrinsically less attractive. It is because they are constantly in danger of being swamped by their larger neighbors culturally, economically, and in every other way. Americans in the 1980s worried about Japanese corporations buying up American businesses, property, and icons, such as Rockefeller Center. The worry was always fanciful. The danger is real, however, that small cultural communities living next door to powerful, expansionist neighbors will lose their identities, becoming absorbed by their neighbors, even vanish. It is no answer to say that *another* culture or community stands ready to incorporate members if their own collapses. Cultures and communities cannot be exchanged like hats. Human beings need stable—not unchanging—communities and cultures to thrive.

Should authorities allow a threatened cultural community to use any means necessary to keep its culture intact, especially given the importance of growing up and living in a strong culture? Not any means necessary, but some means. Minimally, those living in endangered cultures need *tolerance,* that is, not to be denounced or intentionally interfered with simply because those in a neighboring culture dislike or disapprove of aspects of their way of life. The tolerant will not only answer this call but make it themselves. They will do so not for their own good but for the well-being of those who would bear the brunt of intolerant reactions. While they might not *accept* them, neither will they simply put up with them. They will, instead, reach out and seek to accommodate their ways to the extent that their ways are not intolerable. This means that they will enter into conversation with them. These conversations might not always be pleasant, but it will involve a "frank and candid exchange of views," as diplomats of bitterly opposing sides often say. They will, in short, explore the terrain between mere forbearance and full acceptance.

Notice how unlike this is from the approach championed by Locke and Walzer. They address their arguments primarily to those who tolerate, not those who suffer because of intolerance. While each recognizes that tolerant policies benefit objects of toleration, this is not their rationale. Appeals to the enlightened self-interest of the powerful might (or might not) be a good strategic argument, as we have seen. Unfortunately, it fundamentally misdirects the arrow of justification.

Tolerance advances the well-being of the Inuit, Old Amish, Hassidim, Gypsies, and so on, not the well-being of the powerful, except incidentally. By redirecting the arrow of justification, we look first to the well-being of the weak, not the powerful.

Why should the powerful heed this call? Note that the question is not, Will they? but, Should they? The answer rests on twin pillars. It builds, first, on the preconditions of a good life, whether understood in terms of autonomy or some other moral ideal. If self-respect is necessary for well-being and strong cultural communities are, in turn, necessary for self-respect, then to intervene in the affairs of a cultural community in massively disruptive ways demands particularly strong justification. It builds, second, on substantive liberalism's recognition that tolerance must be more than a policy. As a *virtue,* tolerance motivates people to show forbearance for the good of others. To the extent that those with power also accept autonomy as a moral ideal, then logic directs that they should themselves be concerned with the autonomy of others, even those whose beliefs, ways of life, and so on they find unattractive. Because of this concern, they will be motivated to inquire from and interact with those they could dominate, for they will wish to learn what is of value in alien cultures, find what can and cannot be tolerated. They will do so not primarily for their own well-being but for the well-being of those who would suffer if their beliefs and practices were disallowed.

PROTECTING CULTURAL COMMUNITIES

Earlier I remarked that no culture could demand or expect protection from all blows. What they might ask and expect is that they not suffer gratuitously damaging blows. Liberal states must therefore provide some protection to cultures that face pressures from the dominant society. Aboriginal cultures, such as those of the Inuit and Native Americans, have a special claim, based only partially on their being unjustly conquered. Such cultures tend to be small, highly distinctive, geographically threatened, and therefore in danger of inundation by outsiders. All cultures need tending to flourish. Because of their small size and vulnerability, however, aboriginal cultures need the disproportionate, concentrated energy and devotion of their members to keep their cultures vibrant. And this—from a liberal perspective—makes it more difficult for individuals in those cultures to shape their own lives in any way other than as a response to threats from larger outside economic and social forces. Legal and social protection inappropriate if guaranteed to the dominant culture might well be proper to threatened cultures and communities.

This is not primarily an argument from fairness. Instead, it looks to making it easier, where feasible, for members of an endangered people to shape their lives without worrying incessantly and exclusively about the very survival of themselves as a people with their own distinctive art, religion, customs, and ways of life. Without some shielding from outsiders and some protection by the powerful, indigenous people would have to spend all their energy and resources just to keep their cultures and communities viable. Tolerance therefore requires that states take measures to protect aboriginal cultures from such blows. The state may, for example, allow restrictions on property sales to outsiders, or curtail emigration, or impose differential property laws, including rights of inheritance. The state might also delegate extensive self-government to aboriginal communities, for example, allowing hunting exemptions and the use of hallucinogenic plants in religious ceremonies. As long as cultural communities remain part of states, however, their de jure independence can never be more than partial.

We should not limit such measures to aboriginal cultures or Gypsies in Europe. Old Amish and Hassidim, for example, are not indigenous to North America. Yet they face similar problems. And because their culture sustains them, too, tolerance warrants special treatment. That they demand a certain type of special treatment, however, is not dispositive. Before adopting any measure, tolerant individuals and states will examine how allowances and exemptions meet needs of minority cultures and the larger society alike.

Where Amish live, for instance, the state might build wide shoulders adjacent to roadways so that Amish can continue to use horse-drawn carriages safely. Since they use the state's roadways, however, the state might oblige them to install electric signals on their buggies for everyone's safety. States might modify or even waive other health, safety, and education regulations. All will be subject to give-and-take as tolerant and tolerated alike struggle to find principled ways of accommodation, ways that understand and respect the moral demands of the other. While requiring that Amish children receive schooling sufficient to enable them to be good and productive citizens, the state might nonetheless permit them to end their schooling earlier than generally mandated by state law.[39] If an Amish school is small, all on one level, and used only during daylight hours, the state might not require the installation of electric exit signs—though it might require regular fire drills.

It might appear that in requiring Amish to meet certain safety standards, tolerant subjects exact a quid pro quo from them for granting exemptions. Horse trading of this sort undoubtedly happens. At least from the perspective of substantive liberalism, however, it cannot be the dominant approach. Instead, liberals make demands of, say, the Amish so that they can be true to their *own* values. Because they value individual well-being, substantive liberals will have to balance issues pertaining to autonomy against cultural values threatened by certain regulations. Because they value autonomy, for instance, substantive liberals cannot tolerate practices of some cultural communities (at least where they have jurisdiction) that prevent members from leaving.[40]

Substantive liberals can impose these limits even if doing so leads to the demise of a vulnerable culture, for though cultural communities provide a needed context for its members to live well, none has a right to continue its existence no matter what. Its members, for instance, might find their home culture unattractive or other cultural destinations more enticing. If enough members are dissatisfied, the community will gradually wither and die. For those few who remain until the end, this will be a catastrophe. But because cultural communities are neither prisons nor zoos, however, no one can require individuals to remain in a culture that they urgently wish to leave. Throughout history, ancient communities, traditions, and cultures have reached the point where they could no longer sustain themselves, even with outside help. Their passing is always regrettable since it involves the extinction of distinctive human ways of life that once provided sources of value. And for those who hang on until the end, it will be an unmitigated disaster. Recognizing the signal importance of cultural communities does not guarantee their survival. Each culture must earn its continued survival. All that tolerant substantive liberals will wish to ensure is that their survival is not arbitrarily swamped. Further, once individual members reach young adulthood, their home culture has had its chance to win them over. Cultural ties are strong. If, despite many years and strong ties, a cultural community cannot hold on to its young, then it will wither and die. Liberals certainly will not support measures that prevent anyone from leaving.

Substantive liberals, furthermore, need not support cultural communities that behave intolerantly to their own members. The Ottoman Turks largely ignored the significant intolerance within millets since it did not affect the vital interests of the imperial center. Tolerant individuals and groups, however, will take an intense interest in just this, for when a community calls for tolerant treatment, we need not answer that call if the community itself exhibits various forms of intolerance to its own members or members of other groups.

The Inuit and Amish represent two types of cultural communities. There are others, some clearly demarcated, some not; some whose boundaries are porous, some not. Membership is sometimes voluntary, sometimes imposed, and often somewhere between. Membership based on race, ethnicity, national or regional origin, and sexual orientation illustrates these complex, often ambiguous and perplexing, community identities. Many racial and ethnic communities result from immigration. African Americans, whose ancestors were sold into slavery, must be placed in a different category. And, for altogether different reasons, homosexuals fall into yet another category. Governments have an important role to play in supporting and protecting members of each of these communities beyond protection provided for everyone.

Neutralist and procedural liberals must either oppose such measures—or see them as required. Such measures are either forbidden because they violate equal rights or procedures or required because they ensure rights or fair procedures. Tolerance does not figure in the justification, for neither permits arguments unless couched in terms of rights or procedures. There is no room for any other moral arguments. By relying only on narrow procedural or rights-based neutralist premises, liberals too often get themselves into contortions defending what look like special provisions. It would be better to make a direct, substantive argument in favor of tax advantages of indigenous communities, affirmative action, the right to modify uniforms for religious reasons—or oppose them for substantive, moral reasons.

The role of tolerant individuals and nongovernmental organizations is often more significant than state support for groups that mix with the broader society, even when these groups strive "to keep to themselves," for unlike aboriginals or Old Order Amish, they typically do not occupy their own territory, run their own schools and social services, or have their own distinctive religion or distinctive criminal justice system. Everyone rubs shoulders much more. Protective regulations and laws, while necessary, cannot overcome persistent intolerance without the aid of tolerant individuals and groups.

I must stress again that tolerance, even full tolerance, does not entail acceptance. We will find objectionable features in every way of life. How could we not, since we find them in our own? Tolerant individuals and groups will not look away from these aspects but look beyond them. They will try to discover how what they find objectionable fits into the culture, what it contributes, and—even if ill-fitting and destructive—what the community as a whole makes possible for its participants despite its objectionable elements.

By interacting with participants of different ways of life, tolerant individuals will not rest easily at the level of "bare" or "mere" toleration, for tolerance disposes us to look at the well-being of possible subjects of tolerance. To do this honestly and nonpatronizingly, the tolerant must try to see how things look from the perspective of objects of toleration. There is no expectation of either full tolerance or acceptance. Yet in recognizing the value of a culture to its members, the tolerant are likely to take a position closer to full tolerance than to mere forbearance if the culture offers its members the resources for a life worth living. And that will be most cultures, though clearly not all.[41] If I am right, the primary intention informing tolerance is not keeping the peace but helping those tolerated to realize their own conception of a good life, always provided that it is a good way of life.

Tolerance does not require that we accept another cultural community as embodying a conception of the good life on a par with our own. This is but one possible conclusion. Neither logic nor moral common sense requires us to think that every cultural community is equally good. That may be a desirable heuristic principle to adopt until proven otherwise in a particular case, but it *will* be mistaken in some cases. Yet even when seriously objectionable, cultural communities are usually desirable, *all things considered.* For all things considered, they provide the wherewithal, the sources of value and the concrete material and support, for people to live lives worth living. Further and to reiterate, tolerance does not require that we accept the reasons others give for why they believe they must live as they do. Tolerance requires that we look for the good in other ways of life and communities, not accept their own accounts of this.

Not every community is a cultural community. A community of believers, for example, might themselves participate in many different cultural communities in which religion is integral yet not definitive. This is true of all world religions. Roman Catholics the world over will feel (more or less) at home at worship—though not necessarily at home far from the church itself, away from its comforting, common rituals. Religions find themselves integrated in distinctive ways in different cultures. Aspects of older, native religions might become blended into the newer, dominant religion or facets of a religion might be highlighted in one place but not another.

Locke gives one set of reasons for tolerating religious diversity. Substantive liberalism gives another, and more persuasive, reason, for whether we ourselves participate in any religion, it is not hard to see that they are sources of great moral and spiritual value for their adherents. Without the values, hopes, rituals, and stories religion provides, many would be lost, hopeless, and decentered. There is, for example, something deeply reassuring about "religiously" sticking to rituals no matter what. This, again, does not imply that we need to accept the stories each religion tells about itself, their doctrines, rituals, or pathways to salvation. That would be impossible anyhow. Religions conflict doctrinally and practically. We cannot coherently accept all their doctrines or coherently follow all their pathways, or we would bump into ourselves. This in itself does not matter. What matters is that we, if are outsiders, can come to see that religions provide deep, indispensable value for their adherents. Because this is so, they deserve our tolerance.

This might sound like a defense of religious tolerance addressed only to religious skeptics. It is not, for the devout of one religion are typically equally outsiders vis-à-vis other religions. If anything, it fits them better, for, as we know from the sorry history of religious wars, devout adherents of one religious persuasion are often sorely tempted to demand that believers of other persuasions convert. Tolerance, however, should lead them to see that other religions also provide sources of value to their followers. Devout Protestants, say, can see that Catholicism provides its followers with deep moral and spiritual values, resources without which many would be lost, and conversely. The difference is this: Tolerant religious skeptics will give this as their reason for tolerating religions *generally*; tolerant followers of one religion will give this as their reason for tolerating all *other* religions. Of their own religion believers make additional claims, namely, that their doctrines are true, that their values are superior, and that their spirituality is not marred by superstition or other intellectual and moral errors. To the extent that they are tolerant, however, they will be prepared to find the *value* implicit in competing religious outlooks.

We must keep in mind that both skeptics and religious believers can move beyond tolerance altogether, for although skeptics will not embrace any religion and believers only one, both might come to see that (with certain qualifications) any number of religious approaches are fully acceptable—at least as providing good ways to live—none having features one regards as especially objectionable. This would be close to what Bernard Williams describes as the "broad church" view. Since (nearly) all religions provide ways to live rich and fulfilling lives and none have serious moral or social deficiencies, (nearly) all are fully acceptable. Religious skeptics, while remaining skeptical, can arrive at this conclusion depending on what standards of morality and reasonableness they think must be met. No paradox arises unless one assumes that "fully acceptable" means "altogether true." But it does not. To be fully acceptable from a justificatory point of view means only that one has no serious objection, moral or otherwise, to the culture, practice, community, and so on.

One will of course continue to reject many metaphysical and epistemological claims the devout make. Nothing bars the devout of one religion from holding that other religions with conflicting doctrines and practices are all fully acceptable while simultaneously rejecting the thought that all competing *doctrines* are true and all *rituals* or *practices* fully warranted. Here, however, we are examining what tolerance, not acceptance, entails. Because living in a secure cultural community matters greatly, because many find life empty and pointless without the centering religion provides, tolerant subjects will do more than grudgingly restrain negative reactions. Tolerance calls for sympathetic, yet sometimes critical, support. Tolerance calls for support because so much is at stake. Equally, tolerance calls for critical engagement, and for the same reason; namely, so much is at stake. If we are to reach principled accommodations between *our* views, practices, and so on and *theirs,* then we *must* engage each other in vigorous but thoughtful discussion. Accommodation will otherwise be little more than a modus vivendi where it is not patronizing. If we are to accommodate the interests of those we tolerate in nontrivial ways, then we must understand those interests. If we rely solely on our own understandings of those interests, we are certain to misunderstand, misinterpret, and misvalue what they regard as crucial.

But what if a culture or a community just wants to be left alone, does not want to engage in "discussions" about its beliefs, attitudes, and way of life? That should be respected, *provided* that we learn enough about them to know, first, that this is what they want and, second, that they are not engaged in intolerable practices, for one reason that the powerful in some communities wish to be left alone is so that they can tyrannize others or those in a neighboring community. As always, exploration of the field of tolerance calls for enormous cross-cultural understanding and deep appreciation—from the point of view of others—of what is at stake in dialogue, criticism, and other exchanges.

More broadly, tolerance mandates cross-"X" understanding, where "X" is anything that leads to misunderstanding and enmity. So tolerance leads us to cross-national, cross-generational, cross-gender, cross-religious understanding. Locke and Walzer underplay this because their arguments are directed at tolerance's subjects (i.e., tolerators), not objects (i.e., tolerated). Once we give priority to objects of tolerance, however, cross-X understanding becomes a moral necessity, not just a matter of wise policy. Tolerant individuals and groups must try to understand and appreciate what is good about others whose otherness seems threatening in various ways: as unnatural, debased, wicked, or evil. To do this adequately goes far beyond forbearance. It urges learning about others, preferably in their own words—and on their own turf. This, in turn, will often lead to a call for protection, not intervention. And this typically moves tolerant individuals and groups beyond bare toleration to full tolerance.

Since the argument no longer looks to the best interests of tolerators but to the well-being of objects of toleration, the value of tolerance as a virtue becomes apparent. The reason is simple. To pursue enlightened self-interest, one needs the virtues of patience, persistence, courage, and clear thinking. There is little need to develop strong other-regarding virtues. When we justify tolerance primarily in terms of the well-being of others, however, we need the other-regarding virtue of tolerance, and this for two reasons. First, without it, we are more likely to surrender to our initial negative reaction to what we dislike or disapprove. Second, we are unlikely to motivate ourselves to gain needed understanding and appreciation. As a consequence, we are likely to inflict serious wrongs on innocent others. The virtue of tolerance is an other-directed companion to the self-directed virtues of patience and persistence.

This understanding of tolerance encourages subjects and objects of toleration to engage each other in efforts at mutual understanding, though not acceptance. Tolerant subjects will refrain from using their built-in power advantage out of a concern for those who would suffer because of intolerant responses. By mutually engaging, the tolerated can try to show why an aspect of their cultural community should be immune from intervention. Tolerant subjects, in turn, will be inclined to look for what is valuable in whole ways of life, aspects of which remain objectionable.

Once mutually engaged, nothing precludes either from pressing their own concerns about the other in "full, frank, and candid exchanges." In particular, tolerant people might conclude, however reluctantly, that what they find objectionable is intolerable. The limits of tolerance will then be reached. Tolerance is therefore not a free pass. It does not allow us, like Pontius Pilate, to ask dismissively, "What is truth?" and leave others to their own devices. Usually, the truth will leave cultural communities to their own devices. Usually, they can take care of themselves without outside help or intervention. Yet in some circumstances, as we have seen, tolerance demands support. In still other circumstances, however, truth may justify, even demand, forceful intervention, not support. To make any of these moral judgments requires understanding, not approval.

If practiced conscientiously, tolerance becomes something more than a grudging virtue. It becomes something far more admirable, a virtue that builds bridges to others instead of contemptuously walling them off. One reason some feel deep resentment at regimes of toleration, I believe, is not that they crave approval so much as they demand *recognition*. Tolerant individuals and groups do this by opening themselves to the real possibility of moving far beyond bare or mere toleration to full tolerance—and even acceptance. Once genuine understanding of another becomes part of what it is to be tolerant, we might find that the other is not as bad, as disgusting,

and as repellent as we first thought. Familiarity, of course, may breed even greater
contempt, and we need to be alive to that possibility, too.

Tolerance clearly does not imply that everything in another culture or community or way of life is admirable. To see this we need only to think of our own society, our own cultural structures and forms, for every attentive person everywhere can point to features of his or her own society, culture, and so on that are
utterly appalling. If we can see this about ourselves, others can see it about us—
and we about them. There is this important difference. We can far more readily
justify addressing what is wrong in our own cultural community than correcting
deficiencies in others.

This difference does not entail that outsiders may not openly criticize aspects
of another cultural community. Recognition entails neither approval nor silence.
Critics should often mute their negative comments, however, because they are either pointless, cruel, or oppressive. In avoiding oppressive comments, tolerance
generally mandates respectful criticism, even when it needs to be made forcefully. Despite mandating great caution, tolerance does not preclude intervention.
One reason tolerance mandates caution should be clear. However much we think
we understand another cultural community, intimate knowledge will often elude
us. So, even when we find an aspect of another culture deplorable, tolerance leads
us to think carefully about what we plan on doing and why. Intervention will be
a reluctant last resort.

I cite one reason in chapter 3: the "Sweater Principle." The features, structures,
and so on of cultural communities are intertwined. We often learn just how inextricably intertwined after the fact. The more tightly knit, the greater the danger of
unraveling. Cultures do not consist of discrete modules that can be added or removed at will. Elements and structures making them up are usually connected dynamically. Changes in one typically lead to surprising changes in others.

There is a further reason for caution. Throughout history those intervening in
other cultures for "the best of reasons" have done so patronizingly, paternalisti-
cally, and crudely. They assumed, without good reason and often witlessly, that
members of these cultures were either unable or unwilling to act in their own interests. Anthropologists no longer have the hubris to speak of "primitive cultures"
or "the savage mind." Too many, however, still look on other cultures as if they
were populated by people too ignorant, malicious, or corrupt to tend responsibly
to their own affairs. Given how difficult it is to change objectionable features in
our own societies, traditions, and practices, a modicum of humility might give us
pause before adventuring beyond our own cultural borders.

The centrality of autonomy to liberal cultures provides a third reason for re-
sisting interventionist temptations. All who treasure well-being conceived as living autonomously will not frustrate others making something of their lives. Not
all participants in these cultures need be committed to the value of autonomy.
Some might celebrate and realize substantially different ideals. If we ourselves
value autonomy, however, we will see that values others pursue are best realized

in letting them live their lives as they see fit, even if the ways of life chosen are illiberal. Liberals are not inconsistent in living their own values by tolerating values they do not share. They do so precisely because autonomy is so central to their own conception of a good life. From a liberal perspective, even members of nonliberal cultural communities are part authors of their lives, even if they do not think in these terms or, if they do, think it especially significant. More importantly, substantive liberals see the value in protecting whatever gives life meaning, provided that, on balance and in the circumstances, it is worthy.

None of the reasons for tolerance, therefore, hold absolutely and without qualification. Because some practices are destructive of self-respect and well-being, we can sometimes justify intervention. On occasion, intervention can stop great evils without significant loss. Indeed, intervention can prevent loss and create conditions for changes to the good. Tolerance does not demand that anyone stand idly by while great evils are committed, as happens when cultural communities spin out of control or when powerful forces within behave cruelly to their own members. Participants come to see themselves as victims of their own culture, even its prisoners. Perpetrators of cruelty seldom see it this way, but no one's self-understanding is controlling.

We do not throw caution to the winds when we intervene in such cases. Instead, we overcome it. How best to intervene when we conclude we must is another story, one that demands further caution and good judgment. Intervention takes sundry forms. Because tolerance mandates cross-cultural understanding, it helps to engage in open discussions with those whose conduct we find objectionable. Since tolerance does not preclude candid disagreement, we can spell out why we find something abhorrent; others, with equal candor, can explain why we are mistaken—or why it is none of our business. If we are not persuaded on either point, engagement need not stop. We can help victims within a group articulate their concerns, help create educational programs, provide incentives to lure misguided wrongdoers from their harmful activities, and apply political and economic pressure.

Sometimes only highly invasive interventions will succeed, yet—out of an abundance of caution—that will be a last resort for substantive liberals. Circumstances are difficult to imagine where we could justify massive intervention where unacceptable conduct is not involved or where individuals can easily avoid victimization. More particularly, appalling sentiments or vile beliefs will almost never be sufficient to trigger invasive interventions. This is not because beliefs do not matter; they matter enormously. It is, instead, that ugly attitudes and contemptible beliefs are better fought with reasoned argument than with suppression. The considerations Mill adduces in chapter II of *On Liberty* against restrictions on free expression remain compelling. Even so, borderline cases might arise. Malicious propaganda, for example, can create an immediate danger in some circumstances, preventing reasoned counterargument. Further, powerful forces within a group might effectively prevent challenges, making it impossible to mount counterarguments. Here, however, control is itself conduct and creates grounds for intervention if it leads to severe victimization.

As shown in chapter 4, objects of tolerance can be nearly anything: individuals, groups, attitudes, beliefs, specific acts, and practices. Every act of tolerance or intolerance, however, inevitably affects individual human beings. While we may hate sin yet love sinners, we must nonetheless recognize that in attacking sin we affect the sinner. Still, as a last resort, we are justified in intervening to prevent great harm. We should not delude ourselves, however, that we are only attacking intolerable beliefs or practices. We are also affecting the lives of individual human beings. In considering possible interventions in what we regard as intolerable, therefore, substantive liberals need to take this into account.

A further bar to heavy-handed intervention occurs when potential victims can avoid victimization without ruining or seriously damaging their lives. Avoidance might be difficult, but this alone would not justify invasive intervention by outsiders. Outsiders might show the way out, lend various kinds of support, yet not invasively intervene. Here one might object that one man's noninvasive intervention is another's massive attack. We cannot meet the objection by a priori argument. We need in each case to explore possible effects on both communities and their participants. Still, we will not have much trouble distinguishing between, say, refusing to return runaways from oppressive regimes and sending in armies.

Tolerance does not block liberals from demanding the right of exit. No one should be a prisoner in one's own culture. This "should" becomes an enforceable right when the culture or group is itself part of a larger society living under a common political authority. Inuit, Amish, and Scientologists, for example, are also citizens of the states in which they live. Being part of a cultural or religious community or even a cult does not abrogate rights members enjoy as citizens or legal residents. Liberals of all stripes insist on equal citizenship and on preventing violations to basic human rights. All citizens and legal residents, therefore, have the right to sever their connection with communities of their youth or that they joined voluntarily. Cultural communities and voluntary associations exist to serve participants, not the other way around. This is so even for those cultural communities that find themselves living under political authorities not of their own choosing. What one can take if one leaves is more complicated. May authorities forbid émigrés from taking anything more than the clothes on their backs? May émigrés, for instance, take the fruits of their labors that resulted, at least partly, from the material contributions of the community they wish to leave? We cannot answer these hard questions in the abstract. But we can say that what they are allowed to take cannot be so meager that their right of exit is a right in name only.

Some individuals and groups might be neither citizens nor legally permanent residents of the state in which they reside. Refugees lack such status. May they carry on with cruel and barbaric practices they do at home or refuse to permit members to leave? Liberals will rightly insist on protecting certain basic human rights of anyone living under the authority of a host state. Customs tolerated next door might be intolerable in one's own home. This is a moral price that refugees must pay. We cannot require hosts to look the other way at customary practices they regard as cruel and barbaric, however deeply ingrained in the culture they are. Tolerance always has its limits.

Courageous, prudent, and generous individuals try to live courageous, prudent, and generous lives. So, too, will tolerant individuals. In trying to live tolerant lives, they will strive to build a tolerant society, one that goes beyond simply "putting up with" what individuals find disagreeable. This is not easy. It means confronting the intolerant in the sense of asking why they exhibit certain attitudes, or do certain things, to targets of intolerance. Unless they can give good reasons, their intolerance is not justified, and we should make that plain. Again, this is not easy to do. For most, it is easier not to ask but to turn away. But, as argued earlier, all virtues are difficult, or they would not be virtues.

More positively, full tolerance leads individuals to support other individuals and groups in pursuing their conception of the good even when there are aspects of it one finds deficient. The reason is familiar; namely, conceptions of the good—if truly of good and not of evil—give life meaning for those whose conception it is. What this entails concretely depends on context, particularly what would help and be appreciated. It also requires discretion, good judgment, and faithfulness to one's own conceptions of good and evil. A devout, tolerant Catholic, for instance, might contribute to the building fund of a local Protestant church but not to its missionary fund, let alone its programs that support activities regarded as immoral.

NOTES

1. Ronald Dworkin, "Liberalism," in *A Matter of Principle* (Cambridge, Mass.: Harvard University Press, 1988).

2. John Rawls, *A Theory of Justice* (Cambridge, Mass.: Harvard University Press, 1971).

3. Joseph Raz, *The Morality of Freedom* (Oxford: Clarendon Press, 1986).

4. Michael J. Sandel, *Liberalism and the Limits of Justice* (Cambridge: Cambridge University Press, 1982); Charles Taylor, "Atomism," *Philosophical Papers: Philosophy and the Human Sciences* 2 (1985): 187–210.

5. Will Kymlicka, *Liberalism, Community, and Culture* (New York: Oxford University Press, 1989).

6. Robert Nozick, *State, Anarchy, and Utopia* (New York: Basic Books, 1974).

7. Rawls, *A Theory of Justice.*

8. Ronald Dworkin, *Sovereign Virtue: The Theory and Practice of Equality* (Cambridge, Mass.: Harvard University Press, 2000); Raz, *The Morality of Freedom.*

9. Rawls, *A Theory of Justice*; Dworkin, "Liberalism"; Kymlicka, *Liberalism, Community, and Culture*; Bruce Ackerman, *Social Justice in the Liberal State* (New Haven, Conn.: Yale University Press, 1980); Charles Larmore, *Patterns of Moral Complexity* (Cambridge: Cambridge University Press, 1987); Brian Barry, *Justice as Impartiality* (New York: Oxford University Press, 1995).

10. Compare George Sher, *Beyond Neutrality: Perfectionism and Politics* (Cambridge: Cambridge University Press, 1997).

11. Vinit Haksar, *Equality, Liberty, and Perfectionism* (Oxford: Oxford University Press, 1977); Raz, *The Morality of Freedom;* Sher, *Beyond Neutrality.*

12. Ronald Dworkin, *Taking Rights Seriously* (London: Duckworth, 1977), 179–183.

13. See Amartya Sen, *Inequality Reexamined* (Cambridge, Mass.: Harvard University Press, 1995).

14. Alasdair MacIntyre makes this charge in *Whose Justice? Which Rationality?* (Notre Dame, Ind.: University of Notre Dame Press, 1988).

15. Richard Rorty, *Contingency, Irony, and Solidarity* (Cambridge: Cambridge University Press, 1989), 65.

16. See, for example, Daniel Bell, *Communitarianism and Its Critics* (Oxford: Clarendon Press, 1993), and Philip Pettit, *Republicanism: A Theory of Freedom and Government* (Oxford: Clarendon Press, 1997).

17. Immanuel Kant, *The Idea of a Universal History* (Berlin, 1784), as quoted in Isaiah Berlin, *The Crooked Timber of Humanity,* ed. Henry Hardy (New York: Alfred A. Knopf, 1991).

18. Raz, *The Morality of Freedom,* 370.

19. Immanuel Kant, *Foundations of the Metaphysics of Morals* (Berlin, 1785), sec. I.

20. Kant is often (mis)interpreted in ways that make it utterly inexplicable how anyone might have found his theory attractive. For needed correctives, see Onora O'Neill, *Constructions of Reason: Explorations of Kant's Practical Philosophy* (Cambridge: Cambridge University Press, 1989); Christine Korsgaard, *Creating the Kingdom of Ends* (Cambridge: Cambridge University Press, 1996); and Marcia Baron, *Kantian Ethics Almost without Apology* (Ithaca, N.Y.: Cornell University Press, 1995).

21. Aristotle, *Nicomachean Ethics,* Book I.

22. Raz, *The Morality of Freedom,* 370.

23. William E. Connolly, *The Terms of Political Discourse,* 2nd ed. (Princeton, N.J.: Princeton University Press, 1983), 150–151.

24. Sher, *Beyond Neutrality,* 48.

25. See T. M. Scanlon, *What We Owe to Each Other* (Cambridge, Mass.: Belknap Press of Harvard University Press, 1998), chapter 1.

26. For an argument showing that not all values are commensurable, see Raz, *The Morality of Freedom.* An excellent anthology on this topic is given by Ruth Chang, ed., *Incommensurability, Incomparability, and Practical Reason* (Cambridge, Mass.: Harvard University Press, 1997).

27. Raz, *The Morality of Freedom,* 369.

28. Raz, *The Morality of Freedom,* 369.

29. Even exceptions are bounded by reasons. One might vary one's way to and from work by pulling routes out of a hat, for instance, either to ward off boredom or to confuse terrorists.

30. John Skorupski, *John Stuart Mill* (London: Routledge, 1989), 350–351.

31. John Stuart Mill, *On Liberty* (London, 1859), ed. David Spitz (New York: W. W. Norton, 1975), 56.

32. John Stuart Mill, *Utilitarianism* (London, 1863), ed. Roger Crisp (Oxford: Oxford University Press, 1988), chapter 2.

33. Alasdair MacIntyre, *After Virtue,* 2nd ed. (Notre Dame, Ind.: Notre Dame University Press, 1984).

34. See especially Sandel, *Liberalism and the Limits of Justice;* MacIntyre, *Whose Justice? Which Rationality?* and *After Virtue*; Bell, *Communitarianism and Its Critics*; and Michael Walzer, *On Toleration* (New Haven, Conn.: Yale University Press, 1997).

35. In what follows, I adapt the account given by Will Kymlicka in *Liberalism, Community, and Culture.* Kymlicka defends the notion of group rights here and elsewhere (*Multicultural Citizenship: A Liberal Theory of Minority Rights* [New York: Oxford University Press, 1995]). I do not wish to dispute the idea of group rights, but I believe that everything that I need to say here can be said without making use of the idea.

36. Kymlicka, *Liberalism, Community, and Culture,* 165.

37. Rawls, *A Theory of Justice,* 440.

38. Kymlicka emphasizes this point in both *Liberalism, Community, and Culture* and *Multicultural Citizenship.*

39. In *Wisconsin v. Yoder,* 406 U.S. 205 (1972), the U.S. Supreme Court upheld the right of Amish parents to terminate the formal education of their children after eighth grade, about two years earlier than mandated by Wisconsin state law. The Court relies heavily on the religious freedom clause of the First Amendment. Speaking for the Court, however, Chief Justice Warren Burger explicitly mentions factors applicable beyond the peculiarities of U.S. constitutional law.

40. See Joseph Raz, *Ethics in the Public Domain* (Oxford: Oxford University Press, 1994), chapter 8.

41. Colin Turnbull tells the story of the Iks, an unfortunate African tribe whose nomadic hunting life was curtailed by development and the protection of wild animals. It is hard to read Turnbull's account and find anything in the life of the Ik worth saving. His own recommendation was that the children should be physically removed and placed with others. I do not know whether his anthropology is sound, but surely throughout history there have been cultural communities that have disintegrated for innumerable reasons, though it is hard to imagine many facing worse conditions than the Iks. See Colin Turnbull, *The Mountain People* (New York: Simon and Schuster, 1971).

Chapter 9

Objections and Replies

Tolerance as conceived by substantive liberals presents an attractive picture. No longer need we see it as grudging, an attitude we adopt just to keep peace or as a policy to further the interests of the powerful. As conceived here, tolerance moves beyond mere forbearance toward full tolerance. How far will depend on the case. It may lead to full acceptance—even, in a few cases, conversion. In that case, one does not merely *accept* what was once tolerated but *advocates* it as one's own. This prospect frightens those who find comfort in their settled ways. In the pluralist, multiculturalist world in which we live, the fearful worry that tolerance is a virtue they cannot afford.

Tolerance grounded in substantive liberalism raises many objections, not only from cultural conservatives. Many liberals will object that it violates state neutrality since it clearly "takes sides." Others will insist that, denials notwithstanding, tolerance inevitably erodes our own deep commitments. Some will complain that it is smug and complacent: we, though superior, nonetheless deign to tolerate you. Others will detect "bad faith." When pro-life proponents press their case, for instance, some liberals condemn them as intolerant. Yet when pro-choice defenders press their own case, these same liberals regard them as models of tolerance. It all depends, say critics, on whose ox is being gored.

So, tolerance as defended here faces many objections—left, right, and center. That is, the *political* left, right, and center. The Marxist left, for instance, charges that tolerance is "repressive." The conservative right charges that tolerance masks an insidious and far-reaching attack on traditional moral, social, and religious values. Many liberals, too, will object to the defense of tolerance offered here because it clearly violates *neutrality,* a cornerstone of much contemporary liberal theorizing. Finally, the New Left contends that tolerance does not go nearly far enough because it rests on old assumptions about *cultural pluralism* instead of *multiculturalism*, which mandates that we move beyond liberalism and tolerance altogether. These objections, and replies to them, will occupy us for the remainder of this chapter.

TOLERANCE AS REPRESSIVE

Objections

That toleration can be repressive and excluding is argued in *A Critique of Pure Tolerance,* an influential book published in 1965 with individual essays by Robert Paul Wolff, Barrington Moore Jr., and Herbert Marcuse.[1] Although they make no attempt to integrate their objections into a single, sustained argument, all agree that "the prevailing theory and practice of tolerance turned out on examination to be in varying degrees hypocritical masks to cover appalling political realities."[2]

Wolff argues that democratic pluralism, at least as developed in the United States, marries liberal principles with conservative sociology. Pluralism presses for tolerance and noninterference in the private sphere, but only between groups— specifically, religious, ethnic, and racial groups. The consequences are twofold. First, "we find a strange mixture of the greatest tolerance for what we might call established groups and an equally great intolerance for the deviant individual."[3] But, second, the pluralism as it actually exists in democratic states works itself out as a "give-and-take" process among already *legitimated* pressure groups. This version of pluralism grants claims of recognition in theory to *all* groups, but not in practice. Claims of unlegitimated groups are, in practice, ignored or peremptorily dismissed. These two consequences, Wolff contends, are generated by liberal pluralists' hypocrisy. Urging everyone to "attend the church or synagogue of one's choice," for instance, disguises the ways deviant, nonbelievers, disappear. Further, we are not urged to worship at just *any* church or synagogue, only those that are properly recognized. Some will be denigrated as "cults," for instance, and so made ineligible to play the give-and-take game cultivated by pluralist liberalism. Consequently, members of these "churches" disappear, both as individuals and as a body. The government—which liberals assign the role of neutral referee—instead acts as a conservative, repressive force. It does this by refusing recognition to weaker groups, so keeping stronger groups in power.

Barrington Moore worries that tolerance can also become a mask, this time for "intellectual cowardice and evasion."[4] Those who argue for tolerance because people have different world views come in for a blistering attack: "Tolerance for different 'interpretations' based on different *Weltanschauung* merely befuddles the issue [of which interpretation is better]."[5] Science, for Moore, provides us with the model of clear, hardheaded thinking. To use a previous example (not Moore's), tolerating the teaching of creation science in public schools because fundamentalist Christians have a different world view is intellectual cowardice. The question for Moore is not whether creationism is part of someone's outlook but whether there is solid evidence for its truth. If there is not, we should not tolerate it.

At the time of its publication, Herbert Marcuse's contribution "Repressive Tolerance" made the greatest impact. Oddly enough, Marcuse begins with the pronouncement that "[t]olerance is an end in itself,"[6] for, he says, the elimination of violence and suppression are preconditions of a humane society. It is only an end in itself, however, when universally practiced by those in power and not only the powerless. As found in liberal democracies as well as authoritarian regimes, however, we are forced to tolerate the intolerable, for all contemporary governments, he believes, engage in violence and suppression on a massive scale. They then ask those whom they govern to extend tolerance to what they do, though their intolerable policies, conditions, and modes of behavior impede, even destroy, chances of creating an existence without fear and misery:

> This sort of tolerance strengthens the tyranny of the majority against which authentic liberals protested. The political locus of tolerance has changed, for while it is more or less quietly and constitutionally withdrawn from the opposition, it is made compulsory behavior with respect to established policies. Tolerance is turned from an active to a passive state, from practice to non-practice, laissez-faire toward the constituted authorities. It is the governed who tolerate the government, who in turn tolerates the opposition within the framework determined by constituted authorities. Tolerance to that which is radically evil now may appear good because it serves the cohesion of the whole on the road to affluence or more affluence.[7]

Like Wolff, Marcuse contends that the apparent nonpartisan or "pure" tolerance that is the official ideology of liberalism—that is, that the state should not take sides—in fact "protects the already established machinery of discrimination."[8] Bluntly put, tolerance as practiced by modern nation-states destroys. The market, for instance, absorbs art, antiart, and nonart in addition to all conflicting styles of art, providing (in the words of the art historian Edgar Wind) a "complacent receptacle, a friendly abyss."[9] Marcuse, the radical Hegelian, joins ranks with contemporary conservative opponents of tolerance when he says,

> [S]tupid opinion is treated with the same respect as the intelligent one, the misinformed may talk as long as the informed, and propaganda rides along with education, truth with falsehood. This pure toleration of sense and nonsense is justified by the democratic argument that nobody, neither group nor individual, is in possession of the truth and capable of defining what is right and wrong, good and bad. Therefore, all contesting opinions must be submitted to "the people" for its deliberation and choice.[10]

This ignores, however, a fundamental, necessary condition for democracy, if it is to be anything other than the tyranny of the powerful: "namely, that the people must be capable of deliberating and choosing on the basis of knowledge, that they must have access to authentic information, and that, on this basis, their evaluation must be the result of autonomous thought."[11]

We must, therefore, withdraw "tolerance from regressive movements *before* they can become active."[12] Marcuse does not shrink from the obvious implications of his thesis. In a postscript added in 1968, he says, "For this struggle, I proposed the practice of discriminating intolerance."[13] He leaves little doubt that he has in mind the so-called military-industrial complex, advertising, and unfettered markets. Each, in his view, seriously distorts feeling and thought. Tolerance not only reinforces what is twisted but is itself deformed.

However elitist—and dated—these criticisms of "pure tolerance" sound, they do raise the *type* of problems we can expect *any* defense of tolerance grounded in neutrality must face. They echo similar arguments from present-day conservatives. Given that tolerance of absolutely everything is out of the question, how do we judge what deserves the protective umbrella of toleration and what does not? Like some contemporary conservatives, *A Critique of Pure Tolerance* makes a strong case that tolerance rests on *knowledge,* not mere *opinion.*[14] But if knowledge is not to be had—at least not in enough hard cases to matter—then how and where will we draw the line between the tolerable and the intolerable?

As a footnote, we might consider Marcuse's own intellectual fate. When his ardent disciples took Marcuse's words to heart and turned on the university because of its alleged alliances with the sources of oppression, Marcuse denounced them. The university, he said, was the last bastion of civilization. This betrayal, in the eyes of activists, isolated Marcuse from the political struggles of the late 1960s and early 1970s. What it shows is not that either Marcuse or his disciples were mistaken but how much easier it is to fight for Truth and Knowledge in the abstract than to agree on particular truths and knowledge—as liberal defenders of toleration are quick to point out.

Connected with Marcuse's concerns is another criticism of tolerance. Tolerance often seems not to be virtuous at all. Having been taught from an early age that we should be tolerant makes it easy for us to tolerate the intolerable (e.g., mindless television, manipulative advertising, and much worse). If it is not always virtuous to be tolerant, then becoming tolerant can be undesirable because it is so easy to become tolerant of the intolerable. No one can make the same charge against the classical Greek virtues of justice, self-control, wisdom, and courage. We would never say, for instance, that it is a bad thing for someone to become courageous. Sometimes the courageous will die because of their courage, but we do not think this is any moral fault, merely a cause for deep regret. There are times, too, for a courageous person to make a strategic retreat or even, we can imagine, to appear cowardly. Yet surely (we think) it is never desirable to be cowardly (or unjust, unwise, undisciplined). Often, however, intolerance seems not merely permissible but required. This merely reaffirms the essential elusiveness of tolerance. Either we must be tolerant when we should not be or tolerance differs from other virtues in ways that arouse suspicions that it is not a virtue at all.

Reply

What are we to make of these criticisms? Wolff contends that tolerance as *practiced* in pluralist democracies rests on two operating principles. First, liberals adhere to a strict dichotomy between "public" and "private" and then dogmatically claim that we must tolerate everything done "in private." But, second, liberals apply this standard only to socially approved groups. Pluralist democracies, Wolff contends, typically act intolerantly to deviant individuals and groups.

Liberals rightly distinguish between public and private. We should not open everything to public gaze, let alone public interference. But nothing much follows from this. "Public" and "private" do not come conveniently labeled. Of anything we may always ask, Is this appropriately private and, if so, how private should it be? For privacy is never unlimited. It is said that a man's home is his castle. This does not mean, however, that we must allow absolutely anything and everything to go on inside it. No one may use privacy as a shield, for instance, as protection against charges of abuse, conspiracy, or treason.

Of any proposed distinction we should ask not only *how* to draw it but *why*—and with what *qualifications*? The public/private distinction is no exception. Liberals value privacy as a way of controlling how much others may know about one without that one's permission, for knowledge is power. The more others know *about* individuals or groups, the more they have power *over* them. Liberals strive to protect a sphere of privacy because autonomy depends on freedom from unwarranted interventions. This is why privacy matters. Liberals grant, however, that no one may hide behind privacy to *harm others.* Some *do* hide behind it. This is not, however, defensible on liberal grounds. The limitation explains why privacy does not extend to abuse, conspiracy, or treason. Because groups matter to individuals, privacy applies not only to individuals but also to groups. Unless a group disqualifies itself in various ways—for instance, by engaging in fraud, treason, or violence—it need not divulge information about itself to governments or others. Governments, for example, often use membership lists to keep track and control participants in "deviant" groups. Governments are not the only culprits. Corporations, too, often wish to learn not only the buying habits and activities of possible customers but also the health records of possible employees. Both can limit freedom and thus autonomy.

Wolff rightly remarks that tolerance *as practiced* in pluralist democracies seldom lives up to its own self-image. Pointing this out is salutary, but hardly news. Similarly, it is not news that pluralist democracies do not always extend the right of privacy (or other rights and protections) to groups that are not socially accepted. Yet does this show anything more than that practice and ideals fail to match in pluralist democracies? This does not distinguish pluralist democracies or any other institutions: None live up to their ideals. Wolff needs to show that the political failures of pluralist democracies can be traced to failures of doctrine. This he does not do.

Substantive liberalism does not mandate or even recommend that we should legally protect all groups or that we should legally act tolerantly to all protected groups. No one needs, as a rule, to act tolerantly to *intolerant* groups, even if they enjoy legal protection. Because they value freedom and the personal autonomy it makes possible, substantive liberals will not, for example, go out of their way to further the interests of intolerant groups. Within the limits of law, they might go much further, trying to deprive such groups of members, warning others about them, and using legally permissible economic pressure to undermine their strength through economic boycotts and picketing.

When individuals and groups violate norms that inform liberal democracies, they should not—on substantive liberal grounds—enjoy legal toleration. This is a point held in common with other liberals. No form of liberalism need tolerate individuals and groups whose intent and activities are directed at denying others in the society basic human rights or the ability to lead their own lives unencumbered by terror and persecution. Applications of this principle, however, always provide difficulties. Organizations such as the contemporary incarnation of the Ku Klux Klan, for instance, will go to great lengths to disguise their true purposes (e.g., by raising legal defenses that make them appear less intent on violating basic human rights). This fact of life means that in some instances it will legally be *necessary* to tolerate the intolerable. It is not that substantive liberals wish to balance, say, "free speech" against the right of association. Instead, they are wary of bringing the full force of the state against organizations that can make out a legally compelling case that they are not violent, treasonous, or intent on denying human rights. They will, therefore, reject Marcuse's admonition to stamp out repressive groups before they become active on the simplistic grounds that "we all know what they will do before they try to do it." Without invoking the heavy hand of the state, individuals and nongovernmental organizations can mount vigorous criticisms of the beliefs and practices of bigots and the institutions representing them.

Substantive liberals will take to heart Wolff's warning that we should not limit the state to the role of neutral referee. Given that powerful social and economic forces consign undeserving people to the margins of society, substantive liberals see the need to redress this imbalance. While government intervention is not always the wisest course to take, substantive liberals will look for many ways to help deviant individuals and groups. Active tolerance, for instance, might help keep individuals and groups vital. So, substantive liberals will be far more inclined than neutralist liberals to use governmental powers to discourage various hate groups and to provide support groups where circumstances or intentional forces have pushed them to the margins. They will do so cautiously, however, always sensitive not only to governmental fallibility but also to the permanent possibility that the states often overreach themselves or succumb to political, expedient interventions. Without outlawing them, governments can help discourage hate groups through education, through advertising, and by support of tolerant organizations that themselves criticize intolerant individuals and groups. May governments outlaw hate groups? Legal sanctions are permissible but not always wise since outlawing such groups can do more harm than good. This cautionary note, however, cannot settle the matter. To do so, we need more careful philosophical reflection. Such matters must be thought through in their full particularity and concreteness.

Barrington Moore's charge that tolerance encourages intellectual cowardice rests on a false assumption: Tolerance presupposes skepticism. It need not, and does not, in the justification I offer, for we need not, for example, accept at face value interpretations or world views of those we tolerate. To challenge the soundness or truth of someone's views or challenge their practices is *not* to act intolerantly, unless the challenge is nothing more than verbal harassment. If anything, to criticize shows respect, for in doing so we show that we take what others say, believe, and do seriously. Tolerance requires that we appreciate the role played by faulty attitudes, interpretations, doctrines, and claims about the physical world in the cultural background of those whose views they are—and the implications they have for both participants and neighbors. To appreciate how beliefs and actions came to be and the role that they play in a culture, however, does not require that we accept them as sound or valid. Tolerance and vigorous criticism, therefore, go hand in hand.

Not every case of legislation that denies a request amounts to intolerance. In certain school districts in the United States, for example, Christian organizations are lobbying to have creation science given a place in the classroom along with evolutionary biology. Authorities who refuse to grant this demand are not necessarily intolerant. Tolerant authorities still need to make judgments about the wise use of time, money, and teaching resources. That authorities are acting tolerantly in keeping creation science out of public classrooms, however, would not justify preventing its teaching elsewhere, either in the home or in private schools. Whether it would be *prudent* to teach about it in state-funded schools is yet another matter, but not giving it "equal time" in the classroom does not manifest intolerance, for authorities always have to make decisions about what is worthy and what is not. It would be preposterous to think that each time anyone in authority denies an urgent demand ipso facto they are acting intolerantly. It would be intolerant, however, if those charged with curricular matters did not give those pressing for the introduction of creation science a thorough and respectful hearing. This is because the demand grows out of a way of life worth living. And this distinguishes the case from demands that do not grow out of tolerable ways of life, either because they are bankrupt or because they are deeply harmful to others.

We already have seen that liberal tolerance disallows a minority culture within a larger society from preventing its members from leaving. One way that cultures cement cultural solidarity is by teaching clear falsehoods and lies about neighboring cultures or the larger society. This, too, cannot be defended on grounds of tolerance, even if it means weakening cultural ties, for such teachings are harmful, both to those outside and to those inside a group. If those in authority nonetheless judge that it is best not to interfere, it will be for reasons other than liberal tolerance (e.g., the comparative harmlessness of the untruths, the risk of governmental overreaching, and the likelihood that the powerful simply wish to impose their own views). It needs emphasizing, however, that tolerance does not require standing by while others tell lies.

Not all falsehoods are lies, and not all falsehoods are demonstrably false. When we judge that falsehoods fall into that vague category of "matters about which reasonable people can disagree," tolerance suggests that we limit ourselves to verbal interaction. This may be sound advice even when we judge that reasonable people could not disagree. It will depend on how much harm the views cause. We need not tolerate false views about others, for instance, that poison relations. Still, there are innumerable cases that come close to the border but do not cross it. Judging whether the border has been irrevocably crossed requires knowledge, sensitivity, and an ability to place oneself in another's shoes—never easy.

But who are we to judge? The simple answer is, Who else? *Someone* will judge, even if the judgment is not to pass judgment. There is no place to stand that does not take a position. It falls to each of us to make that determination. Judging, however, presupposes grounds or standards of judgments. A judge who drew verdicts out of a hat, for instance, would be a judge in name only. He would not be using any standards on which to base his decisions. He would not, in short, be exercising any *judgment.*

Yet maybe this is not the point of the question. In asking, Who are we to judge? the questioner might instead be asking why the powerful have the right to pass judgment or sit in judgment. The answer lies in the circumstances of tolerance. Recall that tolerance calls on the strong not to act on their intolerant impulses. The weak are in no position to do so. So if "we" are the powerful, then "we" do sit in judgment, and we do pass judgment every day. If we have acquired the virtue of tolerance, however, we will base judgments on the best available reasons, reasons that can withstand rational scrutiny. For substantive liberals, these reasons will enable all to be partial authors of their own lives, including those whose beliefs, attitudes, and ways of life we find undesirable, even detestable. Yet this, too, needs to be tempered by the thought that toleration does not require that we permit adults to indoctrinate their children with crippling thoughts and attitudes. Where, and how, to draw the line is always difficult because the temptation to overreach is difficult to resist.

Marcuse's complaint that Western powers in the late 1960s withdrew tolerance from oppositional groups but required it of established policies would, if true, show only that Western powers behaved badly. Nothing in his argument tells against the defense of tolerance offered here. If, as he contends, "that which is radically evil now appears as good because it serves the cohesion of the whole on the road to affluence or more affluence,"[15] this shows only that appearances often deceive and that tolerance as a virtue requires sound judgment and moral perceptiveness. No one, for instance, should tolerate that which is "radically evil." Similarly, his contention that "pure tolerance" requires that we accept without comment every attitude, every idea, every policy shows only the bankruptcy of "pure tolerance." What is less clear is that anyone defends pure tolerance, as Marcuse understands the term.

Any society can become repressive. Those giving lip service to tolerance often do so hypocritically. This is intolerable. A philosophical account of tolerance cannot hope, by itself, to change society or rid it of hypocrisy. It can, however, aspire to explain how we should understand tolerance and why. Change requires that people absorb the lessons of tolerance and make it part of their everyday life.

TOLERANCE AS INSIDIOUS

Objections

Some cultural conservatives make a different argument. They contend that tolerance—so far from being a virtue—is a vice foisted on the world by hegemonic liberalism. Those advocating open-minded tolerance have their own narrow political agenda, namely, to turn everyone into liberals. If we claim to know that our beliefs are true, that our attitudes are sound, and that our way of life is best, why should we tolerate what we sincerely believe or know is deeply mistaken, even corrupt and depraved? Those advocating tolerance, the argument continues, then urge us to adopt a generally skeptical stance, one that undermines our deepest convictions.

Critics need not put the argument in skeptical terms, however. Doubt will suffice, for if advocates of tolerance can get us to doubt what we believe or doubt the value of our practices, they will succeed in making us timid, tentative, and ineffectual. This will have the desired liberal effect of getting us to tolerate that which we once abhorred. For how can we not tolerate divergent beliefs or practices when we have no confidence in our own?

Gradually, the conservative critic continues, we will lose confidence even in ourselves. This is something other than skepticism or indifference. It is the unhappy state where we become so filled with doubt that a generalized tolerance is our only refuge. Sowing seeds of doubt effectively turns us into a society of (self-) Doubting Thomases. As we come to lack confidence in our own judgments about the value of what we believe and do, it seems only natural to tolerate everyone and everything. We surely would not wish to impose our doubt-plagued judgments on anyone else. Doubt cannot support tolerance directly, of course, since a Doubting Thomas can no more pass judgment on the value of toleration than anything else. Still, he does not have to. It is enough that he slides into diffident toleration.

Whether through skepticism or doubt, once we become tolerant—even if we initially hold on to our own commitments—it will not take long before the acid of skepticism and doubt eats away at our confidence. We will lose that which now gives our lives meaning and substance. We will become jaded and rootless, without a sense that our lives any longer have a center. Tolerance, the argument continues, is just a genteel way for liberals to undermine the solidarity that comes with utter and complete commitment to one's religion, ethnic community, aesthetic sensibility, sexuality, and so on. Tolerance is fine for liberals, the conservative critic continues, since they celebrate only abstract principles, keeping their distance from any deep commitments to particular beliefs and communities. But, he concludes, we rightly resist liberal attempts to foist tolerance on the rest of us. And they surely should not try passing it off as a universal value, a value to which all would happily subscribe if only they were open-minded.

There is more to the objection. Tolerance provides covert encouragement to unwholesome attitudes, beliefs, and practices. It does so in several ways. When we tolerate something, we imply—because it is not intolerable—that it is somehow "OK." It is no answer to reply that tolerance does not imply acceptance. It does not have to. All it needs to do is provide covert encouragement, and this tolerance does only too well. First, many will not be able to draw the fine distinctions between mere forbearance, full tolerance, and acceptance. Just as corrupt politicians too often get away with saying that they did nothing wrong because they did not violate the law, so many will conclude that tolerance is tantamount to acceptance. And why not? Where is the consequential difference? Only by refusing to put up with what we find seriously deficient can we prevent its spread. Tolerance has a place in conservative practice, but only for matters judged deficient but beneath notice, or not seriously deficient, or when toleration is the best we can do, at least for the present.

Second, toleration provides room for the growth of abominable ideas and practices. Even when they cannot succeed completely, efforts to suppress what is undesirable put objectionable beliefs and practices on the defensive, making it more difficult for them to thrive. If abhorrent beliefs and practices do not have legal protection, for instance, they are less likely to spread. By making the price of engaging in objectionable practices high, we can both return casual practitioners to the fold and isolate the rest.

When we tolerate the seriously deficient, thirdly, we provide indirect support for what is unacceptable. Some, for instance, will infer that those in authority lack power or resolve. This can only provide encouragement for tawdry beliefs and deplorable conduct. Others will infer that those in authority no longer hold their own beliefs with any conviction. This makes them easy to ignore. Over time, we are likely to witness a sea change in the moral climate of a society. What people once shamefully felt, said, and did behind closed doors, for example, becomes just another object of accepted choice. This is especially true when we exchange intolerant policies for tolerant ones, for most will yield to the inference that those in authority now admit that their previous policies were mistaken or misguided. This undermines authority. It encourages people to ask, What else are they wrong about? Protestations to the contrary will not blunt the subtle changes brought about in shifting from a stance of intolerance to one of tolerance.

Once liberals succeed in establishing their own regime of toleration, fourthly, they will require far more than simply forbidding violence and overt discrimination. They will require students to explore once rejected beliefs and ways of life, leading them inexorably to adopt sympathetic attitudes. This only increases the likelihood that deplorable beliefs and ways of life will become acceptable. Religious and cultural conservatives in the United States, for example, often complain that teaching sympathetically about homosexual life does just this. In mandating that students learn what it is like for gay people to be the object of ridicule and how negative attitudes and practices affect homosexuals, liberal educators subtly turn gays, and gay sex, into objects of sympathy instead of contempt.

In their pursuit of "understanding," liberals twist language itself. They will, for example, discourage describing homosexual sex as "perverse"; instead, they will insist on calling it an "alternative lifestyle" or a "sexual orientation." As the young gradually become sympathetic to the "plight" of gays, many "straights" will take up their cause. By effectively requiring us to use such terms as "gay," "orientation," "straight," and "plight," liberals obscure the sinful, disgusting nature of homosexuality. Conservatives say that we can reveal their hypocrisy by noting that liberals would never ask us to consider the "plight" of "same-race preferers." They would justly call them racial bigots and make no attempt to show them in a sympathetic light. Finally, liberal tolerance will tempt some young people to explore deviant ways of life for themselves, with disastrous consequences to their moral and spiritual life. This will be especially true for those who are confused about their sexual identity or are tempted to act out adolescent rebelliousness.

All this shows, the argument concludes, that pleas for tolerance are nothing more than covert pleas for *liberal values.* In short, liberals hide behind a rhetorical fog of tolerance obscuring their own substantive agenda, an agenda that pushes liberal values. Not only do they push their own liberal agenda, but they do not seem to realize their own flagrant intolerance to anyone holding conflicting, nonliberal values. At least, say cultural conservatives, do not force us to accept alien views under false colors: Do not pretend to be doing one thing while doing another. Of course those living sinful or depraved lives should not be objects of vigilante justice or state cruelty. Homosexuals, for example, should not be beaten up, let alone murdered. To prevent such atrocities, however, we only need clear laws that are effectively enforced. We do not, after all, approve of vigilante justice or state cruelty when it comes to punishing serial killers. But hating the sin, preventing the sin, and yet not treating the sinner cruelly is not a matter of tolerance.

Reply

We should not defend liberalism—and with it tolerance—on grounds that it is nothing more than a set of value-free procedural principles. Liberals must enter the arena of contestable value and political doctrines; they cannot stand above the fray. All serious liberal thinkers recognize this, including those who defend neutrality and procedural justice. Liberals defend fair procedures, for instance, because they regard them as integral to their core values, not because they worship value-free procedures. The rule of law provides an instance. It generally forbids taking into account a defendant's character in determining legal guilt or innocence, for instance, not because character "does not matter" for *any* purposes—for instance, fixing suitable punishment—but because of the overwhelming concern that we find guilty only those who actually commit crimes. Notice that many nonliberal views defend the rule of law for the same reason, namely, that it makes just outcomes more likely.

Liberals differ from nonliberals on which procedures must be instituted and their appropriate limits. So, liberal advocates of free expression oppose censorship of content because that serves core liberal values better than allowing state authorities to determine what may and may not be expressed in words and images. Self-expression is only one reason to support free expression, for free expression opens possibilities that less adventurous people might not have thought of or been too timid to explore without trailblazers leading the way. Only a few democracies have as rigid a doctrine of free expression as the United States, but all recognize that it—along with freedom of conscience, religion, and association—is fundamental to individual freedom and hence to personal autonomy. Nonliberals will support many of these same values, but they will be derivative. They will draw other lines because of their differing core beliefs.

True, some people mistakenly think that liberal values, including tolerance, need no defense. This only shows that one can be a liberal without having any deep understanding of what it presupposes or entails. This, however, does not serve to distinguish unthinking liberals from unthinking radicals or unthinking social conservatives. Some cultural conservatives, for example, mistakenly think that every right-minded person must agree with them about what is and is not tolerable. It is simply obvious. In a society where any single political outlook dominates, followers will feel less intellectual pressure to defend their views. We should not, however, interpret efforts to articulate and defend normative views according to the reactions of their least sophisticated followers, however many. That way lies the death of all critical and reflective thought.

Necessarily, liberalism has an "agenda," if by that one means a body of doctrines, values, and political recommendations. It would not be a political philosophy if it did not. Further, liberals believe that they can mount a successful defense of this agenda. This includes meeting certain objections. This is what I am attempting here as it pertains to tolerance. Liberals do indeed wish to offer persuasive reasons to accept liberalism to those living in contemporary political democracies. As political activists, moreover, they will try to concretize their values and recommendations in public institutions and policies. Tolerance occupies a vital, but limited, place in any liberal account of social and political life, so liberals will strive to see it realized in political and social life. A complete account would necessarily develop a liberal account of rights, equality, justice, authority, the nature and limits of political obligation, civil disobedience, conscientious refusal, and so on.

I have spoken of liberalism's core values. These must be disentangled from derivative ideas many liberals have held at one point or another in its long history.

Ronald Dworkin explains the distinction this way:

> We may . . . distinguish, for any full political theory, between constitutive and derivative political positions. A constitutive position is a political position valued for its own sake: a political position such that any failure fully to secure that position, or any decline in the degree to which it is secured, is *pro tanto* a loss in the value of the overall political arrangement. A derivative political position is a position that is not, within the theory in question, constitutive [e.g., that taxes should be raised or lowered].[16]

Walzer's Ottoman Turks clearly think of toleration as a policy of derivative value. They would jettison it instantly were it to prove contrary to the interests of the imperial center. They choose toleration as a strategy, not a core value. Liberals from Locke onward have placed tolerance at the heart of their outlook. For them, tolerance is more than a strategy. Liberals differ, however, about *why* tolerance should have the importance it does. Substantive liberals, unlike Lockean liberals, argue that tolerance makes it possible for people to live their own lives without undue meddling by others. We should tolerate much that we find disagreeable because of its importance to those who find it valuable in shaping a significant life.

Still, substantive liberals will not tolerate everything. In particular, they will not tolerate that which is harmful to others or, if we live in a liberal society, that which is inimical to other core values of political liberalism. Political liberals, for example, will not tolerate abandoning the rule of law to satisfy some alleged higher purposes, or granting citizens differential rights because of race and class, or limiting expression simply because it offends religious sensibilities. I will not further defend these here, but I mention them for two reasons. First, to stress yet again that tolerance is but one core value of liberalism, neither the only one nor even the preeminent one. Second, to raise a fresh point. Core values can conflict, their boundaries are often vague, and they can prove inadequate in extreme situations. Even if the world were tidier than it is, we should surrender the dream — or fantasy — that any political morality consists of a set of principles or values that fit together like a geometrical system. We can have that type of unity only at a price not worth paying. Mill tries to satisfy this demand with his harm principle. Yet, as critics point out, it is not one, unambiguous principle. And even if it were, it leaves out too much. We should expect to find, therefore, that in extreme situations — for instance, wars and emergencies — some core values may defeat others, or at least temporarily eclipse them. Particularly in times of crisis, we might curtail the scope of tolerance because other values become far more pressing.

Contrary to a common charge, liberals do not try to turn everyone into liberals. In particular, they will not generally deny the rights of citizenship or community life to those who defend other values, for it is part of substantive liberalism, at least, not to discourage individuals or groups from pursuing their own intellectual, religious, and value beliefs. Will substantive liberals proselytize? There is no general reason why not, though there may be many occasions on and situations in which it would be inappropriate. Liberalism as a way of life is not for all cultures in all circumstances. It is not suitable, for example, in hypertraditional communities largely isolated from interaction with others. These are rapidly disappearing, not because of liberalism but primarily because of market globalization. Still, they exist, and substantive liberals, ceteris paribus, support them in their way of life. They do so *not* because they accept the self-image or self-descriptions of hypertraditional societies but if they provide a flourishing way of life for their members.

Liberalism is well suited, however, for those living in Western European states, the Americas, the Antipodes, and many other states characterizable by cultural pluralism, democratic forms of government, a modern sensibility, rapid technological change, social mobility, and complex, highly structured economic systems. In such places liberals will try to convince people of the soundness, indeed superiority, of their views. It would be strange if we think our political morality (whatever it might be) is superior to others yet would not try to see it concretized in our institutions and practices. In that sense, liberals will try to create a liberal society. As liberals, they will not use methods that would tend to undermine the very values they champion. Depending on the circumstances, however, there will be some nonliberal views and practices that substantive liberals will actively try to discourage (e.g., racist views and practices).

A further consideration may help allay conservative fears. Those with a liberal sensibility will strive to see tolerance embodied not only in the state but also in those voluntary associations in which they participate (e.g., churches, labor unions, universities, and families). It is no part of the liberal brief, however, that tolerance must be pursued in those voluntary associations in which liberals themselves do not participate. Liberals are committed to tolerating churches and universities, for example, that are themselves intolerant, provided only that they do not violate presuppositions of any constitutional democracy and minimal standards of morality. It would be intolerable, for instance, were a church to imprison or whip its members. It would not be intolerable (however foolish and even wrong) from a liberal perspective, however, for a church that one can leave of one's own free will to excommunicate homosexuals or refuse to ordain women.[17] A university, too, might permissibly require that subjects be taught in ways that most people outside the university think are narrow-minded and even bigoted. What it cannot do, however, is dismiss employees or students without cause or act in certain bigoted ways. More would have to be said, however, were we to explore any particular matter in detail. The general point is that—within constitutional and legal limits—substantive liberalism does not forbid intolerant attitudes and practices, provided that they are confined to voluntary associations that members can join without coercion—and freely leave.

I insisted in the previous chapter on the value commitments of substantive liberalism just to meet many objections mentioned here. Substantive liberalism is not skeptical, nor does it advocate skepticism. Nor does it advocate doubt as a strategy of encouraging tolerance. If substantive liberals sow seeds of doubt, it will be because they argue that attitudes, beliefs, practices, and institutions are either unsound or contestable. If doubts arise as a consequence, that is all to the good. But it is no part of liberalism's brief to mount a general assault on anyone's firm convictions. If there is an assault, it is an assault against those attitudes, practices, and so on that strike at defensible core liberal values.

Further, tolerance as an active virtue should *discourage* anyone from concluding that forbearance amounts to acceptance. Throughout I have tried to show how tolerance generally invites engagement, pointing out reasons for disapproval, weighing counterclaims, and so on. Tolerance, as developed here, insists that there are many resting points, indeed stops, on the way from bare forbearance to full tolerance to full acceptance. True, liberals generally have a high regard for the intelligence and judgment of their fellows, and this issue is no exception. No doubt some may misread tolerance for lack of resolve, but that is a poor reason for acting intolerantly. Liberals do not assume the worst about the ability of their fellows to make distinctions and see their point. There is, therefore, no reason to suppose that tolerant regimes grounded in a substantive liberal outlook need sap anyone's self-confidence. If criticism shakes one's confidence in unreflectively accepted attitudes, beliefs, and practices that are open to criticism, we should find that a benefit, not a liability.

Does liberal tolerance encourage the spread of undesirable views and practices? That is an empirical question, the answer to which will depend on the case. We simply cannot say in advance. Liberals are generally suspicious of "slippery slope" and "camel's nose" arguments. Such arguments adversely affect autonomy by foreclosing possibilities in advance. Those who argue in this way usually concede that an act or practice, though undesirable, is not intolerable. Nonetheless, they say, we must not allow it, for once we do, we will surely slide down a slippery slope to disaster. Before accepting state intervention because of what *might* happen, liberals will ask for solid evidence, not speculation. Our highly technological, highly mobile society only amplifies liberal worries. Could anything short of massive state oppression prevent undesirable conduct from its slide down a slippery slope before it begins? Better, liberals believe, to engage in active tolerance, that is, allow, but engage in other ways (e.g., with serious investigation, persuasive criticism, and discouragement). About some things, this may be of no avail. But then it is not clear that other alternatives can promise more—without seriously undermining the possibility of living an autonomous life.

Further, liberals reject arguments that see *change* as generally *bad.* It is not only cultural conservatives who dislike change; it is, after all, often unsettling to many of all persuasions. That change is unsettling, however, does not provide good reasons to prevent others from exploring it. Cultural conservatives need to provide evidence and argument showing that the change in question creates harm or is so squalid that we must intervene. When they do, liberals should listen, for they are committed to balancing their general inclination for autonomy with the recognition that serious, demonstrable harms can and should be prohibited and that base and despicable forms of life need not be supported.

Does liberal tolerance provide indirect or tacit support for what is unacceptable? It does so only if not trying to stop something counts as indirect support. But liberals should reject this "either/or" thinking. We *allow* many things we think undesirable without *supporting* them. Further, to allow something is far from *endorsing* it. Liberals will not be shy to show what is undesirable about that which they allow, for this is part of what liberal tolerance entails. Liberal tolerance—on the other hand—will sometimes provide not only tacit but overt support for practices, ways of life, and so on, aspects of which one finds undesirable. Every complex practice or way of life has undesirable features, many recognized by participants themselves. Were we to support only those that are faultless, none would find support.

In some cases, as Raz notes,[18] vices mirror virtues. Because what makes someone good at something cannot be switched on and off, behavior outside a special context may manifest the vices. That would not lead us to conclude, however, that we should not support those with special talents. Scholars, for example, are known for their indecision. There is always more evidence to gather, another book to read, one more experiment to perform. For this reason, they may infuriate policymakers who need to make decisions and make them quickly. Surgeons typically exude self-confidence; would we want it otherwise? When they carry this self-confidence outside the operating theater, however, we might very much want it otherwise. In general, character traits that make one accomplished in one endeavor do not always transfer to other endeavors without negative effects.

More general practices and ways of life share this coupling of virtues and vices, the admirable and the detrimental, what is full yet one-sided. This will seem problematic only to those who think that generally praiseworthy practices or ways of life—even in their idealized forms—are both faultless and complete. But, as Kant says, nothing of this sort exists since it would have to be made from "the crooked timber of man." Seeing *both* that a practice or way of life is good *and* that it entails serious deficiencies and lacunae, tolerant individuals and groups will consider providing various support, both direct and indirect.

The charge cultural conservatives make looks more persuasive than it is because they tend to isolate what is admittedly undesirable from its broader context, not acknowledging its embeddedness in otherwise admirable practices and ways of life. We cannot, generally, surgically remove what offends without adversely affecting the whole. Is it worth destroying the whole to rid the world of the offending part? That depends on the overall assessment of the whole—and what would replace it in the lifetimes of participants. If, for example, it would leave a whole people cultureless, then unless the culture is as bad as Colin Turnbull portrays the Iks in the *Mountain People,*[19] the price is far too high. Again, however, this does not mean that criticism is out of place. Tolerance does not require silence. It urges engagement. That, if it goes beyond hectoring, clearly entails attempts at knowledge and understanding *before* engaging in overt criticism. Too often we are all tempted to attack without understanding how what we attack fits into a generally wholesome way of life. And because power belongs to tolerators, we must take care that criticism does not amount to browbeating or implied threats.

Finally, generally and in the long run, understanding and critical engagement change far more minds than invasive interventions. Liberals will recommend invasive interventions only in egregious cases. They will be far less eager than cultural conservatives to intervene in the lives of others to protect or further "what is best" by their own lights. Both cultural conservatives and liberals need to show that the case at hand is egregious and that the moral costs of intervention are not disproportionately high. Clearly there can be disagreements on both counts, even among liberals. The fact that something is deplorable, however, will not suffice. Instead, liberal tolerance urges that we *trust* objects of tolerance, that we treat them with respect. It does this by showing a willingness to engage with those tolerated honestly and candidly about why and where they fall short, what our limits are, why, and so on.

SUBSTANTIVE LIBERALISM VIOLATES POLITICAL NEUTRALITY

Objection

Most contemporary liberal theorists defend the neutrality thesis,[20] namely,

> that the state shouldn't favor, promote, or act on any particular conception of the good. Instead, it should simply provide a neutral and just framework within which each citizen can pursue the good as he understands it. To provide this framework, a government must sometimes interfere with liberty. It must restrict its citizens' options in order to secure security and stability, promote prosperity and efficiency, and make available various public goods. Also, if justice requires more equality than unconstrained markets can provide, the state must intervene to equalize opportunity or resources. But, according to . . . [the neutrality thesis], this is *all* that government should do. If in addition it tries to make citizens more virtuous, to raise their level of culture or civility, or to prevent them from living degraded lives, it oversteps its bounds. Even if some traits or activities are genuinely better than others, no government should promote the better or suppress or discourage the worse. About all questions of the good life, the state should remain strictly neutral.[21]

Advocates of state neutrality forward a cluster of related reasons for their thesis, depending on their more general political philosophy. Neutrality appeals to Rawls, for instance, because rational contractors with sharply opposed conceptions of the good can nonetheless unanimously commit themselves to common principles of justice and a shared constitution. In *On Liberty,* Mill presents a classic defense of the neutrality thesis from a broadly utilitarian outlook:

> [T]he only purpose for which power can be rightfully exercised over any member of a civilized community, against his will, is to prevent harm to others. His own good,

either physical or moral, is not a sufficient warrant. He cannot rightfully be compelled to do or forbear because it will be better for him to do so, because it will make
him happier, because, in the opinions of others, to do so would be wise or even
right.[22]

Others contend that the state is not the right type of institution to pursue any
conception of the good. We should leave that task to individuals and fully voluntary associations, such as churches. Even conceding—for argument's sake—that
states may pursue conceptions of the good, Locke's concern remains. Why suppose that governments will get matters right? Our experience shows conclusively
that those who attain power in any constitutional democracy have no special insight into deep moral truths about how to live. If anything, the reverse seems true.
When we add that conceptions of the good often derive from religious commitments that raise extraordinarily controversial metaphysical and epistemological
problems, governments would seem to be the last place to look for their solution.
No one could defend any constitutional democracy speaking ex cathedra.

Because massive coercive power lies behind state authority, moreover, anything states do to attack a conception of the good will likely overwhelm free and
equal citizens, preventing them from thinking and acting for themselves. As it
stands, those in neutral constitutional democracies who find themselves in disagreement with their church or cultural community can try reform. Failing that,
they have the constitutionally guaranteed right to leave. Once we grant states—
even constitutional democracies—authority to enforce conceptions of the good,
however, experience shows that they will act oppressively. And citizens of one
state typically have nowhere to go since others will not have them. When we look
around the real world, finally, we find that those clamoring that states should enforce conceptions of the good offer conceptions that are invariably pinched and
narrow-minded, where they are not outright racist, sexist, and homophobic.
Dworkin nicely captures many of these fears. Writing in 1983, he says,

> Government must be neutral in matters of personal morality, [and] must leave peo-
> ple free to live as they think best so long as they do not harm others. But the Rev-
> erend Jerry Falwell, and other politicians who claim to speak for some "moral ma-
> jority," want to enforce their own morality with the steel of the criminal law. They
> know what kind of sex is bad, which books are fit for public libraries, what place re-
> ligion should have in education and family life, when human life begins, that con-
> traception is sin, and that abortion is capital sin. They think the rest of us should be
> forced to practice what they preach.[23]

Reply

These are formidable objections. Fortunately, we need not address them in detail
here since others have done so convincingly.[24] It will be enough to show that liberal tolerance, though nonneutral, neither violates core liberal values nor runs a

serious risk of becoming a tool of oppression. As we have seen, liberals of different stripes order the cluster of liberal values differently, some giving pride of place to equality or justice or freedom. Others place rights at the heart of liberalism, while their liberal critics stress the importance of desirable outcomes. These differences hold whether one advocates neutral or substantive liberalism. So, we must proceed carefully, avoiding sweeping generalizations about "liberalism."

Defenders of neutral liberalism fear the heavy hand of the state in pursuit of contestable ends, ends that unfairly and without justification privilege the values, tastes, predilections, and practices of one class, race, gender, caste, or religion. This is not a trivial concern. Since the rise of the state in the early modern period, different groups have tried to capture it to lend support to their own particular causes. When successful, oppression inevitably follows. By placing as many contestable values as they can off the table, neutralists hope to keep the state above the cultural wars besetting so many states today. Liberals advocating neutrality, such as Rawls, Dworkin, and Kymlicka, do not deny that they themselves defend values; far from it. But they argue that the values they defend grow out of the necessities of constitutional democracies and the avoidance of gratuitous cruelty. Consequently, they defend the rule of law, fair procedures, showing through law equal concern and respect to all, and incontestable human rights protecting everyone against torture, rape, arbitrary imprisonment, and unlawful killing.

But it must be pointed out that Dworkin himself does not shrink from making and defending a wide range of substantive moral judgments. He is right to do so. He is also right to worry about life in a state governed by Reverend Falwell; it would indeed be narrow and pinched and undoubtedly oppress many worthwhile ways of living and being. But this means only that his views are *morally unsound*. Dworkin, however, is not willing to commit moral ground troops to that refutation; he prefers his moral bombing from on high. He unnecessarily retreats, I believe, to the high ground on moral rights and abstract principle to secure his position. That, however, makes everything on the moral ground look as fields do from 33,000 feet: perfectly flat and perfectly rectangular. For anyone who is not a moral skeptic and who believes there are better and worse reasons for concrete political proposals—as Dworkin himself is—positions like Falwell's should be refuted point by point. That is not only the way to provide an effective refutation. There is a place for abstract principles, but they must be interpreted and articulated "in the cave" to be convincing.

As the aim here is not to criticize this strand of liberalism but to defend substantive liberalism against charges brought against it, I will say nothing more about the strengths and weaknesses of neutral liberalism. What does need to be addressed is how substantive liberalism can meet the criticisms leveled against *it*.

First and foremost, as long as it remains liberal, substantive liberalism will take comparatively weak forms. It will remain liberal insofar as it supports personal autonomy, that is, insofar as it recognizes—and values—that each individual develops his or her own life path in the cultural context in which one finds oneself.

One person, for example, will find himself immersed in an Amish community; another in a secular, urban artistic community; and yet a third in an orthodox Jewish community. Substantive liberals will see what is good in each of these communities and the life each is living, whether it expresses personal autonomy or not. The latter needs emphasis because substantive liberals need not accept the self-image or self-understanding of the participants as to the *truth* or *objective* value of their various commitments. Instead, substantive liberals will look to the effect of these values on the lives of those living them out. This is not to say that substantive liberals cannot themselves be participants in *some* of these cultural communities; they almost certainly will. There is no reason, for example, why a substantive liberal cannot be a Roman Catholic, though it is factually true that many Roman Catholics are not substantive liberals. Those who are both Roman Catholics and substantive liberals will advocate both the *truth* of their religious convictions *and* the value of personal autonomy—yet also see the value of personal autonomy (but not the truth) in ways of life that are radically divergent from it.

This example might seem to undermine the plausibility of substantive liberalism, for will there not be "hard cases" forcing Roman Catholics to cast their allegiance with either their church or their liberalism? Is not abortion just such a case? The evasive yet candid answer is, It depends. If one concludes that abortion is murder plain and simple, then of course it must be opposed and opposed strenuously, even by illegal means if necessary. But then it is not clear that this conflicts with liberalism, for no liberal countenances murder. Ever since abortions became comparatively safe and inexpensive, the crucial questions concern the moral status of the fetus and the rights and well-being of pregnant women and how, if they conflict, these are to be reconciled.

Still, substantive liberals morally opposed to abortion will be reluctant (though will not rule out) using the power of the state to forbid women from getting medically competent legal abortions. They will see that the overwhelming majority of women seeking abortions—and the physicians and nurses who provide them—are not living *otherwise* immoral and depraved lives, that their defense of abortion is not unreasoned, even if opponents conclude that they are mistaken. Further, they will see how *not* having access to safe and legal abortions would adversely affect women's profound interest in controlling their own reproductive lives, thus seriously and devastatingly affecting their autonomy. It is this aspect of laws prohibiting abortions that angers women most, for it replaces *their* moral judgment with another's. It holds that their moral judgment is so defective in this instance that the state is justified in replacing it with the judgment of others. Finally, substantive liberals will want to know if more death, hardship, and lawlessness will result by driving abortion underground.

Provided, then, that those opposing abortions do not conclude that they (generally or in particular circumstances) are intolerable and to be stopped by any legal (or illegal?) means necessary, they will tolerate both the practice and those engaged in it. This they might do both silently and grudgingly. On the account of tolerance defended here, however, they would be fully licensed to state publicly and forcefully their reasoned convictions and to engage forthrightly with opponents to convince them of the error of their ways, for there is nothing in tolerance that requires critics to do no more than bite their tongues. Nor is there anything wrong with their using political means to pass laws supporting alternatives to abortion and more. When it comes to "more," however, weak substantives will again tread carefully. For, first, it is only too easy to pass laws that make it difficult for poor and frightened women to take advantage of their right to an abortion. And, second, it is only too easy to pass laws that hold up a fig leaf of respectable reasons when the not-so-hidden reasons behind the legislation are unrelated: here, to prevent as many women as possible from having abortions. One way in which liberals can be substantive, therefore, is by being above board about the reasons for advocating or opposing legislation and not hiding behind fictions that they themselves do not think adequately ground their support. Bad faith can affect all parties to a controversy.

Substantive liberals will, like others, believe that it is sometimes necessary to set aside considerations of self-government. This is especially so where it involves identifiable and incontestable harm to others. And these "others" can be animals and the environment. Substantive liberals do not tolerate letting people torture animals for the fun of it or dumping toxic wastes into rivers or groundwater. Harm to the environment harms humans and animals, but it also harms something of intrinsic value. This illustrates that personal autonomy is not the only value held by substantive liberals.

Nor is harm to others the only consideration. Paternalistic acts and legislation also concern liberals. Children, the mentally damaged or disturbed, and those overwhelmed by stressful circumstances cannot always think straight or do not always have the intellectual and motivational resources to guide their own lives. Where possible, the aim of paternalistic acts and legislation is temporary: to permit children to make mature decisions, to restore the disturbed and stressed to normality so that they can live lives that are not only worth living but are worth living *because they are their own*. Where this is not possible—and it is not always—then the aims are more basic. It will be to prevent them from harming themselves and to help them live a life worth living, even if it is not fully their own, but essentially given to them to live by others. Yet even here there are likely to be small accomplishments, achievements made with enormous effort—for instance, feeding oneself, learning to walk after a debilitating stroke, holding down a menial job—that provide a genuine sense of being part author of one's own life, of governing oneself.

Autonomy calls for freedom of choice, but celebrating choice for itself is misplaced. Choice matters because without choices one cannot live one's own life, make of it what one can. But it is *this* that matters, not the sheer fact of choice itself. As mentioned earlier, some choices are choices in name only. Spending one's life in a supermarket choosing among myriad laundry detergents is not to have enough of the right type of choice from which to mold much of a human life. Other choices may be real enough—for instance, an impoverished child scrounging for her next meal—but so constrained that they, too, do not provide enough to provide the makings for an autonomous life.

But does not substantive liberalism, however weak, still permit far too much state intrusion into the lives of others? Will it not, for example, countenance censorship of television, movies, and the Internet? Substantive liberals will find much to abhor in these media. Censorship, however, brings with it follies and evils of its own. Attempts to eliminate just the "really bad stuff," however defined, inevitably become entangled in endless disputes about what is in and out, chill artistic expression, turn otherwise law-abiding citizens into criminals, and involve state bureaucracies that typically hound minor characters—all with little positive effect. Substantive liberals will explore less intrusive, bureaucratic, and state-sponsored ways of expressing moral disapproval. Voluntary associations that excoriate violent television directed at children, for example, have had some influence on programming. Like all liberals, however, substantive liberals will be cautious in using state power because of its tendency to abuse, misdirection, and ineffectiveness.

Neutralist liberals, therefore, have less to fear than meets the eye. Still, it must be granted that substantive liberals will not rule out in advance legislative proposals to discourage morally indefensible programming. More positively, substantive liberals will advocate voluntary and state-sponsored support of morally defensible programming. Noncommercial funding of children's programming is only one example. Substantive liberals can also support tax breaks and other indirect means to support what is valuable in a culture without resorting to the coercive powers of the state to enforce what is valuable or root out what is not. When agencies directly funded by the state *offer* funding for activities, applicants need to make a case that what they offer is not only feasible but also desirable. This will not end controversies, even bigotry, for a state agency might routinely deny applications from "disapproved" minorities or cultures. But then the burden shifts to the agency to justify its intolerance, to show that it is not bigoted. Even when the prejudice persists, those excluded do not have to suffer the added indignity—and real punishment—of having their activities criminalized.

These considerations should allay the fears of neutral liberals. It opens controversial questions to direct moral, religious, and practical debate. That some proposal would violate unfettered expression, for example, will be a strong reason to believe that the state should abandon the proposal, but not a conclusive reason, for there are no conclusive reasons in this area, only better and worse reasons. As proponents of tolerance, moreover, substantive liberals will make efforts to see what can be said *for* attitudes, beliefs, and practices that they find abhorrent. This is part of what it is to *recognize* others and show them respect. It does not entail that they will be convinced that what they antecedently believe is intolerable can be tolerated, let alone move them to acceptance, but on many occasions it might do one or the other. Where it does not—where, that is, our antecedent beliefs remain unchanged—substantive liberals will still ask whether the harm done to the autonomy of others is worth the intrusion, especially given the "Sweater Principle." We need to be especially careful when we tug on errant threads that the community, culture, or group does not unravel, destroying what was originally valuable for those living in them. So, this is a further cautionary note that substantive liberals will bear in mind as they consider intervening in what they may ill-understand. Tolerance, then, will be called for.

TOLERANCE IN A MULTICULTURAL WORLD

Objections

Tolerance, contend proponents of multiculturalism, seems ideally suited for the type of world in which it arose. It is suited for a pluralistic world divided, even bitterly divided, by differences that are family disputes. Those most at home with tolerance in such a world are "cosmopolitan," those who can rise above the family dispute and take a detached stance, although *from* a particular place, they think of themselves as "citizens of the world"—which is to say citizens of nowhere. This is the world of Montaigne. Tolerance appears especially attractive to artists, intellectuals, those on the margins of tightly knit communities (e.g., gays), and those who have never identified strongly with their own culture, people, or ethnicity. This stance, however, is not attractive for the vast majority, whose identities are inextricably tied to their specific families, clans, tribes, cultures, religions, and nationality. Any viable social and political theory must acknowledge this. Liberals in theory and practice are not so obligated. In particular, tolerance as conceived by liberals fails to grant full recognition and full acceptance of others it merely tolerates.

Even those who think of themselves as cosmopolitan, argue multicultural critics, spend their childhood in some community or other, master a native tongue, learn the leading narratives of their people, imbibe its art and religion, and so on. So, it is simply preposterous to suppose that there could be what one might regard as an "Esperanto" culture, a culture that was neither this nor that but some abstraction of all. (This is at least a partial explanation why the artificial language of Esperanto has never made much of an effect.)

Liberal tolerance assumes pluralism of interests, and that, in turn, presupposes a *monoculture*. Divisions in monocultures can be deep but seldom wide, for those divided share so many cultural similarities. Protestants warring with each other in Locke's day, for example, were all good Englishmen with a similar Christian heritage. Tolerance speaks to this condition because both tolerators and tolerated have so much in common. It does not, however, speak to the *multicultural* world we now live in, for the language of toleration always privileges some hegemonic power group.

Today, only a few states are not multicultural (e.g., Iceland). Almost every other state encloses diverse nationalities, ethnicities, cultures, and subcultures. England today is no exception: Devout Muslims live among devout Christians, and neither Catholics nor Jews are excluded from public life. In different countries, cultures occupy distinctive geographical regions; in others, they do not but are found throughout the state. Equally important, most now identify strongly with their group or subgroup and with their diverse heritages. That we now live in a multicultural world, the critic asserts, is thus a sociological fact of enormous importance.

Distinctive normative implications flow from the fact of multiculturalism (sometimes leavened by a postmodern sensibility). First, we can no longer think of controversies as primarily struggles over "issues" or "interests" dividing otherwise like-minded people. True, Pakistani-born Muslims and English-born Christians in the United Kingdom will disagree over the "issue" of women (e.g., the schooling of girls). Those disagreements, however, will be inextricably connected with profound religious and cultural differences—indeed, with a whole worldview. Second, no culture has a monopoly on truth or beauty or goodness. Truth, certainty, meaning, and interpretation are local. Modes of inquiry and interaction, ways of understanding the world, discerning the meaning of life, and so on are largely (though not exclusively) confined to the traditions and communities from which they arose. Different cultures present us with different experiments in living, and, except for a few transient distortions (e.g., Cambodia under the Khmer Rouge, Germany under the Nazis), none is better than any other is. Indeed, the language of "better than" or even "as good as" supposes a stance above the fray from which we can judge as impartial observers. But there is no such place, no view from nowhere.

If this is true, then it would seem preposterous for the powerful in one culture to *tolerate* other cultures and communities or particular views, attitudes, and practices found in them, for it is preposterous to tolerate what cannot be legitimately criticized. And we cannot legitimately criticize that which is as good as what we prefer or that which is nothing more than *different* from what we are used to. As we saw in chapter 4, someone who said that he tolerated people who were honest or courageous would reveal that he had a corrupt moral outlook. Again, something may not be our "cup of tea," but it would be ludicrous to tolerate what is *merely* a matter of taste. *There is simply nothing to tolerate.* We should *accept* what is good or merely different, not tolerate it. Similarly, we should *accept* other cultures—even *embrace* them—not *tolerate* them.

We might not always be able to appreciate strange cultures and their ways— for instance, their musical forms—but we should simply grant that they are valuable for those who live them. While we may have the *power* to crush another culture, it can never be right to do so because all cultures are equally good, morally, religiously, artistically, and in every other way. That we *prefer* our own because of its familiarity and comfort gives us no reason to *tolerate* those that are unfamiliar or make us feel uncomfortable. Instead, we need to accept others as they are. We need to recognize that every culture, community, and so on has its rough edges and that it is not our place to smooth those edges or even criticize them. In an enlightened multicultural society, the critic concludes, cultures will sit easily side by side, members happily enjoying their own cultures, participating as guests in the ceremonies and rituals of others, with no efforts to proselytize or judge.

There is one further point. Because liberal democracies are committed to equal representation of all individuals, they fail to account for our particular identities as Inuit, Catholic, gay, women, and so on. They can *tolerate* individuals pursuing their *private* interests through group identity, but the state will not tolerate their existence at a public level.[25] But liberal democracies have difficulty *recognizing* our various identities in the public sphere, where people rightly want them to be recognized. Why must one's religious convictions, for example, be relegated to the private sphere? If confined to that sphere, the state—not unlike the Ottoman Turks—will tolerate one's being religious (or gay or African American), but only if it does not show its face in public. And this seems wrong.

We therefore need to move *beyond* tolerance. We need to move to *mutual recognition* and mutual *respect*. The language of tolerance and toleration will then be seen for what it is: strategies for coping in a monocultural world but presumptuous anachronisms in our own multicultural world.

Reply

Substantive liberalism can grant many of the points arrayed by proponents of multiculturalism. It should and can acknowledge the needs of individuals as members of specific cultural groups. But, as Amy Gutmann notes, the demand for recognition points in the direction of satisfying needs but also in the direction of protecting basic human rights.[26] And in the type of societies discussed in this book, this means that we must take great care to preserve the possibility of people developing their personal autonomy.

Some proponents of multiculturalism cannot be accommodated by substantive liberalism; namely, those inspired by *some* postmodernists, but only some. Those whose views cannot be accommodated take extreme positions on the social construction of everything, the disappearance of the "subject," and the broad rejection of value judgments that are not tied narrowly and tightly to a specific time and place.[27] It is this kind of postmodernism that worries John Searle.[28] As manifested in the university, it celebrates a mindless "political correctness." This substitutes identity politics, an attitude of resentment and a sense of victimization, and a deep-seated view that authority is nothing but power for critical intelligence that relies on well-established standards of rationality.

There is certainly something to Searle's worry. But we do better to take as models of multiculturalism the best versions, not the worst. And among the best is that championed by Charles Taylor.[29] His criticisms of liberalism for its atom-izing effects and its celebration of "hyperindividualism" are on the mark. But substantive liberalism agrees with much of that criticism and can accept without compromise or embarrassment most of what he defends in *The Politics of Recog-nition,* for substantive liberalism fully acknowledges that autonomy requires cul-tural support and that various cultures provide that support in markedly different ways but drawing on the notion implicit in liberalism that all are equally deserv-ing of respect and equal rights.

I stressed the importance of culture in the previous chapter but did not em-phasize the supposed link between recognition and identity. If identity desig-nates our understanding of who they are, then how we are recognized (or *mis*-recognized) helps shape our identity. Misrecognition, therefore, not only shows a lack of respect but "can inflict a grievous wound, saddling its victims with a crippling self-hatred. Due recognition is not just a courtesy we owe people. It is a vital human need."[30]

Two changes made the preoccupation with identity and recognition inevitable. The first was the collapse of social hierarchies in which *honor* had pride of place. The modern notions of dignity and respect replaced it. Unlike honor, which some have and others do not by virtue of their station in life, dignity and respect is the birthright of everyone. The second change flows from the new emphasis on indi-viduals. It gives rise to an *individualized* identity expressed as a demand for *au-thenticity.* As Taylor puts it, the ideal of "being true to myself and my own par-ticular way of being."[31]

The latter bears certain affinities with the notion of personal autonomy de-fended here, but it is not the same. Authenticity, as Taylor describes it, is not the only way to interpret the move away from social hierarchies to dignity and re-spect. Rousseau and the romantics develop that interpretation, and the strain de-veloped here undoubtedly owes something to it. But as Taylor goes on to argue, there are ways of developing this strain that are both less subjective and do not stress *originality* and *creativity* to the same degree, let alone the thought of the lonely individual fighting conformity and being true to a self he creates. It is therefore far more open to reasoned reflection and criticism than the strain found in romanticism. Here, for instance, is Taylor's fine gloss on the romantic sensi-bility of authenticity:

> It [authenticity] accords moral importance to a kind of contact with myself, with my own inner nature, which it sees as in danger of being lost, partly through the pres-sures toward outward conformity [and partly through taking an instrumental stance toward myself]. . . . Not only should I not mold my life to the demands of external conformity; I can't even find the model by which to live outside myself. I can only find it within. Being true to myself means being true to my own originality, which is something only I can articulate and discover. In articulating it, I am also defining my-self. I am realizing a potentiality that is properly my own.[32]

The politics of recognition, Taylor argues, has come to mean two different things. It has come to mean, first, the politics of universalism, with its equalizing of rights. But it also has come to mean, second, the politics of difference, with its claims to recognition of one's unique identity as a member of a group (e.g., French Canadian) or distinctive grouping (e.g., women, gays). Each reproaches the other:

> The reproach the first makes to the second is just that it violates the principle of nondiscrimination. The reproach the second makes to the first is that it negates identity by forcing people into a homogeneous mold that is untrue of them.[33]

Yet Taylor himself argues that a sensible liberalism can draw on resources that take much of the sting out of each reproach. Adopting substantive liberalism—one that takes a position on the substantive goods of life—makes this even easier, for the kind of substantive liberalism defended here does not restrict liberalism to fair procedures or rights or demand that the state be neutral among conflicting goods. It therefore makes it easier to support ways of life that are good, even when they are not themselves particularly liberal. In short, substantive liberalism will not negate identity by forcing people into a homogeneous mold.

Substantive liberals can further agree with Taylor that a community can be organized around a definition of the good life whether or not liberal (with certain provisos) and seek to attain that good as a matter of public policy. What are the provisos? That depends on many things. If, for instance, the community is itself part of a larger constitutional democracy, then it cannot withhold basic constitutional rights and liberties from its members. Consistent with such constitutional rights and liberties, however, it can seek to preserve its cultural identity. Foremost in Taylor's own thinking is the fate of French culture in Quebec, especially the preservation and use of the French language. Substantive liberals can support those policies because it enables French-speaking Quebecers to live a flourishing life *as individual men and women.* This does not entail, however, that "anything goes." For instance, French-speaking Quebecers cannot forbid the speaking of English or make it virtually impossible for English-speaking inhabitants to live their own lives. Where and how to draw lines is exceedingly important and difficult and can be thought through responsibly only after a thorough knowledge, even immersion, in the history and details of the problems presented. Only in this way can we resolve the tensions—or mutual "reproach"—Taylor mentions.

Taylor further notes that liberalism—because it is substantive—cannot embrace every possible conception of the good, especially those that violate the principles articulated in Western liberal constitutional democracies. So, to cite his example, it cannot tolerate (within its own borders, certainly) the sort of standing death threat issued against Salman Rushdie for his *Satanic Verses,* for that would be contrary to liberalism's own core values. As Taylor says, liberalism is itself a "fighting creed"[34] and so has its own values to champion and protect.

Where I disagree with Taylor and side with Kymlicka concerns whether liberalism, substantive or otherwise, must make every effort to *guarantee* the survival of a subculture within a broader political society. Taylor rightly notes that a liberalism that recognizes the importance of culture for identity (and hence for the possibility of realizing one's autonomy) nevertheless "doesn't justify measures designed to ensure survival through indefinite future generations. For the populations concerned [e.g., Indian bands in Canada, French Canadians], however, that is what is at stake."[35]

That demand cannot be met. Measures *ensuring* cultural survival would be inconsistent, for example, with liberal demands that permit people to leave, with liberal demands that the education of the young not be grotesquely distorted by tales about the dominant culture, and with any claim that members of such cultural communities lose their rights and liberties as *citizens* of the broader political society. Substantive liberalism can make things *easier* in ways discussed earlier. But it can offer no guarantees of survival, and it cannot abrogate either fundamental civil or human rights in helping endangered cultures and communities.

Multiculturalism is too often portrayed as a mindless acceptance of every self-declared identity. Because substantive liberalism is neither *neutral* nor purely *procedural,* however, it must reject this stance. And here it finds an ally in Taylor, for it accepts Taylor's "presumption that all human cultures that have animated whole societies over some considerable stretch of time have something important to say to all human beings . . . [but that] the validity of the claim has to be demonstrated concretely in the actual study of the culture."[36] Whether every culture, every proclaimed identity, is "equally good" remains to be *shown,* not merely asserted. And the beginning of wisdom in this regard is to admit that no one, including liberals, can be confident that we have the principles and standards to make such sweeping judgments. What we can do as substantive liberals, however, is show tolerance to cultures that we do not understand, to open up space so that understanding and critical appreciation can occur. That might lead to acceptance—or rejection—or all the resting points in between.

NOTES

1. Robert Paul Wolff, Barrington Moore Jr., and Herbert Marcuse, eds., *A Critique of Pure Tolerance* (Boston: Beacon Press, 1965).
2. Wolff et al., eds., *A Critique of Pure Tolerance,* vi.
3. Wolff et al., eds., *A Critique of Pure Tolerance,* 37.
4. Wolff et al., eds., *A Critique of Pure Tolerance,* 54.
5. Wolff et al., eds., *A Critique of Pure Tolerance,* 60.
6. Wolff et al., eds., *A Critique of Pure Tolerance,* 82
7. Wolff et al., eds., *A Critique of Pure Tolerance,* 82–83.
8. Wolff et al., eds., *A Critique of Pure Tolerance,* 85.
9. Edgar Wind, *Art and Anarchy* (New York: Alfred A. Knopf, 1964), 101.

10. Wolff et al., eds., *A Critique of Pure Tolerance*, 94.

11. Wolff et al., eds., *A Critique of Pure Tolerance*, 95.

12. Wolff et al., eds., *A Critique of Pure Tolerance*, 107.

13. Wolff et al., eds., *A Critique of Pure Tolerance*, 123.

14. See, for example, Robert George, *In Defense of Natural Law* (Oxford: Clarendon Press, 1999).

15. Wolff et al., eds., *A Critique of Pure Tolerance*, 82.

16. Ronald Dworkin, "Liberalism," in *Public and Private Morality*, ed. Stuart Hampshire (Cambridge: Cambridge University Press, 1978), 116, note 1.

17. This needs some qualification, for it might be that in some circumstances, excommunication is tantamount to a life outside society.

18. Joseph Raz, *The Morality of Freedom* (Oxford: Clarendon Press, 1986), 404.

19. Colin Turnbull, *The Mountain People* (New York: Simon and Schuster, 1972). Turnbull tells the tragic story of the Iks, an unfortunate African tribe whose nomadic hunting life was curtailed by development and protection of wild animals. It is hard to read Turnbull's account and find anything in the life of the Ik worth saving. He recommends that someone physically remove the children and place them with other tribes. I do not know whether his anthropology is sound, but surely throughout history there have been cultural communities that have disintegrated for innumerable reasons.

20. Defenders include John Rawls, *A Theory of Justice* (Cambridge, Mass.: Harvard University Press, 1971), and *Political Liberalism* (New York: Columbia University Press, 1995); Robert Nozick, *Anarchy, State, and Utopia* (New York: Basic Books, 1974); Bruce Ackerman, *Social Justice in the Liberal State* (New Haven, Conn.: Yale University Press, 1980); Ronald Dworkin, *A Matter of Principle* (Cambridge, Mass.: Harvard University Press, 1985); Charles Larmore, *Patterns of Moral Complexity* (Cambridge: Cambridge University Press, 1987); D. A. Lloyd-Thomas, *In Defence of Liberalism* (Oxford: Basil Blackwell, 1988); and Will Kymlicka, *Liberalism, Community, and Culture* (Oxford: Oxford University Press, 1989).

21. George Sher, *Beyond Neutrality: Perfectionism and Politics* (Cambridge: Cambridge University Press, 1997), 1–2.

22. John Stuart Mill, *On Liberty*, ed. Elizabeth Rapport (Indianapolis: Hackett Publishing Company, 1978), 9.

23. Ronald Dworkin, "Neutrality, Equality, and Liberalism," in *Liberalism Reconsidered*, ed. Douglas MacLean and Claudia Mills (Totowa, N.J.: Rowman and Allanheld, 1983), 1.

24. Sher, *Beyond Neutrality;* Vinit Haksar, *Equality, Liberty, and Perfectionism* (Oxford: Oxford University Press, 1977); Raz, *The Morality of Freedom*.

25. There are a few exceptions. Certain indigenous peoples in Canada, for example, negotiated treaties giving them some protection that they would not otherwise enjoy. And affirmative action strays from the neutrality of liberal democracy, but not without attacks that it is contrary to both the letter and the spirit of constitutional, liberal democracies.

26. Amy Gutmann, ed., *Multiculturalism: Examining the Politics of Recognition* (Princeton, N.J.: Princeton University Press, 1994), 8.

27. Postmodernism comes in many guises. Among the most influential are Jean-François Lyotard, *The Postmodern Condition: A Report on Knowledge* (Minneapolis: University of Minnesota Press, 1984; originally 1979); Michel Foucault, *Discipline and Punishment* (New York: Vintage Books, 1979); Michel Foucault, *Power/Knowledge* (New

York: Pantheon Books, 1981); Jacques Derrida, *Of Grammatology* (Baltimore: Johns Hopkins University Press, 1976); Jacques Lacan, *Ecrits* (New York: W. W. Norton, 1977); and Luce Irigaray, *This Sex Which Is Not One,* trans. by Catherine Porter with Carolyn Burke (Ithaca, N.Y.: Cornell University Press, 1985). They are not, however, responsible for all the excesses of their devotees.

    28. John R. Searle, "Rationality and Realism: What Is at Stake?" *Daedalus* 122, no. 4 (1993): 55–83, and "The Storm over the University," *New York Review of Books* 37 (December 6, 1990): 34–42.

    29. Charles Taylor, "The Politics of Recognition," in *Multiculturalism*, ed. Gutmann.

    30. Taylor, "The Politics of Recognition," in *Multiculturalism,* ed. Gutmann, 26.

    31. Taylor, "The Politics of Recognition," in *Multiculturalism,* ed. Gutmann, 28.

    32. Taylor, "The Politics of Recognition," in *Multiculturalism,* ed. Gutmann, 30–31.

    33. Taylor, "The Politics of Recognition," in *Multiculturalism,* ed. Gutmann 43.

    34. Taylor, "The Politics of Recognition," in *Multiculturalism,* ed. Gutmann 62.

    35. Taylor, "The Politics of Recognition," in *Multiculturalism,* ed. Gutmann 41.

    36. Taylor, "The Politics of Recognition," in *Multiculturalism,* ed. Gutmann 66–67.

Epilogue

I have tried to show that tolerance need not be elusive or even grudging if placed at the heart of substantive liberalism. To be at the heart of something, however, is not to be the whole of it. In a fuller study, I would have to show how tolerance fits in with, and supports, other claims and values of substantive liberalism, especially justice, equality, and rights. Even without this, however, we can see the possibilities a defense of tolerance as part of substantive liberalism offers. Clearly, for liberals who take personal autonomy as essential to their flourishing, this task, though arduous, can be successfully undertaken. Developing tolerant attitudes, acquiring the virtue of tolerance, and encouraging tolerant practices radiates outward, making it possible for most members of pluralist, multicultural societies to live flourishing lives—whether liberals or not.

I say "most" because substantive liberals must make their own judgments about what is intolerable, what lies beyond the pale. They cannot, for example, tolerate those who would undermine their own tolerant practices. And it will be intolerant of any group that lies within its jurisdiction that denies its members fundamental human rights or typical constitutionally guaranteed civil rights of constitutional democracies. Provided that intolerant groups avoid these intolerable wrongs, however, substantive liberals will tolerate intolerant communities and traditions in their midst. They will do so not because they are indifferent or skeptical or because they do not find them seriously objectionable. They will do so because and to the extent that intolerant but voluntary communities are sources of genuine values enabling individuals to live good lives if they are willing to keep the traditions and stay in the communities.

Tolerant members of societies shaped by substantive liberalism will not shy from engaging with those with whom they disagree. They will not do so in a hectoring way. They will do so mainly to understand and appreciate the value others find in their ways of life, beliefs, attitudes, and practices. Mutual discussion and exploration will often be vigorous and contentious, as they should be when mat-

173

ters of substance are at stake. They need not, however, be threatening. Often they will urge support, direct and indirect, for ways of life they do not share or much like. This support can take both governmental and nongovernmental forms. And, as far as possible, they will honor the request to be left alone. True, sometimes liberals will conclude that the practices of a certain community or group are intolerable. Far more often, however, exploration, dialogue, and argument will lead to a greater appreciation of the real values available in traditions liberals themselves cannot share or communities they would not dream of joining, even if invited.

The values discovered in traditions, communities, religions, and cultures might not always be those stated. We need not accept anyone's claims at face value, including our own. We need not, for example, accept views about the supernatural or rituals that pay homage to god(s) or (false) historical claims. Yet we can still fully appreciate how much beliefs and rituals and historical narrative give shape and substance to many genuine values: a sense of a shared fate, a close community, loyalty, friendship, self-sacrifice, courage in the face of hardship, and so on.

By its very nature, philosophical reflection is abstract, even if done in the cave, as Walzer recommends. But we can never settle by abstract argument where to draw the line between the tolerable and intolerable in concrete cases. No philosophical exploration and defense of tolerance can substitute for the hard work that we must do within each society to fashion satisfactory practices of toleration. These will vary according to circumstances. Because of its recent history, for instance, Germany will not tolerate neo-Nazi groups. Because of America's struggles over free expression and fears of unbridled attacks on it, the rigid First Amendment jurisprudence of the Supreme Court might be just right—for Americans. Neither Germans nor Americans are wrong in their response to their peculiar circumstances. But their solutions to particular questions of tolerance might not be right for others. Each has to work through its own history, its own traditions, and its own capacity for mischief and even evil. Where tolerance begins and ends will thus shift as circumstances change. For it is only by working through the implications of tolerance in concrete cases that we can, in the end, determine both the possibilities and the limits of tolerance.

As we acquire greater understanding and appreciation of beliefs, attitudes, communities, traditions, and practices of others, we might come to see what they contribute to those whose beliefs, attitudes, and practices they are. We might even find that they offer something valuable to us. Even where what they offer is something we find deplorable, there might be valuable elements that make it tolerable, if only barely so. With few exceptions, it would be surprising to find *nothing* of genuine value that a deplorable community, say, offers its members. Whether it is enough to overcome our intolerance is often a very real question. But before surrendering to our understandable temptation to lash out and intervene, we need to ask whether intervention—even if successful—would not simultaneously destroy prospects to live flourishing lives. The thought that we could "surgically remove" an offending practice without seriously damaging what was valuable makes about as much sense as surgical bombing; both lead surely and inexorably to unacceptable "collateral damage." So sometimes—especially where we ourselves are not implicated—we will have to accept "mere" tolerance: putting up with what we find disgusting. More often, however, we can range more widely between forbearance and acceptance, exploring possibilities that we will overlook if we think of tolerance as nothing more than a grudging virtue, if a virtue at all.

Raising children to see the good in what we find strange or offensive is not easy, though children seem to do this more easily than the adults who teach them. But the effort is worth it if tolerance is not to remain elusive and grudging. And it is necessary if our impulses do not cause us to sink back into a raging intolerance that sweeps away everything before it.

Bibliography

Ackerman, Bruce. *Social Justice in the Liberal State.* New Haven, Conn.: Yale University Press, 1980.

Allen, Anita L., and Milton C. Regan, eds. *Debating Democracy's Discontent: Essays on American Politics, Law, and Public Philosophy.* Oxford: Oxford University Press, 1988.

Aquinas, Thomas. *Commentary on the Nicomachean Ethics.* Vol. 2. Translated by C. I. Litzinger. Chicago: Regnery, 1964.

———. *Summa Theologiae.* Translated by English Dominicans. London: Burns, Oates, and Washbourne, 1912–36. Reprint, New York: Benziger, 1947–48.

Aristotle. *Nicomachean Ethics.* Translated by Martin Ostwald. Indianapolis: Bobbs-Merrill Company, 1962.

Baron, Marcia. *Kantian Ethics Almost without Apology.* Ithaca, N.Y.: Cornell University Press, 1995.

Barry, Brian. *Justice as Impartiality.* New York: Oxford University Press, 1995.

Bell, Daniel. *Communitarianism and Its Critics.* Oxford: Clarendon Press, 1993.

Bentham, Jeremy. *Principles of Morals and Legislation.* Edited by J. H. Burns and H. L. A. Hart. London: Athlone Press, 1970.

Berlin, Isaiah. *The Crooked Timber of Humanity.* Edited by Henry Hardy. New York: Alfred A. Knopf, 1991.

Best, Steven, and Douglas Kellne. *Postmodern Theory: Critical Interrogations.* New York: Guilford Press, 1991.

Chang, Ruth. *Incommensurability, Incomparability, and Practical Reason.* Cambridge, Mass.: Harvard University Press, 1997.

Connolly, William E. *The Ethos of Pluralization.* Minneapolis: University of Minnesota Press, 1995.

———. *The Terms of Political Discourse.* 2nd ed. Princeton, N.J.: Princeton University Press, 1983.

Cranston, Maurice. *John Locke: A Biography.* London: Longmans, Green, 1957.

Derrida, Jacques. *Of Grammatology.* Baltimore: Johns Hopkins University Press, 1976.

Dewey, John. *Experience and Nature.* Chicago: Open Court Publishing, 1925.

———. *Human Nature and Conduct: An Introduction to Social Psychology.* New York: Henry Holt, 1922.

————. *Individualism: Old and New.* New York: Minton, Balch, 1930.

————. *Intelligence in the Modern World: John Dewey's Philosophy.* Edited by Joseph Ratner. New York: The Modern Library, 1939.

Donagan, Alan. *The Theory of Morality.* Chicago: University of Chicago Press, 1977.

Dworkin, Ronald. *A Matter of Principle.* Cambridge, Mass.: Harvard University Press, 1985.

————. *Sovereign Virtue: The Theory and Practice of Equality.* Cambridge, Mass.: Harvard University Press, 2000.

————. *Taking Rights Seriously.* London: Duckworth, 1977.

Fotion, Nick, and Gerard Elfstrom. *Toleration.* Tuscaloosa: University of Alabama Press, 1992.

Foucault, Michel. *Discipline and Punishment.* New York: Vintage Books, 1979.

————. *Power/Knowledge.* New York: Pantheon Books, 1981.

George, Robert. *In Defense of Natural Law.* Oxford: Clarendon Press, 1999.

Gutmann, Amy, ed. *Multiculturalism: Examining the Politics of Recognition.* Princeton, N.J.: Princeton University Press, 1994.

Haksar, Vinit. *Equality, Liberty, and Perfectionism.* Oxford: Oxford University Press, 1977.

Harvey, David. *The Condition of Postmodernity: An Enquiry into the Origins of Cultural Change.* Oxford: Blackwell, 1990.

Heyd, David, ed. *Toleration: An Elusive Virtue.* Princeton, N.J.: Princeton University Press, 1997.

Hobhouse, L. T. *Liberalism.* New York: Henry Holt, 1911.

Horton, John, ed. *Liberalism, Multiculturalism and Toleration.* New York: Macmillan, 1993.

Humbolt, Wilhelm Freiherr von. *The Sphere and Duties of Government.* Translated by J. Coulthard. London, 1854.

Hume, David. *Enquiry concerning Principles of Morals.* London, 1751.

Hurka, Thomas. *Perfectionism.* New York: Oxford University Press, 1993.

Kamen, Henry. *The Rise of Toleration.* London: Weidenfeld, 1967.

Kant, Immanuel. *Foundations of the Metaphysics of Morals* (London, 1785). In *Immanuel Kant: The Groundwork of the Metaphysic of Morals.* Translated by H. J. Paton. New York: Harper, 1956.

————. *Metaphysical Elements of Justice: Part I.* 2nd ed. Translated by John Ladd. Indianapolis: Hackett Publishing, 1999.

Korsgaard, Christine. *Creating the Kingdom of Ends.* Cambridge: Cambridge University Press, 1996.

Kymlicka, Will. *Liberalism, Community, and Culture.* New York: Oxford University Press, 1989.

————. *Multicultural Citizenship: A Liberal Theory of Minority Rights.* New York: Oxford University Press, 1995.

Lacan, Jacques. *Ecrit.* New York: W. W. Norton, 1977.

Larmore, Charles. *Patterns of Moral Complexity.* Cambridge: Cambridge University Press, 1987.

Lecler, Joseph. *Toleration and the Reformation.* 2 vols. Translated by T. L. Westrow. New York: Association Press, 1960.

Locke, John. *An Essay concerning Human Understanding* (London, 1689). Edited by Peter H. Nidditch. Oxford: Oxford University Press, 1975.

——. *John Locke: A Letter concerning Toleration in Focus.* Edited by John Horton and Susan Mendus. London: Routledge, 1991.

——. *The Works of John Locke: A New Edition.* Vol. VI (corrected). London, 1823.

Lyotard, Jean-Françoise. *The Postmodern Condition: A Report on Knowledge.* Minneapolis: University of Minnesota Press, 1984.

MacIntyre, Alasdair. *After Virtue.* 2nd ed. Notre Dame, Ind.: University of Notre Dame Press, 1984.

——. *A Short History of Ethics.* New York: Macmillan, 1966.

——. *Three Rival Versions of Moral Inquiry: Encyclopaedia, Genealogy, and Tradition.* Notre Dame, Ind.: University of Notre Dame Press, 1990.

——. *Whose Justice? Which Rationality?* Notre Dame, Ind.: University of Notre Dame Press, 1988.

Mendus, Susan, ed. *Justifying Toleration: Conceptual and Historical Perspectives.* Cambridge: Cambridge University Press, 1988.

——, ed. *The Politics of Toleration in Modern Life.* Durham, N.C.: Duke University Press, 2000.

——. *Toleration and the Limits of Liberalism.* Atlantic Highlands, N.J.: Humanities Press International, 1989.

Mill, John Stuart. *On Liberty.* London: J. W. Parker and Son, 1859.

——. *On Liberty.* Edited by David Spitz. New York: W. W. Norton, 1975.

——. *On Liberty: In Focus.* Edited by John Gray and G. W. Smith. London: Routledge, 1991.

——. *Utilitarianism.* London, 1863.

——. *Utilitarianism.* Edited by Roger Crisp. Oxford: Oxford University Press, 1998.

Nederman, Cary, and John Christain Laursen, eds. *Beyond the Persecuting Society: Religious Toleration before the Enlightenment.* Philadelphia: University of Pennsylvania Press, 1998.

——, eds. *Difference and Dissent: Theories of Tolerance in Medieval and Early Modern Europe.* Lanham, Md.: Rowman & Littlefield, 1997.

Nidditch, P. H., ed. *David Hume: Enquiries concerning Human Understanding and concerning the Principles of Morals.* Oxford: Clarendon Press, 1974.

Nozick, Robert. *State, Anarchy, and Utopia.* New York: Basic Books, 1974.

O'Neill, Onora. *Constructions of Reason: Explorations of Kant's Practical Philosophy.* Cambridge: Cambridge University Press, 1989.

Pettit, Philip. *Republicanism: A Theory of Freedom and Government.* Oxford: Clarendon Press, 1997.

Popkin, Richard. *The History of Scepticism from Erasmus to Spinoza.* Berkeley and Los Angeles: University of California Press, 1979.

——, ed. *Skepticism and Irreligion in the Seventeenth and Eighteenth Centuries.* Leiden: Brill, 1993.

Proast, Jonas. *The Argument of the Letter concerning Toleration, Briefly Consider'd and Answer'd.* Oxford, 1690.

Rashdall, Hastings. *The Theory of Good and Evil: A Treatise on Moral Philosophy.* 2 vols. Oxford, 1907.

Rawls, John. *Political Liberalism.* New York: Columbia University Press, 1993.

——. *A Theory of Justice.* Cambridge, Mass.: Harvard University Press, 1971.

Raz, Joseph. *Ethics in the Public Domain.* Oxford: Clarendon Press, 1994.

——. *The Morality of Freedom.* Oxford: Clarendon Press, 1986.

Rorty, Richard. *Contingency, Irony, and Solidarity.* Cambridge: Cambridge University Press, 1989.

———. *Philosophy and the Mirror of Nature.* Princeton, N.J.: Princeton University Press, 1979.

Sandel, Michael J. *Liberalism and the Limits of Justice.* Cambridge: Cambridge University Press, 1982.

Scanlon, T. M. *What We Owe to Each Other.* Cambridge, Mass.: Belknap Press of Harvard University Press, 1998.

Sen, Amartya. *Inequality Reexamined.* Cambridge, Mass.: Harvard University Press, 1995.

Sher, George. *Beyond Neutrality: Perfectionism and Politics.* Cambridge: Cambridge University Press, 1997.

Taylor, Charles. *Human Agency and Language.* Vols. 1 and 2. Cambridge: Cambridge University Press, 1985.

———. *Philosophical Arguments.* Cambridge, Mass.: Harvard University Press, 1995.

———. *Sources of the Self: The Making of the Modern Identity.* Cambridge, Mass.: Harvard University Press, 1989.

Turnbull, Colin. *The Mountain People.* New York: Simon and Schuster, 1972.

Wallace, James. *Virtues and Vices.* Ithaca, N.Y.: Cornell University Press, 1978.

Walzer, Michael. *On Toleration.* New Haven, Conn.: Yale University Press, 1997.

———. *Spheres of Justice.* Oxford: Martin Robertson, 1983.

Williams, Bernard. *Shame and Necessity.* Berkeley and Los Angeles: University of California Press, 1993.

Wind, Edgar. *Art and Anarchy.* New York: Alfred A. Knopf, 1964.

Wolff, Robert Paul, Barrington Moore Jr., and Herbert Marcuse, eds. *A Critique of Pure Tolerance.* Boston: Beacon Press, 1965.

Index

About the Author

Hans Oberdiek is Henry C. and Charlotte Turner Professor at Swarthmore College, where he has taught moral philosophy, social and political philosophy, and philosophy of law since 1965. He has been a visiting lecturer at Oxford University and visiting professor at Temple University, the University of Florida, and the University of Pennsylvania. In addition to articles in moral philosophy and jurisprudence, he is the coauthor (with Mary Tiles) of *Living in a Technological Culture.*